THE HE
by H

Owing to production difficulties it is impossible to maintain large stocks of our publications, and the titles available change so rapidly that the complete catalogue is of little value as a means of knowing what books are in print. If you are not already on our mailing list and would like to know when new books or reprints are added, please send in your name and address on a post card.

Suggestions for additions are welcomed.

The Hero of Delhi

A LIFE OF JOHN NICHOLSON
SAVIOUR OF INDIA
AND
A HISTORY OF HIS WARS

BY

HESKETH PEARSON

PENGUIN BOOKS
WEST DRAYTON MIDDLESEX ENGLAND
245 FIFTH AVENUE NEW YORK U.S.A.

First published 1939
Published in Penguin Books 1948

MADE AND PRINTED IN GREAT BRITAIN
FOR PENGUIN BOOKS LTD., BY HAZELL, WATSON AND VINEY, LTD.
LONDON AND AYLESBURY

To

C. R. A. Hammond

Tributes to Nicholson by some Contemporaries

'I have never seen any one like him. He was the beau-ideal of a soldier and a gentleman.'

Field-Marshal Lord Roberts

'A tower of strength. . . . His name cowed whole provinces while he was yet scores of miles away.'

Lord Dalhousie

'Without John Nicholson Delhi could not have fallen. . . . The memory of his deeds will never perish so long as British rule endures.'   *Sir John Lawrence*

'The idol of all soldiers.'   *General Sir Hugh Gough*

'After all, Nicholson is the general after my heart.'

Major Hodson (of Hodson's Horse)

'The greatest of men amongst us . . . the pride of the whole army of India.'

The Chaplain of the Army before Delhi

'He was a grand fellow. He had a genius for war.'

General Sir Henry Daly

'The foremost man in India.'   *General Younghusband*

'Nicholson was undoubtedly the most remarkable of those heroic men who became famous in the days of our humiliation.'   *Field-Marshal Sir Evelyn Wood*

'The most successful administrator, the greatest soldier, the most perfect master of men, in India.'

Colonel Malleson

'A nobler spirit never went forth to fight his country's battles. . . . I never saw another like him, and never expect to do so.'   *Sir Herbert Edwardes*

I wish to thank Mr. Sydney Maiden for the help he has given me, also Mr. W. Angelo for allowing me to read the unpublished autobiography of his father, who served with Nicholson in the second Sikh war and the Indian Mutiny.

Contents

7

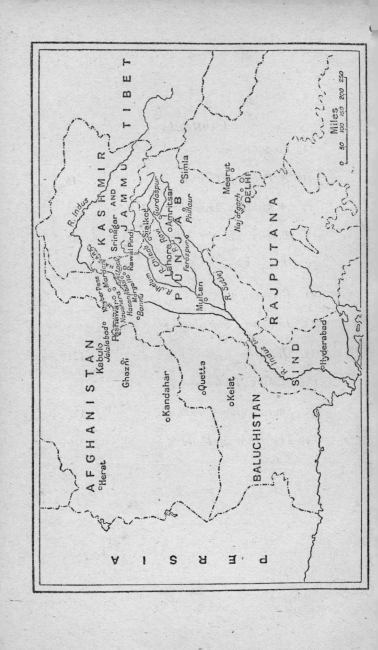

CHAPTER I

Preparation

A BOY aged three was alone in a room lashing the air savagely with a knotted handkerchief. His mother, entering suddenly, asked what he was doing.

'I am trying to get a blow at the Devil,' answered the lad gravely. 'He wants me to be bad. If I could get him down I'd kill him.'

A good deal of the boy's future life was to be spent in lashing the devil without and checking the devil within.

He was born in Dublin on the 11th of December, 1822. His father, Alexander Nicholson, was a doctor, the descendant of a Cumberland family of Quakers resident in Ireland since the 17th century. His mother belonged to the Ulster family of Hogg which had also lived in Ireland from the 17th century. As she was a member of the orthodox church, Alexander's marriage resulted in his expulsion from the Quaker community. He sustained the blow with equanimity and they spent ten happy years together, reading the Bible and producing a family of five boys and two girls. John, who began to fight the devil at such an early age, was their eldest son. By the time he was four he could both read and write.

The doctor's practice was increasing when he died of a fever caught while attending to his patients, and his widow was left with a family of seven and a slender income derived from the rents of several small estates. For a year she resided at Lisburn, where her mother still lived; then she went to Delgany in County Wicklow, where the older boys attended a day school run by the clergyman of the parish. It is a common saying that remarkable men take after their mothers, but there are grounds for believing that in John Nicholson's case it was the other way about, and that Mrs. Nicholson took after her son. At Delgany she worked as a district visitor and she made a habit of letting one of her children accompany her as a reward for progress at school. Once, when John was the chosen companion, she happened to pass a cottage without calling at it and he wanted to know why.

'They are such bad people that I do not go near them,' she replied.

John's comment on this, she afterwards asserted, altered her future line of conduct as a district visitor:

'God makes His sun to rise upon the evil and the good, and sends His rain upon the just and the unjust,' said the lad of nine.

Mrs. Nicholson was a Spartan woman with a stately carriage, a dignified manner and a resolute countenance. Occasionally her financial difficulties weighed upon her, and noting the troubled look on her face, John comforted her as best he could. 'Don't fret, Mamma,' he once said with a kiss; 'when I'm a big man I'll make plenty of money and I'll give it all to you.' His own patience under affliction was demonstrated in a manner that deeply impressed her. During a holiday at Lisburn he was experimenting with gunpowder when it exploded and blinded him. Covering his face with his hands, he went to his mother and said, 'Mamma, the gunpowder has blown up in my face.' Having thus warned her, he removed his hands and she saw that his face was black and bleeding and that he could not open his eyes. He lay, closely bandaged and in total darkness, for ten days without a murmur, only expressing his anxiety for his mother's state of mind. When the bandages were at last removed his sight was unimpaired.

But at the Delgany school his mind was being inflamed by the thrilling stories of campaigns told him by the drill-sergeant, and in his twelfth year his mother sent him to the Royal School at Dungannon in County Tyrone, where he remained for four years. He soon gained a reputation for fighting bullies and protecting the weak, not because he had any particular sympathy with weakness, but because he thoroughly enjoyed fighting. He was good at games, but his temper was quickly aroused by meanness and he would break off a game in order to fight someone who was playing unfairly. He could not have been very popular with his schoolfellows because, though reasonably idle in class, he was of a retiring disposition and awkwardly honest. It is even recorded that he was never known to tell a lie, which, if improbable, is more likely to have been true of him than of others who have earned a like reputation.

At the age of sixteen he left school, and his uncle, James Hogg, who had made a fortune in India and was about to become a director of the East India Company, was able to get him a cadetship in the Bengal Infantry. This was very fortunate for John, who without his uncle's influence would have had to go through a period of training at Addiscombe, the Military College of the East India Company. He said good-bye to his mother, whose parting words were 'Never forget to read your Bible, John,' and left home for London, where he stayed a month or so with Uncle James, who paid for his journey and bought his outfit. Towards the close of February, 1839, he sailed in the *Camden* for India, where he hoped to make money for his mother, to achieve distinction as a soldier, and to read the Bible daily. The Old Testament in particular was an ideal book for Empire-makers, for it encouraged them to smite Amalekites of every description.

On the long sea-journey via the Cape Nicholson was picked out from a boisterous batch of cadets by the ship's captain, who was much struck by his aloofness from his companions, his disciplined demeanour, his studiousness of disposition. The other lads probably thought him a pious prig; the captain found him restful. He did not regret his behaviour on the boat, for when two years later his brother Alexander was about to follow him to India John (aged 18) wrote a few lines of advice: 'You should endeavour to improve your manners on the passage, as without good manners you can never advance yourself. Be reserved and prudent in your communications with your fellow-passengers and those with whom you may be associated on your arrival in this country.'

He reached Calcutta in July and stayed for a while with one of his uncle's friends. In August he was temporarily posted to the 41st Regiment of Native Infantry at Benares, where for the first time he felt lonely. Living by himself in a small bungalow, surrounded by natives who could not understand a word of English, unable himself to speak more than fifty words of their language, and cut off from the social pleasures of his brother-officers by temperamental disaffinity and the need for economy, he filled in his spare time by studying Hindustani, reading as many books as he could obtain, writing letters to his mother and wondering what his brothers and sisters were doing: 'I often, when I am sitting alone here in the evening, think of you all at home, and say to myself, there is no place like *home*.' Fortunately for him a paternal uncle was staying at Benares just then and gave him a horse, which enabled him to take exercise in the heat and to attend his parades in comfort. Though able to live within his pay, he was worried by the thought that when permanently posted to a corps up-country he would have to raise 400 rupees for a tent and hire camels for transport. But in spite of heat, solitude, drills, courts martial, financial worries and Indian servants, he did not forget his mother's admonition: 'I go to church every Sunday, and read my chapter every day. . . . I find dear Mary's Bible very useful.'

In December he was posted to the 27th Native Infantry, stationed at Ferozpur on the Sutlej river, and wrote to tell his mother that the journey there would take three months and that the march would be an unpleasant one. His prophecy was fulfilled in a way he had not anticipated: at Meerut a servant stole his forks and spoons; at Karnal his tent was cut open in the night and he woke up to find that his trunk, pistols, dressing-case, several other articles and £10 were missing; and at Karnal, too, not content with losing his property, he lost his temper with a senior officer who had dared to remind him of his duty. He was so furious that he wanted to fight a duel and asked the doctor to carry his challenge; the doctor refused and he tried someone else, who also refused. While storming round the camp in search of challengers his temper cooled off and honour was ultimately satisfied with hand-shaking.

At Ludhiana he was introduced to the political agent, Colonel Wade, who gave him a note to the heads of all the villages en route, ordering them to supply him with provisions on payment. Instead of helping him the production of this authority aroused feelings of independence in the breasts of the Sikh headmen, who spoke contemptuously of Colonel Wade and told him that he could whistle for his food. However, he had a corporal's escort with him, and by threatening the village notabilities with a good flogging he made them see reason.

Ferozpur, a recently-established frontier post, was 'a perfect wilderness,' wrote Nicholson to his mother; 'there is not a tree or blade of grass within miles of us, and as to the tigers, there are two or three killed in the neighbouring jungle every day.' The soldiers had to start building huts for themselves the moment they arrived, and as the construction of a habitable bungalow cost an officer at least £40, Nicholson shared a stable with another officer until he could afford better quarters. When the hot winds began to blow the atmosphere in the stable became too oppressive for the study of oriental languages, but it did not keep him from the study of oriental literature: 'I have not forgot your parting advice to read my Bible daily,' he wrote to his mother in July, 1840; 'I have just recovered from a severe attack of fever, brought on by the want of proper shelter; but my new house will soon be finished, and then I hope I shall enjoy my usual health. You can have no idea how the hot weather enervates the body, and, if you do not take special care, the mind also. I am just finishing a most interesting work, which, if you have not already read, I strongly recommend you to do so; it is Faber's *Fulfilment of the Scriptural Prophecies.'*

He had scarcely settled in the 'new house' before his regiment was ordered to relieve another in Afghanistan. Early in 1841 it marched to Peshawar, penetrated the Khyber Pass and reached Jalalabad, where after a brush with one of the hill tribes Nicholson again settled down to learn Hindustani. His work was interrupted by an order which sent his regiment back to Peshawar in order to safeguard Shah Suja's harem of six hundred ladies, who were being threatened by mutinous Sikhs on their journey to the Afghan capital. Having frightened the Sikhs and escorted the ladies to Kabul, the regiment was then ordered to relieve the garrison at Ghazni. Nicholson now had time on his hands and resolutely attacked the languages he wished to learn, writing home to say that he would like to enter the service of Shah Suja, 'whom we have lately restored to the throne of Kabul, and whose army is officered by Europeans, who receive a much larger salary than they do when serving with their regiments. However, I shall soon pass in the language, and perhaps through my uncle's interest may obtain some appointment in Hindustan better worth having.'

Among the officers who were being relieved by the arrival of Nicholson's regiment at Ghazni was a young subaltern named Neville Chamberlain, who wrote of his meeting with Nicholson: 'We became friends at first sight, as is common with youth, and we were constantly together during the short time that intervened between his regiment taking over the fort and my regiment leaving for Kandahar. . . . He was then a tall, strong, slender youth, with regular features, and a quiet, reserved manner.'

CHAPTER II

A Political Comedy

WHILE John Nicholson is struggling with native dialects at Ghazni, we must consider the men whose policies sent him there.

In the early years of the 19th century the rulership of Afghanistan had been disputed by three brothers of the reigning family. One of them, Shah Suja, more by luck than good management, had eventually gained the throne of Kabul. Not by nature a man of action, he was never popular with his bellicose fellow-countrymen, and his hold on the state was insecure. He loved to read, to converse and to meditate; occupations which did not promote his efficiency in governing a people who loved to kill, to murder and to mutilate. After long periods of indolence he would sometimes prove worthy of his ancestry and order a wholesale massacre of his opponents, but by comparison with most of his race he was gentle and merciful. As a ruler he lacked vigour, firmness, judgment, and his failure as a leader of barbarians may be explained by the fact that he wrote an autobiography wherein his conduct on all occasions appears exemplary.

Towards the close of Shah Suja's brief reign a British Mission was dispatched to his court by Lord Minto, Governor-General of India, in order to counteract French influence in Persia. It was felt by the English authorities in London and Calcutta that Napoleon I might at any moment decide that Europe was too small for him and descend upon India with his invincible army. They did not pause to consider the difficulties in his way; they merely thought that as Alexander the Great had done

it Napoleon might do it, and that it would be as well
to have an ally of England on his line of march to the
Indian frontier. Early in 1809 Shah Suja received the
deputation at Peshawar, where the bad impression made
by the personal appearance of the Englishmen, whose
shaven faces aroused the contempt of the shaggy Afghan
warriors, was quickly removed by the costliness of the
presents they brought. Seated on a gilded throne, his
person ablaze with jewels, his turban sparkling with the
Koh-i-noor, Shah Suja informed his visitors that 'England and Kabul were designed by the Creator to be
united by bonds of everlasting friendship.' An agreement
between the two nations was duly signed; but a generation later, the Creator having reconsidered His design,
the English and Afghans were at war, an uncertifiable
number of men and women of both races were butchered,
and the 'bonds of everlasting friendship' were severed.

Shortly after the departure of the British Mission
from Peshawar Shah Suja was driven from his kingdom
by his brother Mahmud and became a prisoner in what
was then the Afghan province of Kashmir. Advised by
his brother's chief minister, Fateh Khan, to visit the great
Sikh ruler Ranjit Singh, who was anxious to have him
as a guest, Suja left Kashmir and journeyed to Lahore.
It soon appeared that Ranjit Singh was more desirous to
own the Koh-i-noor than to entertain the ex-King, for
he instantly demanded it as the price of his hospitality.
Suja demurred, but his host did not wish to argue the
point, made him a prisoner, starved him into subjection,
and then, as a pledge of eternal friendship, courteously
exchanged turbans, that of Suja's being decorated with
the Koh-i-noor. In this way the most famous diamond
in the world, which had once graced the headgear of the
Mogul emperors, came into the possession of the Sikh
Maharajah; while the royal fugitive, fearing that the
pledge of eternal friendship flavoured too much of the

next world to make his life secure in this, escaped via
the main sewer from Lahore, and after many vicissitudes,
which included a disastrous attempt to conquer Kashmir,
found an asylum and a pension in British territory.

Meanwhile life had not been dull in Afghanistan,
where another leading actor in our drama was about to
make his entrance on the stage. Preferring the luxuries
to the responsibilities of kingship, Suja's brother Mahmud left the management of the country in the hands
of his chief minister Fateh Khan, whose power was resented by the other members of the royal house. They
eagerly awaited an opportunity to encompass his down-
fall, and when it occurred they made the most of it.
Fateh Khan was ambitious; he wished to beat the
Persians, who were encroaching upon the western border
of Afghanistan, and he wished to gain control of Herat,
which was governed by Mahmud's brother. Encamping
outside the walls of Herat, he received the chiefs of the
place, while his young brother took advantage of their
absence, paid a friendly visit to the city with his followers,
murdered the palace guards, seized the governor, looted
the treasury, violated the harem and stripped the jewelled
waistband from the person of a royal princess. These
acts, especially the last, aroused the indignation of the
reigning house, and when Fateh Khan returned from
Persia he was taken prisoner by Mahmud's son, who
pierced the pupils of his eyes with a dagger. Resolutely
refusing to betray the whereabouts of his young brother,
Fateh Khan was condemned to death. He was brought
before Mahmud and other members of the royal family,
all of whom were inspired with the hatred born of
jealousy. After accusing the blind man of the many
insults and injuries they had suffered in the days of his
greatness, one of them stepped up to him and, seizing
his left ear, sliced it off with a knife, another removed
his right ear, a third hacked off his nose, a fourth his

right hand, a fifth his left hand. Fateh Khan received these attentions with dignity, merely requesting that the business should be expedited; but when his beard, sacred to a Mohammedan, was cut off his fortitude forsook him and he burst into tears. A slash with a sabre now took off his right foot, another blow severed his left foot, and finally his throat was cut.

An account of these unreasonable and erratic proceedings reached Fateh Khan's young brother, who had fled to Kashmir, and from that moment the reigning family of Afghanistan was doomed. The young brother's name was Dost Mahomed Khan. He had started life as a sweeper at the sacred tomb of the father of the prophet Noah. Later he was allowed to serve his famous brother, whose water he carried and whose pipe he bore. Closely observing everything, but taking care not to push himself forward, he at last gained the favourable notice of Fateh Khan by slaying one of that minister's enemies. Thereafter Dost Mahomed never looked back. He was given a military command and quickly became notorious not only for courage as a fighter and skill as a leader, but for his many cruelties and excesses. All of these qualities were exercised to the full during the war which followed his departure from Kashmir to avenge his brother's murder. He collected an army, marched on Kabul, won it by a stratagem, punctured the eyes of the governor—an Afghan habit hallowed by tradition—and succeeded, after many trying adventures and treacherous murders, in gaining control over the entire country.

From 1826 until 1838, although Shah Suja made several attempts to regain his lost throne, Dost Mahomed was the supreme ruler of Afghanistan. His government was a great improvement on that of his predecessors. A complete reformation of his moral character seems to have taken place from the moment be became Amir. Before that he had been a persistent drunkard and

lecher, a robber and murderer, too busy scalping his
opponents and ravishing their harems to pay due attention to the mysteries of religion. But once in possession
of power he announced his determination to turn over
a new leaf, and turned it. He became abstemious and
moderately chaste; he attended closely to the business
of government; he taught himself to read and write;
he studied the Koran; he redressed wrongs, relieved the
poor, helped the suffering, listened patiently to com-
plaints, was accessible and courteous to all. His manners
were affable, his habits simple, and such was his equity
that an act of harshness by one of his officials would be
met with the query: 'Is Dost Mahomed dead that there
is no justice?' As a fighter he was intrepid, as a ruler
he was shrewd; in both capacities he showed no mercy
when his sovereignty was disputed by war or intrigue,
and his chieftains knew what to expect when they received such hints as this: 'In the event of your not
attending to my advice, such circumstances will happen
as will make you bite the finger of repentance.' But his
self-discipline, his frank dealing, his ready sympathy
and his eagerness to be fair, made him popular with his
people, and his reign would have been both happy and
prosperous but for the capture of Peshawar by Ranjit
Singh.

This extraordinary personage, quite the most remarkable Indian of the 19th century, now claims our attention. He was one of the four principal characters in the
political comedy which had such a tragic finale. Object-
ing to the exercise of any authority but his own, he
asserted his independence at the age of seventeen by
murdering his mother and taking control of his property.
An unusual endowment of cunning and common sense
was his from the start, his ambition being well seasoned
with sagacity. The power of the East India Company
was growing and the steady march of the English was

heard along his borders. In order to realise his dream
and to build a great Sikh empire he knew that he would
have to fight or make friends with his white neighbours;
so he visited their camps in disguise, noted the efficiency
of the British-trained native troops, decided that they
were more than a match for his own, concluded an
alliance of "perpetual friendship" with the Company,
and began to create an army by attracting deserters from
the British ranks with offers of good pay and engaging
French, Italian and Dutch officers to train his troops.
With this army the dominions of the Khalsa (the "elect"
or "chosen people," as the Sikhs called themselves) were
rapidly extended. As time went on Ranjit Singh acquired
many territories that were once part of the Mogul
Empire—Multan, Kashmir, the Derajat, Peshawar—and
he became known as "the Lion of the Punjab." He even
had his eye on Sind, but the English were too quick for
him there.

His achievements were the result of adroit statecraft.
They were attained rather by the show of force than by
the use of it. If artifice failed, he tried bullying, and if
bullying failed he resorted to arms; but when he had
got what he wanted he usually managed to soften the
blow by some little device designed to make the result
appear like a gentleman's agreement, as in the case of
Shah Suja and the Koh-i-noor. In political astuteness and
tenacity of purpose he was unapproached by his rivals.
Before the age of forty he was supreme throughout the
Punjab and had made a sect numbering about half a
million the strongest nation in India, every Sikh enjoying
all the privileges of Khalsa citizenship: exemption
from taxation, freedom to oppress, liberty to live like a
brigand.

Having welded his people together and obtained
complete personal ascendancy over them, having carved
out an empire for himself and held it securely through a

long reign, this almost fabulous figure made no attempt to devise a system of government and was wholly indifferent to the welfare of his subjects, being firmly convinced that self-interest was the mainspring of all action. He was proud of the fact that he could neither read nor write, yet his memory was phenomenal, and he knew the name, position and history of about twelve thousand villages in his kingdom. There were no law courts, no schools, no prisons throughout the Punjab in his time; the only punishments were fines for the rich and mutilation, the lopping of an arm or a leg, for the poor. He never made or repaired a road, a bridge or a canal; he did not construct a single work of public utility, unless forts may be so called; the towns were allowed to crumble, the villages to decay; the inhabitants of the former, always excepting the Sikhs, were treated as slaves, while the peasantry in the latter could die of starvation. He was incredibly greedy, mulcted Sikhs and Moslems alike of their wealth, and though he permitted his revenue collectors to cheat him and make their fortunes he balanced the account by plundering their families when they died or were disgraced. He allowed the pay of his troops to fall into arrears, and when they became mutinous he gave them something on account. His vaults were crammed with cash and jewels, and in later life he began to bury his money underground.

To European visitors he appeared 'a bit mad,' for his curiosity was limitless and he would ask innumerable questions on unconnected subjects, such as God, Napoleon Bonaparte, hell, artillery, paradise, the soul, horses, Satan, salt, opium, monogamy and the ten commandments, which he thought ridiculous, especially the tenth. He could be very amusing, his witticisms being pointed by a very expressive single eye, which looked extremely droll in his pox-pitted, much-puckered face. He was a superstitious atheist, for though by nature a complete

sceptic, he went to the holy city of Amritsar every year
to perform his devotions and sometimes even visited the
tombs of the Moslem saints. He had a passion for horses
and occasionally waged war in order to seize an animal
to which he had taken a fancy and which had been refused him by a neighbouring rajah; but his favourite
hobby, apart from the fun of accumulating wealth, was
drinking. He loved to circulate the cup and to keep it circulating, his only serious complaint being that he could
not drink like a fish and remain sober enough to continue
indefinitely drinking like a fish, just as it grieved him that
he could not eat like an elephant without vomiting. His
feasts invariably ended in drunken orgies and the promis-
cuous bestialisation of host, guests and nautch-girls. In
the enjoyment of women, too, he felt himself ill-used, for
the time came when a serious ailment, which he referred
to as a weak digestion, lessened his appreciation of the
beautiful Kashmir girls who surrounded him. Lament-
ing that he was now deprived of much innocent pleasure,
he solaced himself with less normal forms of indulgence,
and some of his European visitors were shocked at the
influence acquired over him by the effeminate son of his
prime minister.

Until the age of fifty his iron constitution withstood
great hardships in the field and prolonged debauches in
the palace. Then he had a paralytic seizure, followed by
a period of enforced abstinence. Recovering partially,
he went back to the bottle and the dancers, but his great
days as a toper were over and the only amusement he
could get out of his nautch-girls was to mount them on
horses and make them gallop. Great age seemed to
overtake him suddenly; his beard went white, his body
became frail, and he could not walk without support;
but the little broad-browed, one-eyed warrior refused to
be lifted into the saddle and surmounted the difficulty by
stepping on to the neck of a kneeling attendant, who then

rose slowly and transferred his load to the back of a horse, on which the Maharajah sat like a centaur. Even in this physical condition he was eager to add to his kingdom and begged the English Governor-General to let him have fifty thousand muskets. 'The constitutional restlessness of the old man of Lahore seems to increase with his age,' grumbled the Governor-General, who declined to send the arms, but offered instead a doctor and a dentist.

Our fourth leading actor has now appeared on the scene, and we must take a look at him before he begins to play the rôle for which he was so utterly miscast.

In his youth Lord Auckland had imbibed whiggish ideas from his father, and when the party came into power he was appointed President of the Board of Trade and Master of the Mint. In 1834 he became First Lord of the Admiralty, and about a year later, on Lord Melbourne's recommendation, the court of directors of the East India Company made him Governor-General of India. He arrived at Calcutta in February, 1836. It was hoped that he would pursue a policy productive of peace with dividends, and certainly there was nothing warlike about him. It was his ambition, he declared, to do good to his fellow-creatures; but like so many men with a similar ambition it would have been better for a large number of his fellow-creatures if Lord Auckland had never been born.

He was a gentle, pleasant, kind-hearted person, beloved by his family, among whom he was known as "the comical dog," and popular with his servants. His manners were beyond reproach; he was industrious, not in the least pompous, and there was nothing about him to which anyone could take exception save perhaps an addiction to playful punning. His consideration for the native servants and soldiers in India won their affection and respect. He was the first Governor-General to adopt an entirely human attitude towards the natives; he frequently admonished British magistrates for the callousness and indifference with which they judged the unprotected and oppressed; he did not think it "sporting" of English landowners to hunt "niggers" with bloodhounds; and when he visited the north-west provinces during the famine of 1838 he not only subscribed handsomely to the relief fund from his private purse but instituted an inquiry concerning preventive measures that led to excellent results and marked an epoch in the history of the Indian people. He was in fact an able and conscientious administrator, and within the limits of his work as a civil servant his sister Emily Eden was not far wrong when she wrote: 'If he *has* a fault (I don't think he has but *if* he has) it is a slight disposition to trifle with the English letters'—in other words his dispatches were usually a day too late for the steamer. Unfortunately he was not content with being a good civil servant, and to cover up his grave mistakes in other fields he suppressed facts and tampered with official correspondence. It must be admitted that few public men in English history have had more urgent personal reasons for editing their records with unscrupulous care.

He arrived in India at an inauspicious moment. Like their predecessors a generation earlier, the English politicians of the eighteen-thirties were nervous about the influence of a foreign power in Persia. This time it was not France, for Napoleon was dead and buried and shortly to be reburied, but Russia. It was the shadow cast by this vast and incalculable power over Persia that once more reminded the British authorities that Afghanistan lay on the direct road from Persia to India and forced them to read books by travellers who had visited Kabul and Herat. There could be no doubt that Russia, in order to excuse her territorial acquisitions in the west of

Persia, was encouraging the Shah to make similar depredations to the east of his dominions. The Shah was only too eager to accept the help and advice of Russia, for his ancestors had once possessed Afghanistan, and in any case it would be more profitable to fight the Amir than to fight the Tsar. He therefore decided to commence operations by laying siege to the city of Herat, which was the key to Kabul and commanded the only route whereby a formidable army could march on India from the north-west.

Dost Mahomed regarded the Shah's policy with mixed feelings. The territory of Herat was the only part of Afghanistan still in the hands of the ruling family he had dispossessed, the governor being one of the murderers of his brother Fateh Khan. Furthermore, he would have welcomed the Shah as an ally in a religious war against the Sikhs, who had taken Peshawar from him. In these respects the prospect of the fall of Herat left him calm. But there was no knowing where the Shah would stop, with Russia pushing him on, and the Dost felt that an alliance with the English would be safer for him, especially as they were friendly with Ranjit Singh and might influence that ruler to relinquish Peshawar.

Anxious to lose no time in coming to a friendly understanding with the Indian Government, Dost Mahomed wrote to Lord Auckland: 'The field of my hopes, which had before been chilled by the cold blast of wintry times, has by the happy tidings of your Lordship's arrival become the envy of the garden of paradise. The late transactions in this quarter, the conduct of reckless and misguided Sikhs, and their breach of treaty, are well known to your Lordship. Communicate to me whatever may suggest itself to your wisdom for the settlement of the affairs of this country, that it may serve as a rule for my guidance. I hope that your Lordship will consider me and my country as your own.'

The kind invitation conveyed in the last sentence was in due course accepted by his Lordship, but at the moment he had other engagements and restored the temperature referred to in the first sentence with the frigid reply that it was 'not the practice of the British Government to interfere with the affairs of other independent states.' Nevertheless he hinted that he would send 'some gentlemen' to Kabul to discuss business matters with the Amir; and towards the close of 1836 a Mission, headed by an officer named Alexander Burnes, set out for Afghanistan with the ostensible object of working out the policy of 'opening the River Indus to commerce.'

Burnes was regarded as an authority on the country through which he was about to journey. Some years previously he had taken a gift of horses to Ranjit Singh and had travelled up the Indus, where his presence was bemoaned by a native in the words 'Sind is now gone, since the English have seen the river which is the road to its conquest.' Later he had visited Afghanistan and Persia, published an account of his wanderings and become the lion of a London season. Incidentally he had made the acquaintance of Shah Suja and Dost Mahomed and had formed an opinion of the latter as favourable as his opinion of the former was unfavourable.

Now he again took the route through Sind and was hospitably entertained by the Amirs of that province at Hyderabad. He then proceeded, via Peshawar, to Kabul, where in September, 1837, the Mission was received with pomp and housed in splendour. Dost Mahomed welcomed them with enthusiasm and Burnes displayed the presents he had brought, describing them as 'some of the rarities of Europe.' The Dost replied courteously: 'You yourselves are the rarities, the sight of which best pleases me.' He did not mean to be ironical, but his court made unfavourable comparisons between the pins, needles, pistols, telescopes and such-like knick-knacks brought by Burnes—chosen in order 'to exhibit the superiority of British manufacturers'—and the costly gifts which had been showered on Shah Suja nearly thirty years before.

As the English make a stern rule never to meddle in the affairs of another country unless a handsome profit can be made out of it, Burnes went to Kabul as a 'commercial agent'; but he soon became involved in diplomacy. Dost Mahomed expressed his wish that Peshawar should be restored, Burnes agreed to mediate between him and Ranjit Singh, and the Dost promised not to receive Russian or Persian representatives at his court. But Burnes could not say anything definite until he had received instructions from Calcutta, so he kept the Amir quiet with phrases of amity and optimism. All was going swimmingly between them when Burnes, overcome by the importance of his mission and the part he was acting, made a false step. In the event of Persian and Russian aggression in western Afghanistan, he promised financial backing to Dost Mahomed's brother, who was governor of Kandahar. He was promptly censured by Lord Auckland for exceeding his powers, the promise was withdrawn, and as there was every reason to believe that Herat would be taken by the Shah of Persia, Dost Mahomed's brother made an alliance with the Persians and Russians in order to save his skin.

But Dost Mahomed himself remained steadily pro-British. He was really anxious to come to an agreement with the Indian Government, and when a Russian emissary arrived at Kabul with friendly assurances and advantageous promises from the Czar he refused to treat with him, even offering to expel the emissary from his kingdom if Burnes desired it. Lord Auckland, however, seemed determined to antagonise the Dost, for he refused to allow Burnes or any one else to mediate between the Amir and Ranjit Singh for the return of Peshawar to the former. This placed Burnes in a very awkward position; his hands were tied; he could now promise nothing in return for the friendship of Dost Mahomed, whose continual refusal to form an alliance with Persia was so vital to British interests. There were protracted interviews between the two men and in many passages of his letters Burnes did his utmost to persuade the Governor-General of the reasonableness of the Dost's demands and of his eagerness to remain on terms of friendship with the British. Beyond suppressing or garbling such passages when the letters were published in a blue book, Lord Auckland took no notice of them and at length issued his fiat: the proposals of the Amir were rejected, Peshawar would remain in the hands of the Sikhs, Dost Mahomed must refuse to ally himself with any other state; and in return the British Government would prevent Ranjit Singh from attacking the Dost's dominions. But as Ranjit Singh had no intention of attacking Afghanistan, and as he would certainly have been defeated if he had made the attempt, the Dost received this offer with a 'Thank you for nothing' and his chief minister pertinently asked whether the Afghans were to provoke the hostility of Persia and Russia by adhering to the British and yet receive no protection from the latter? Nevertheless Dost Mahomed persevered in his offers of a friendship based on a reasonable quid pro quo and wrote personally to Lord Auckland begging for 'a little encouragement and power.' The answer was a flat negative, and Dost Mahomed opened negotiations with the Russian emissary; while Alexander Burnes, his mission a failure, left Kabul for India at the end of April, 1838.

Throughout these exchanges Lord Auckland had

been at Simla, described by the historian John Kaye as
'the cradle of more political insanity than any place
within the limits of Hindostan,' and had not been in
touch with his Council in the capital. His companions
at the hill-station were William Macnaghten, chief
secretary to the Government, Henry Torrens, Macnaghten's assistant, John Colvin, private secretary to the
Governor-General, and Lord Auckland's two sisters.
Macnaghten was an extremely able civil servant, whose
knowledge of oriental languages and customs was
profound and whose reputation as a steady, cautious
diplomat was considerable. Torrens was of a type easily
recognisable, predestined to attract a man of Auckland's
chaste and rather old-maidish disposition; the type that
knows something about everything, that can with equal
ease quote a poem or act in a charade or write a state
paper or plan a campaign or play the piano or pay a
compliment or amuse the ladies without shocking them;
he was gay, graceful, airy, mercurial, charming, pleasant
to have about the house, one who could always be
depended upon to invent distractions and keep things
going. Colvin was not so versatile, but made up for his
lack of drawing-room accomplishments by the quickness
of his judgments and the tenacity of his character; he
was extremely vain, but his vanity was that of the
puppet-master, of the man who likes to control without
being seen. Of Auckland's two sisters it need only be
said that they worshipped him and that it would have
required a stronger nature than his to prevent such
adoration from going to his head. He did not lack sense
and such opinions as he had were sound and humane,
but he wanted firmness, was easily influenced by his
environment, and too readily listened to the more
resolute and irresponsible views of his companions. In
these circumstances and in such an atmosphere was the
Afghan War hatched.

The official mind does not change, does not adapt itself to new conditions, and because the Indian Government had remained friendly with Shah Suja, had pensioned him and had even encouraged him to recover his lost throne, there seemed no particular reason why Dost Mahomed should now be helped or encouraged, though every one who knew all the circumstances strongly advised such a course of action. In spite of the fact that the Afghans had shown again and again that they did not want Suja and had been equally emphatic in their allegiance to the Dost, Lord Auckland could not get it out of his head that Suja had a legitimate claim to the throne of Kabul, possibly because the right of the English to their Indian possessions resembled too closely the right claimed by Dost Mahomed to his own conquests. Besides, the Dost was an independent man, a fellow of spirit, and it would better serve British interests were a puppet to rule Afghanistan, one who would be entirely amenable to advice and even subject to orders.

The promptings of Lord Auckland's official mind were strengthened not only by the forceful Colvin and the effeminate Torrens, but by the warnings of the British Government, which advised strong measures to deal with Russian intrigue and the menace of the Persian ruler's army before Herat. It was believed that if Herat fell, the Shah, egged on by the Tsar, would overrun Afghanistan and possibly descend upon India. At length Lord Auckland acted, but he was still guided by caution. He sent Macnaghten at the head of a Mission to Ranjit Singh for the purpose of cementing an alliance between the Maharajah and Shah Suja, the object being to recover the latter's possessions with the aid of a Sikh army, the Indian Government supplying the necessary cash and providing officers to direct operations. Ranjit Singh received the Mission with much ceremony and at once began to talk of war, women, wine, the weather, Sanskrit, shrapnel, poetry, hunting and Herat, passing from one subject to another with bewildering rapidity and displaying an equal interest in each. For example:

'Are you a good huntsman?' asked Ranjit.

'No,' answered Macnaghten.

'Do you know Arabic?'

'Yes.'

'Then recite a couplet in that language.'

It was difficult to discuss business during this flood of small talk, but the next day Ranjit listened patiently while Macnaghten expounded the policy of the Governor-General. The Maharajah was reminded that some years previously he had made a treaty with Shah Suja. 'Do you think it would be still for your benefit that the treaty should stand good, and would it be agreeable to your wishes that the British Government should become a party to that treaty?' asked Macnaghten. 'This would be adding sugar to milk,' replied Ranjit; and although Macnaghten made it plain that the Governor-General would have preferred independent action on the part of the Sikh ruler, the wily Ranjit refused to listen to such a proposal and insisted on British co-operation. He also requested that British troops should take part in the expedition. Macnaghten made a guarded reply, merely suggesting that 'circumstances might compel us,' etc. Having satisfied himself that he would be handsomely in pocket over the transaction, Ranjit signed the treaty, which was then submitted to Shah Suja, who after some haggling added his signature to it.

At this point in the proceedings it was perfectly clear that, backed by the authority and the treasury of the Indian Government, a force of Sikhs was to march on Kabul from Peshawar, and that a force of Suja's followers, with a few English officers, was to march on Kandahar, Suja having insisted that he should lead his own troops and not appear among his people as the puppet of the British or the Sikhs. But now the policy of the Governor-General took a wider sweep. During the absence of Macnaghten, who was busy arranging the treaty, and under the influence of Torrens and Colvin, who were fascinated by the vista of conquest opening out before them, Auckland's native caution forsook him and he determined to send a large British-Indian army to Afghanistan in support of Suja. He appointed Macnaghten as 'Envoy and Minister' for the Government of India at the court of Suja, with Burnes to assist him. After which he issued a proclamation in which Dost Mahomed's character was blackened, Shah Suja's was whitened, and the possibility of the capture of Herat was given as the main reason for the expedition.

But the proclamation had scarcely been distributed throughout India before the news arrived that, largely owing to the heroic fortitude displayed by a young Englishman named Eldred Pottinger, the Shah of Persia had been forced to raise the siege of Herat, which had lasted for ten months, and had returned to his capital with what he called 'our world-subduing army.' The one excuse for the invasion of Afghanistan by a British-Indian army had now gone, but Lord Auckland was soon ready with another and publicly stated that the army would march in order to substitute a friendly for a hostile power at Kabul.

The 'Army of the Indus,' as it was napoleonically named, assembled in November, 1838, at Ferozpur, where a meeting between Ranjit Singh and Lord Auckland had been arranged to give the expedition a good 'send-off.'

To the thunder of artillery, the rumbling of drums, the roar of the crowd, the blare of brass instruments and the trumpeting of elephants, Ranjit Singh arrived. To the accompaniment of less hubbub, the Governor-General went forth to greet him. There was a day of

H.D.—2

festivity, of gift-presentation and gift-appreciation, of crowds and colours and din and disorder. Although the Maharajah had to be assisted as he tottered along, his limbs being almost powerless, the magnetism of his bright, rolling eye and quick, questioning tongue was felt by every one, and it was generally agreed that, mentally at least, he was still very much alive. His visit was returned and Ranjit Singh's reception of the Englishman outshone the Governor-General's reception of the Sikh. In the matter of light entertainment, too, the contortions of the Maharajah's dancing girls and the strange antics of his male performers seemed to emphasise the formality of Lord Auckland's evening party. The military skill of the two armies was then displayed; the Sikhs showed that they had not learnt their tactics from European instructors for nothing, and the British army fought a brilliant battle against an imaginary foe and won it.

The celebrations were continued at Lahore, whither Ranjit Singh had repaired, followed by Lord Auckland, after the junketings at Ferozpur. As a guest of very special honour, Auckland had to drink the heady blend favoured by Ranjit Singh, who pressed it to his lips: a brandy distilled from raisins and sugared with powdered pearls. At the conclusion of the final night's entertainment they took leave of one another; or rather Lord Auckland, bending formally over the horizontal and unconscious figure of the drunken Maharajah, uttered the conventional words of farewell that etiquette demanded. Meanwhile Shah Suja, his white beard dyed black, was leading his troops into Sind, and the Afghan War had begun.

CHAPTER III

A Military Tragedy

I n the beautiful December weather of 1838 the Army of the Indus, reduced in size since the good news had arrived from Herat, began its march towards Kandahar. The British-Indian force was 9,500 strong, with 38,000 camp-followers and 30,000 transport camels, while Suja's levies numbered about 6,000.

The roundabout route through Sind was undertaken for two reasons. Firstly Ranjit Singh would not allow the British-Indian troops to traverse the Punjab, and secondly it had been decided that the Amirs of Sind should finance the Governor-General's policy. Many years before the Amirs had paid tribute to Kabul, and though Shah Suja had renounced all his claims the present circumstances necessitated a revival of them. Ranjit Singh demanded fifteen lakhs of rupees, Suja a further ten, and in addition the troops had to be supplied with provisions. The Amirs naturally objected to this arrangement and incidentally reminded the British authorities of their promise that the River Indus should only be used for commercial traffic. Both of these objections were met with the stern warning that if the Amirs placed any obstacles in the way of 'the just and necessary undertaking' in which the Indian Government was engaged, they would be deprived of their possessions. The Amirs still demurred, but gave way when a British force marched on Hyderabad; after which the independent province of Sind was peacefully plundered and the natives watched with growing resentment the passage through their villages of what to them was a multitude of marauders.

The army, spreading dismay and provoking hostility as it went, leaving hundreds of dead camels and bullocks in its track and baring the country of supplies for man and beast, passed through Sind and entered Baluchistan, where the Khan of Kelat was not as helpful in the matter of provisions as he might have been and even suggested that the war was an error of judgment on the part of the British. At a later date he paid for this lack of enthusiasm with his life. Sixty miles of the Bolan Pass exhausted the troops, and when the army reached Quetta the men were on quarter-rations. Hearing that their march was not likely to be opposed in the south-western parts of Afghanistan, the Commander-in-Chief, Sir John Keane, decided to push on without delay, and on April 25th, 1839, Dost Mahomed's brother having fled before the oncoming force, Shah Suja entered Kandahar with Macnaghten the Envoy riding close behind him.

The populace was excited and noisy and Macnaghten reported that the Shah had been 'received with feelings nearly amounting to adoration,' but when a fortnight later a grand demonstration of welcome was staged on the plain before the city not more than a hundred Afghans went out to see the show. This was partly due to the Shah's exhibitions of petulance whenever his new adherents clamoured for places in the government: 'Since it took God Almighty six days to make heaven and earth,' he told them, 'it is hard that you will not allow me, a mere mortal, as much time to settle the affairs of a kingdom.' But the sudden decline in the restored monarch's popularity was primarily due to the presence of his infidel allies, who were making themselves comfortable in the royal palaces and whose very presence was deemed sacrilegious in a city where the shirt of the Prophet Mohammed was enshrined in a mosque.

Owing to lack of provisions the army was forced to remain at Kandahar till the crops ripened, and two months elapsed before it set out for Ghazni. Leaving his siege guns behind at Kandahar, the British Commander-in-Chief advanced upon the strongest fortress in the country with a few field guns; but thanks to the assistance of a traitor from within the walls, who explained how the main gate could be blown in with gunpowder, the assault was successful. A fierce resistance was overcome at the cost of much carnage and Shah Suja took possession of the place. He did not celebrate his triumph with clemency. A number of Mohammedan veterans known as Ghazis, inflamed by their priests and convinced that they would enter paradise if they slaughtered the infidels or were slain in the attempt, had attacked the Shah's camp. They were routed and fifty of them were taken. Brought into the Shah's presence, they were tactless enough to taunt the monarch over his allegiance to infidels, and one of them, not content with criticism, stabbed a royal attendant. The Shah, who did not share their extreme views on infidels, ordered them to be destroyed, and for an hour or more, to the accompaniment of much merriment, the executioners hacked and maimed these religious enthusiasts, killing most and leaving the remainder to bleed to death from the wounds thus inflicted. John Nicholson and others had cause to regret this incident at a later date.

The defection of his brother at Kandahar had not surprised Dost Mahomed, but the fall of Ghazni, which he thought impregnable, shook him. After one attempt at negotiation he put himself at the head of his followers and marched forth to beard the British. But the Afghans were never at their best on a losing side and they began to desert him. He besought them to be true to their creed and to make one stand against the infidels. 'You have eaten my salt these thirteen years,' he reminded them. 'Grant me but one favour in requital for that long period of maintenance and kindness—enable me to die with honour. Stand by the brother of Fateh Khan while he executes one last charge against the cavalry of these Feringhee dogs; in that onset he will fall; then go and make your own terms with Shah Suja.' There was no response. He discharged them and rode off with a few loyal followers to the mountains beyond the border.

On August 6th the British army reached Kabul and the next day, after thirty years of exile, Shah Suja entered the capital of Afghanistan. But not even Macnaghten, who rode with Burnes in the monarch's company, could have described the feelings that animated the crowd as 'nearly amounting to adoration.' A little curiosity was aroused by the presence of the British, but the inhabitants scarcely deigned to leave their doorways as the procession passed by. A month later the motley crew of Sikhs and Hindus, which had been conducted through the Khyber Pass by Captain Wade under the nominal leadership of Suja's son, trickled in. Wade had not had an easy journey. As was common in Ranjit's army, some of the troops had received no pay for almost two years and were in a state of open mutiny; to make matters worse, no sooner had Wade solved the financial problem than Ranjit Singh died, senile at 58. The Maharajah's debauches during Lord Auckland's visit had resulted in a stroke and during the last month of his life he lay supine and speechless, giving orders by signs and asking for information by movements of hand or eye. With the arrival of fever and dropsy he threw over all his native and European doctors and sent for priests of every denomination, just to be on the safe side. He endowed temples, gave elephants, horses, golden chairs and bedsteads as propitiatory offerings to various deities, lavished his hoarded treasures on the holy men of every persuasion, in order to win a few more hours of mental consciousness. On the last day of his life, June 27, 1839, he scattered a million sterling and issued an order that the Koh-i-noor should be sent to adorn the idol of Juggernaut. But apparently the intention was not good enough for the deity in question: Ranjit died and was duly cremated in company with his four wives and seven slave-girls specially selected for the honour. Wade's difficulties now increased. No one in the Sikh kingdom except Ranjit had any interest in the Afghan expedition and from the moment of his death every effort was made to frustrate it. At a later period the Sikh rulers conspired with the Afghans to expel the British, but they had not yet laid their plans and Wade managed, somehow, to get through to Kabul.

The news that the Afghan capital had fallen was received with enthusiasm in England. Sir John Keane was made a baron, Lord Auckland an earl, Macnaghten became a baronet, Wade a knight, and a number of lesser people were able to put letters after their names. But the Duke of Wellington was right when he said that the real difficulties would begin after the conclusion of the major military operations. The Shah was unpopular because he had regained his throne with an army of infidels, and it was realised at once that if the British left him he would lose it again. Nevertheless it was impossible to keep such a large army at so great a distance from India, and in the middle of October Sir John Keane marched off with a portion of the troops, saying to an officer just before his departure: 'Mark my words, it will not be long before there is here some signal catastrophe.' The rest of the army was stationed at Kabul, Kandahar and Ghazni, with small isolated detachments in various parts of the country.

From the autumn of '39 until the autumn of '41 there were innumerable punitive expeditions against marauding chieftains whose right to rob was questioned by the British authorities or whose objection to being governed by foreigners had to be overcome. Despite the warnings sent in by political officers in charge of different districts, Macnaghten believed that all was well, reproved his "alarmist" subordinates and sent reassuring messages to Lord Auckland. For a while the guerrilla tactics of Dost Mahomed were troublesome. Defeated in several minor engagements, he reappeared in another part of the country and became the rallying-point of disaffected tribes. 'I am like a wooden spoon,' said the Dost; 'you may throw me hither and thither, but I shall not be hurt.' He flitted from place to place, a will-o'-the-wisp. Shah Suja wanted to "hang the dog" and even Macnaghten began to think that hanging would be too good for him.

Towards the close of 1840, on the 2nd of November to be exact—a dark date in the story of the British occupation of Afghanistan—the Dost beat his opponents in open battle. But he realised that the victory was only a flash in the pan and decided that he could now surrender with honour. On the evening of November 4th Macnaghten and his military secretary, Captain George Lawrence, were returning from their customary ride beyond the British cantonments, which were situated outside the city of Kabul. They were both feeling depressed by the news of Dost Mahomed's victory. Suddenly, just as they were approaching the residency, a horseman rode up from behind and pushing his way between them asked if Macnaghten was 'the Lord Sahib.' On Lawrence's reply in the affirmative the horseman caught hold of the Envoy's bridle and exclaimed, 'The Amir, the Amir!' Macnaghten, amazed and agitated, called out, 'Who, who? Where, where?'

They turned and saw another horseman, a robust power-ful man, with sharp aquiline nose, highly-arched eye-brows and grey beard and moustache much in need of trimming, who rode up, flung himself from his saddle, seized the Envoy's stirrup-leather, took his hand and put it to his own forehead and lips as a sign of submission. Macnaghten instantly dismounted and said to the Amir, 'You are welcome, you are welcome.' He was indeed welcome, and a week later he went under a strong escort to India, where he was received with open arms and given a handsome pension at the expense of the Indian people.

Yet calmness did not descend upon the country with his departure, and the directors of the East India Com-pany were faced with the prospect of spending over a million a year in order to secure the allegiance of that relatively small section of the Afghan people who were 'within range of our guns and cavalry.' The cry of re-trenchment was soon heard in the council-chamber and Macnaghten was forced to reduce expenses. He began with the Ghilzyes, a tribe that was able to cut the com-munications between Afghanistan and India and so had been bribed into good behaviour. The moment they heard that no more cash was forthcoming the Ghilzyes occupied the passes south and east of Kabul and recom-menced their time-honoured practice of plundering. The subsidies paid to other chieftains were also curtailed and before long the entire country was leagued against the infidel who had only been tolerated on account of his purse. Urgent warnings of tribal hostility were received from officers on outpost duty; but Macnaghten, who had been appointed Governor of Bombay in the early autumn of 1841 and whose desire to leave a tranquil country behind him overmastered his judgment of current events, reported that 'everything was quiet from Dan to Beersheba' and that all was *couleur de rose.*

Yet, while his luggage was being packed in the early morning of November 2nd, '41, the storm which others had prophesied and he had disregarded suddenly banked up and burst over Kabul.

At this time Shah Suja, with his bodyguard and attendants, was housed in the fortress that overlooked Kabul, the famous Bala Hissar, while the majority of the British-Indian troops were in the cantonments beyond the city walls, where the residency was also situated. The cantonments had been placed and planned in such a way as to be completely at the mercy of an enemy occupying the hills, forts and villages in the vicinity. If some Afghan leader of genius, in an inspired moment, had hit on the ideal place in which to entrap and slaughter the invading army, he would have chosen the cantonments which had been approved by a British General, Sir Willoughby Cotton. In this vulnerable but pleasantly airy spot the British had made themselves reasonably comfortable, riding races, fishing, shooting, organising concert parties, playing cricket during the summer and skating in the winter, to the amazement of the Afghans, who failed to understand how a slide could be continued indefinitely. Some of the officers had managed to get their wives from India to live with them, but the majority made free with the Mohammedan zenanas, and this was one of the causes of the bitter hatred which burst forth on that November morning.

Incited by the chiefs whose allowances had been docked, a mob of looters and infidel-haters surrounded the house of Alexander Burnes, which was in the centre of the city, and howled for his blood. Dispatching a note to the Envoy for help, Burnes ineffectually harangued the multitude from an upper gallery. By an act of treachery he was lured down to the garden, where he and his brother were hacked to pieces. Owing to the dilatoriness of the chief military authority nothing was done that day. Swift action would have saved Burnes and his friends and restored order in the city. But the officer in command of the troops was General Elphinstone, who had been chosen to succeed Sir Willoughby Cotton on account of his pleasant manners and easy-going nature and who was old, gouty, feeble-minded, a physical wreck and quite incompetent. 'We must see what the morning brings,' he wrote to Macnaghten, 'and then think what can be done.' Nearly the whole of his character was contained in that sentence.

Unrepressed revolts soon grow, and by the next day a riot had become a revolution. Enemies sprang up in every village and concentrated on Kabul. In time Dost Mahomed's son, Akbar Khan, arrived at the capital and became the focal personality of the rebellion. He had what would later have been called an artistic temperament, his behaviour being wholly unpredictable. Charming at one moment, ferocious at another, he would murder to-day and repent to-morrow. He was quite capable of receiving a joke with roars of laughter and cutting the joker's throat when his mirth had subsided; and however barbarous his actions he would apologise for them with the utmost sincerity.

The idea of entering into an agreement with such a man was repugnant to Macnaghten, who in the early days of the rising did his best to separate the revolting chiefs by bribery; but as there was not enough money for all of them, and as the chiefs did not trust one another, his attempts were fruitless. Nevertheless he persevered, for it soon became clear that the British commander was more of a menace to the safety of the force than the Afghan knives and bullets. Elphinstone spent his time in giving orders and countermanding them. He would listen to the advice of an officer, take it, and promptly repudiate it when a contrary opinion was proffered. In this manner all his resources were frittered away. Following an urgent appeal he would order an attack on a fort, and following an equally urgent appeal he would send insufficient troops to take it. The fort which contained the provisions and medical stores for the army was soon in the hands of the enemy and the soldiers were repeatedly beaten in the field. Owing to his vacillation and the gloom imparted to the officers by his obvious incapability, the soldiers fought with little heart and bad discipline. Though there were many acts of individual bravery, there were many more of collective cowardice. Distant outposts were attacked, their defenders were massacred, and the victors helped to swell the ranks of the Kabul insurgents. 'We must hope for the best,' was the burden of Elphinstone's messages to Macnaghten. It was not entirely the General's fault; he should have been in a bath-chair at some pleasant seaside resort. He was sent there by Lord Auckland, who believed he would work smoothly with Macnaghten and to whom it had not occurred that, in a crisis, smoothness accelerates a slide into the abyss.

At length the food shortage became grave, and there was no hope of relief. General Sale was beleaguered at Jalalabad (between Kabul and Peshawar), Colonel Palmer was shut up in Ghazni, attempts to send a force from Kandahar had been foiled by the enemy, while the terms offered by the Kabul chiefs for the capitulation of the army were too humiliating to be accepted. The men in the cantonments were reduced to eating the animals that had died of starvation and all the trees had been stripped of their bark and branches to feed the cattle. Macnaghten strongly advised that the army should evacuate the cantonments and occupy the Bala Hissar, where they could have withstood a long siege, but his advice was vetoed by Elphinstone and his associates on the ground that such a movement would imperil the safety of the wounded and risk the loss of artillery. Apparently it had not crossed their minds that risks and perils were inseparable from wars.

This refusal was the last straw, and Macnaghten, loathing the necessity thus forced upon him, opened negotiations with the refractory chiefs, who agreed to a treaty whereby the British-Indian troops at Kabul, Ghazni, Kandahar and Jalalabad should quit the country unmolested, Shah Suja should stay at Kabul or go with them as he desired, and Dost Mahomed with his family should return to Afghanistan. The retiring troops were to be assisted with carriage and provisions and four British officers were to remain behind as hostages until the arrival of the Dost.

There followed a period of procrastination, during which the chiefs increased their demands and Macnaghten tried to divide them by bribery. The chiefs began to suspect that the Envoy was playing one against the other and laid a trap for him. Akbar Khan secretly suggested that his people and the Ghilzyes should unite with the British and attack a chief who was supposed to be inimical to their interests, after which the British could voluntarily withdraw from the country, leaving Suja on the throne with Akbar as his chief minister, the latter to receive a large cash payment and a permanent pension. Macnaghten, whose morale had been sapped during the past six weeks by an exhibition of military incompetence without parallel in English history and whose brain had been affected by diplomatic association with a treacherous enemy, fell into the trap and accepted Akbar's proposal. His associates warned him, but he was desperate. 'I would rather suffer a hundred deaths than live the last six weeks over again,' he said. A conference between himself and Akbar was arranged and on December 23rd he rode out of camp accompanied by three of his staff officers. They met the Afghan chiefs, who were surrounded by many followers, about 600 yards from the cantonments and were asked to sit down on the side of a hill. Hardly a dozen words had been spoken before the English were seized from behind. The three officers were dragged off and each was made to mount a horse ridden by a chief; two reached the city, but the third slipped from his insecure seat and was cut to bits by the mob. When last they saw Macnaghten he was struggling with Akbar Khan, 'consternation and horror depicted on his countenance.' It was afterwards learnt that exasperated by his prisoner's resistance Akbar had drawn a pistol and shot Macnaghten, whose body was then slashed by the knives of fanatical Ghazis. In due course Akbar expressed regret that he should have lost his temper, which, however, he thought excusable on the ground of the Envoy's obstinacy.

Elphinstone, of course, did nothing to avenge Macnaghten's death, and Eldred Pottinger, whose courage and heroism have inspired several works of romance, was asked to conduct future negotiations with the chiefs. He hated the job, argued against acceptance of the degrading terms and urged that a great effort should be made to occupy the Bala Hissar. But the military command was utterly demoralised and Pottinger was forced to approach the chiefs with Macnaghten's original treaty. After a number of further concessions, mainly of cash, hostages and artillery, the treaty was ratified.

The retreat of the British army from Kabul did not proceed according to plan. On the 6th of January, 1842, a force of over four thousand fighting men and twelve thousand camp-followers, accompanied by many women, children, camels and ponies, straggled out of the cantonments. The ground was thickly covered with snow and the cold was intense. Although they had agreed in the treaty to supply a strong Afghan escort, the chiefs omitted this detail and left the retiring army to the

mercy of every marauding and fanatical element in the
country. The futility of Elphinstone, now actually
dying from worry no less than senility, was at no time
so strikingly apparent. He stopped when he should have
pushed on, and pushed on when he should have stopped.
There was no order, no discipline on the march; the
fighting men were mixed up with the camp-followers,
who rushed to the front when the rear was being
attacked and rushed to the rear when the front came
into action; an army was converted into a rabble. The
Indian troops, their women and children, could not
withstand the cold; they dropped off in twos and threes
and then in dozens and hundreds, the lucky ones being
frozen to death, the others being incapacitated by frost-
bite and mutilated by the hostile tribes that hovered by
night and day on the flanks of the hated Feringhee,
equally ready to plunder and to murder. Occasionally
Akbar Khan with his horsemen appeared on the scene,
asked for more hostages, got them, promised his protection, withdrew, and the attacks by the Ghilzyes
recommenced. Partly to save their lives, but primarily
with an eye to the future, Akbar took under his protection the English women, their husbands, General
Elphinstone and several other officers. The only hope for
those who were not surrendered to Akbar was to reach
Jalalabad, where General Sale commanded a garrison
that had repeatedly beaten its besiegers. But in the giant
defiles which had to be penetrated by the Kabul troops
the slaughter was tremendous. The British soldiers
fought with the strength and courage of desperation;
the Indians were panic-stricken and the Afghans
butchered them like sheep. Of the sixteen thousand
human beings who had left Kabul a mere remnant got
through the last of the cavernous passes that separated
them from safety; and when, on January 13th, a sentry
on the ramparts of Jalalabad saw a solitary rider droop-

ing over the neck of a pony that could scarcely keep its feet, a party rode out to meet the sole survivor of that terrible retreat, Dr. Brydon, who had been very nearly killed by a blow on the head from an Afghan knife and whose life had been saved, not, as was usual in those days, by a Bible, but by a copy of *Blackwood's Magazine* in his forage cap. The retribution that had thus over-taken the policy of Lord Auckland has been described by certain historians as the judgment of God. But it might be argued that if the judgment of God had always fol-lowed the iniquity of man, the world would long ago have been depopulated.

Two other important towns in Afghanistan were still holding out against the angry tribes. Like General Sale at Jalalabad, General Nott managed to retain possession of Kandahar until relief came from India; but unfortunately the one man who could and would have held Ghazni against all odds was a youthful ensign named John Nicholson, who had to obey the orders of his commanding officer, Colonel Palmer. The garrison consisted of one weak regiment of Indian soldiers. Cold weather and the enemy arrived together shortly after the outbreak at Kabul, but when the enemy heard that a force was marching from Kandahar to relieve Ghazni they departed, leaving the garrison to enjoy the cold weather, of which the English officers made the most by skating on the ditch beyond the walls. The force from Kandahar failed to get through and the enemy returned early in December, cutting off Ghazni from all succour. It was believed that the townsmen were well disposed towards the garrison, but their true disposition was manifested on December 16th when they dug a hole beneath the outer wall and admitted several thousands of Ghazis, who had not forgotten Shah Suja's treatment of their fellow-fanatics. Colonel Palmer withdrew his regiment to the citadel and there maintained a sturdy

defence in spite of the temperature, which sank to fourteen degrees below zero and which soon incapacitated
the Indians. Every day there were casualties from the
enemy's rifle-fire; the hospital was overcrowded; there
was a shortage of food and water, and frequently
the men had to quench their thirst with snow, which
seemed to burn their stomachs and was 'like fire in
the inside.'

In the middle of February a chieftain named Shamsudin arrived before Ghazni with an order signed by
Elphinstone that the town should be evacuated, pursuant
to the treaty between the Afghan and British leaders.
Similar orders had been dispatched to Sale at Jalalabad
and Nott at Kandahar, both of whom refused to obey
them; but owing to lack of water and provisions Palmer
was in a more difficult position, and still hoping for
assistance from Kandahar, he played for time, sending
various sums of money to keep Shamsudin quiet. This
suited the Afghan, who was not roused to action till the
money ceased to flow, when he demanded the surrender
of the citadel. On March 6th, after extracting a solemn
oath from the local chiefs that his troops should be
conducted safely to Peshawar, Palmer marched the
regiment out of the citadel into the quarters that had
been assigned to them until the snow should have melted
in the passes. But on the very next day, while the Indians
were cooking their midday meal, the Ghazis made a
sudden rush on the houses occupied by Palmer's men.
Nicholson with another officer and two companies of the
regiment found themselves separated from headquarters,
and the enemy set fire to the house they were in. Forced
from one room to another by the heat of the blazing
building, by the persistent rifle-fire and violent assaults
of the Ghazis, they at last found themselves with no
more rooms to fall back into. From noon on the 7th till
midnight of the 9th they fought with nothing to eat or

drink, surrounded by dead or dying men, and when their ammunition was exhausted they still held the enemy off with their bayonets. There was only one way of escape from an untenable position. Taking advantage of the darkness, they made a hole through the back wall of the house with their bayonets and then, one man at a time, dropped into the street below and escaped to headquarters. On the morning of the 10th all the survivors of the attack were in the two houses held by Colonel Palmer, every room of which was crowded by soldiers, camp-followers, women and children, all struggling to avoid the round shot which came crashing through the walls from the citadel guns.

Having thoroughly enjoyed this diverting interlude, Shamsudin sent a message to say that if the British would lay down their arms they would be honourably treated and given safe conduct to Shah Suja at Kabul. Colonel Palmer, in a grave predicament, agreed to treat with the enemy and ordered his officers to cease operations. Nicholson, like Nelson when a similar order was given, pretended not to be conscious of it and drove the enemy back three times at the point of the bayonet. At last the command was repeated in a way that not even an officer who had suddenly become blind and deaf could mistake; and a feeling of shame and grief spent itself in a burst of tears as he gave up his sword.

Shamsudin then informed Palmer that the lives of the British officers were in danger from the Ghazis and urged that they should take refuge in the citadel where he could afford them protection. Nicholson was violently opposed to such a course and implored Palmer not to leave his Indian soldiers. Palmer obtained a promise from Shamsudin that the Indian troops would be allowed to retire to Peshawar, and given every assistance on the way. Again Nicholson criticised his Colonel's decision, said that he would remain with the men, and offered to recapture the citadel if Palmer would give him the command of four companies. But all his threats, offers and entreaties were wasted on Palmer, who once more reminded him that his duty was to obey orders. The humiliation of this surrender to a treacherous foe had a permanent effect on Nicholson, who would always have preferred death to failure and whose nature flowered in action but withered in quiescence.

The officers re-entered the citadel under a strong escort on the night of March 20th. As Nicholson had foreseen, Shamsudin immediately removed the guard he had sent to protect the Indian troops and their wives; whereupon the Ghazis massacred all but a few pretty women, for the possession of whom they quarrelled, and several fortunate men who could rapidly remember the Mohammedan creed and repeat it verbatim, an accomplishment which saved their lives but condemned them to slavery.

And now John Nicholson, at the age of nineteen, was to undergo an experience which gave him an insight into oriental character and coloured his thought and behaviour for the rest of his life. At first the prisoners were treated well, Shamsudin sympathising with them on their bad luck and regretting that he had been unable to control his fanatical followers. But they were soon left to the mercy of gaolers, who relieved them of their watches, penknives, money and everything they possessed. They were confined in a room, 18 feet by 13, and as there were ten of them the whole floor was occupied when they lay down to sleep, while for exercise they had to take it in turns to walk the six paces backwards and forwards. Having no change of linen, their bodies were soon covered with vermin, the catching of which gave them an hour's entertainment each morning, and their shirts were worn until they were black and rotten.

On April 7th the news came that Shah Suja had been murdered at Kabul and from that moment the confinement became more rigorous. The solitary window was darkened and kept shut, the door was only opened when food was brought in and the air became foul beyond description. A fortnight later, in the belief that the English had concealed some money, Colonel Palmer was encouraged to disclose the hiding-place by torture "with a tent-peg and rope." The other officers were forced to witness the process and one of them wrote of it as 'something on the principle of the Scotch boot described in *Old Mortality*.' They were informed that if the money was not given up all of them would be tortured in turn, after which, should they continue obstinate, they would be blown away from guns.

It was an uncertain sort of life, made no easier to bear by the kindly inquiries of the gaolers, who seemed really concerned about the private affairs of their victims, asking such questions as 'Have you a mother?' 'Have you any brothers and sisters?' 'How many?' and so on. Even in such circumstances Nicholson could not bridle his temper, for when a chieftain ordered him to hand over the little locket in which he kept his mother's hair he threw it at the man's head, thereby endangering his own. But curiously enough the Afghan admired his action, giving strict injunctions that the locket was not to be taken away from him. 'Alas! alas!' said one of their captors to him frequently, 'what a state of mind your poor mother must be in about you now; how I pity both you and her!' This warm-hearted sympathiser would have cut any one's throat for an onion, said Nicholson, who at a later date summarised his views on the Afghans: 'They are, without exception, the most blood-thirsty and treacherous race in existence . . . with all that, they have more natural innate politeness than any people I have ever seen.'

At the end of April their guards became more affable and their food improved. This was because news had arrived that a force under General Pollock had marched from Peshawar and relieved Jalalabad, that Akbar Khan had been defeated and that a movement on Kabul was expected. A little later the guards reverted to their former demeanour and the food was not so good. This was because the British army remained inactive at Jalalabad. Henceforth the advance or delay of the British troops could be guessed from the behaviour of the guards and the quality of the food.

On May 12th, probably because Kandahar had just been reinforced, the Ghazni prisoners were allowed to walk for an hour on the terrace of the citadel. To breathe fresh air again and to see from a distance a few fields of clover was a blessing which only those who had lived for weeks in darkness and a polluted atmosphere could appreciate, and as it was to be repeated once a week they used to count the hours between each event. On the 15th June one of the ten prisoners, Lieut. Davies, went down with typhus fever. 'We had no medicines, no comforts for him,' wrote a fellow-officer, Lieut. Crawford, 'and he lay on the ground delirious, raving about home and his family, and every hour proving worse, till, on the 19th, death put an end to his sufferings. We read the burial service over him, and then made his body over to the guard to bury; but I am afraid they merely flung the poor fellow into a ditch outside the gate.' On the 20th, to their unspeakable joy, they were removed to another building and given several rooms and a court-yard to breathe in. Shamsudin began to treat them in a friendly manner, no doubt because he felt the reinforcements at Jalalabad and Kandahar meant business, and for two months they were relatively comfortable. Then, on the 19th of August, without warning, they were rushed on camels to Kabul and taken straight to the quarters of Akbar Khan, who received them with the utmost courtesy, asked after their healths, hoped they were not too fatigued by the journey, regretted that no attention had been paid to his previous orders that they should be brought to Kabul, and assured them that they would in future be treated as officers and gentlemen. He was, they decided, a delightful fellow, good-humoured, frank, considerate, polished. They dined with him and his chiefs and while they enjoyed the best meal they had eaten for months Akbar chatted and joked away on a dozen different topics. 'I never was in the company of more gentleman-like, well-bred men,' wrote Nicholson. '. . . As I looked round the circle I saw both parricides and regicides, whilst the murderer of our Envoy was perhaps the least bloodstained of the party.'

The next morning Akbar sent them an excellent breakfast, horses to carry them to the fort where all the other British prisoners were congregated, and asked for a list of their clothing requirements, which should promptly receive attention. They found their country-men—some of whom had been given as hostages to Akbar, some taken prisoners by him during the retreat—in what to the Ghazni new-comers appeared a paradise. The fort, a few miles from Kabul, contained comfortable quarters and a beautiful orchard; the officers and ladies were waited on by servants; the guards kept at a respectful distance; and John Nicholson was given the first clean shirt he had had for months. Reminiscences were exchanged and the latest arrivals heard how General Elphinstone, overcome by infirmity, mortification and hardship, had died during the forced marches to which the hostages had been subjected.

The party from Ghazni were not suffered to enjoy their repose for long. A few days after they arrived all the prisoners in the fort who were in a fit condition to travel were sent under a strong escort towards the

mountains of the Hindu Kush. News had just reached
Akbar Khan that General Pollock was moving out of
Jalalabad and commencing his march to Kabul. The
presence of this new British force in Afghanistan must
now be explained.

When the story of the disaster that had overtaken the
Kabul army reached Lord Auckland, he gave vent to an
outburst of indignation, which gave place to a period of
prostration, during which he seemed to age ten years in
as many days. His term of office was drawing to a close
and he was nervous of giving orders that might be dis-
approved and countermanded by his successor. But even
in the semi-paralysed condition to which he had been
reduced it was clear to him that General Sale's garrison
at Jalalabad must be relieved and withdrawn. For this
purpose General Pollock was placed in command of an
army which was slowly formed at Peshawar and then
went through the Khyber Pass to Jalalabad. Troops were
also pushed forward from Quetta to help General Nott
to retire from Kandahar. While these two Generals were
awaiting further instructions a new Governor-General,
Lord Ellenborough, arrived at Calcutta. He was a man
with an inflated sense of his own importance and
thoroughly mistrusted the advice of every one about
him. The governing classes of India, both military and
civil, were loud in their outcries that the British reverses
in Afghanistan should be avenged. Ellenborough stiffened his jaw and declined to be stampeded. He was
anxious for his own greater glory to wipe out the stain
of his predecessor's policy, but for the same reason he
dared not risk the danger of another reverse. His instructions to Pollock and Nott were therefore couched in
contradictory terms; he shilly-shallied, advising them
almost in the same sentence to go forward and to come
back. Eventually he hit upon an expedient, popular with
many politicians since his day, whereby he would gain

credit for courage in the case of victory and credit for
caution in the case of defeat: he advised Pollock and
Nott to advance in order to retreat. In other words,
he suggested that it might be convenient for Nott to
retire from Kandahar to India by way of Kabul, which is
like retiring from London to Brighton by way of Bath,
and for Pollock to assist Nott's retreat by advancing on
Kabul. Thus if the Generals failed the odium would be
entirely theirs; if they succeeded the glory would be
chiefly his.

The hint was sufficient for Pollock and Nott, who
wished to redeem their country's reputation. Desirous
to act in concert with his confederate commander,
Pollock sent message after message to Nott asking when
he intended to march; but the distance between Jalalabad and Kandahar was great, the country bristled with
hostile tribes, and at length Pollock determined to ensure
the safe receipt of a letter by writing a few common-
places in ink, dispatching it to Akbar Khan at Kabul and
requesting him to forward it to Nott, who applied
iodine to the paper and read the important information
which had been written in rice-water. Had he known
that he was being employed as the medium for his own
destruction, Akbar would have complained that Pollock
was not a gentleman.

At last the two Generals, one from the east, the other
from the south-west, began their forward movements
on Kabul. Akbar, having dispatched his prisoners to the
northern borderland, mustered his forces and went to
dispute Pollock's progress through the passes. But this
time he had not to deal with a demoralised force under
an incompetent commander, and he was thoroughly
beaten, fairly and squarely, on his own ground and in his
own style of mountain warfare. He fled, and on September 15th, 1842, the British force under Pollock
arrived at Kabul, to be augmented on the 17th by the

force under Nott, who had destroyed Ghazni on the way.

Meanwhile John Nicholson and the other English prisoners were travelling towards Turkistan with the prospect of being sold as slaves to some chieftain beyond the Hindu Kush. They were treated as a rule with kindness by the inhabitants of the districts through which they passed, though their discomforts were considerable. At one halting place an officer of their party went into a serai to beg for a room for the ladies and children, but was asked how he, an infidel, dared to enter the place with his shoes on. Nicholson remembered this repulse many years later. After travelling for a number of days along lovely valleys, where the green cultivated fields were interspersed with clumps of willow and poplar trees, and over rough bare mountains, where the eye found no relief from rocks and stones, they came to Bamian.

The commander of their escort, a trusted lieutenant of Akbar Khan, was one Saleh Mahomed, who had served under the English, but had deserted them because 'he was disgusted with the abusive language used towards him by the European non-commissioned officers.' At least that was the reason he gave when taxed on the point; but he was really a soldier of fortune who fought for any one with money to pay him and who entertained no hostility towards his temporary enemy, because the enemy of to-day might be the employer of to-morrow. He was a jolly, good-humoured fellow, who thought himself a hero and loved to brag of his exploits. The prisoners listened to his tales of personal valour with marked appreciation, hoping thereby to gain his partisanship when the opportunity should be ripe. At first a suggestion of bribery—or rather reward—was thrown out as a joke and was instantly repelled. But the news that Kabul had been retaken by the British weakened

Saleh Mahomed's allegiance to Akbar and caused him to approach the question of compensation from a different angle. On September 11th he informed three of his prisoners that he had received instructions from Akbar to convey the party to Kulum, where they were to be handed over to the chieftain as slaves. Allowing time for this piece of news to sink in, he relieved their despair by saying that he had been offered, on the authority of General Pollock, a life pension of 1,000 rupees a month and a present of 20,000 rupees if he would release the prisoners. 'I know nothing of General Pollock,' he continued, 'but if you three gentlemen will swear by your Saviour to make this offer good, I will deliver you over to your own people.' The oath was given, an agreement was drawn up and signed, its terms guaranteed by all the prisoners, a Union Jack displaced the Jolly Roger (or its equivalent) on the fort they occupied, and on September 16th they set out on the return journey, being met the next day by Sir Richmond Shakespear who had been sent by Pollock to rescue them with a party of friendly Afghan horsemen, and on the 20th by General Sale's column, which escorted them back to Kabul.

While in camp there Nicholson met an officer named Henry Lawrence, who had obtained such an ascendancy over the Sikhs that he had quelled a mutiny and then led some hundreds of them through the dreaded Khyber Pass with Pollock's force. Lawrence was much struck by the young ensign and later on became the chief influence in Nicholson's life. Someone else was struck by him in a different way. 'As I was passing not far from a tent surrounded by Afghans,' reported Neville Chamberlain, 'I was struck by a stone. I put my hand to my sword and approached the man, who was stooping to pick up another stone, when to my surprise who should my assailant prove to be but John Nicholson, surrounded by other rescued officers, dressed in their Afghan prisoner's dress, when of course we both burst out laughing and shook hands heartily.'

Having razed a large number of towns and villages to the ground, destroyed the food supplies of the Afghans and killed as many of them as possible, it was still felt that a mark of displeasure should be left upon the land, and what so effective as the obliteration of the chief centre of commerce? Accordingly the great Bazaar of Kabul was blown to bits by gunpowder, and, though this was unauthorised, the town was burnt and pillaged and many of its inhabitants killed by soldiers and camp-followers. The army then marched back to India, where every one agreed it would now be possible 'to look a native in the face again with confidence,' and where Lord Ellenborough had staged a tremendous reception for the conquering heroes at Ferozpur.

But before leaving the country where he had endured so much Nicholson was to receive one more blow from fate, least expected and hardest to parry. On November 1st, near the Afghan mouth of the Khyber, he met his brother Alexander, who had come straight from school to India and had just been posted to a regiment in Pollock's army. Both were delighted. His brother then went on ahead with his regiment and two days later John, while riding through the Pass, saw what looked like an Englishman's naked body some distance off. Against orders he left the line of march with a friend and galloped off to inspect it. Stripped of clothing, the genitalia slashed away in orthodox Afghan fashion, lay the corpse of Alexander. At first Nicholson could not speak; then his feelings found release in tears. A few days later he tried to comfort his mother: 'It is with a sorrowful heart that I sit down to write to you now, after a silence of more than a twelvemonth. Indeed I should scarcely dare to do so now, were I not encouraged by the knowledge that God will enable you to bear your sad loss with Christian resignation, and comfort you with His Holy Spirit. Poor Alexander is no more. He was killed in action when on rear-guard on the 3rd instant; but I know that you will not sorrow as one without hope, but rather rejoice that it has pleased the Lord to take him from this world of sorrow and temptation. . . . Now, my dearest mother, let me entreat you not to grieve more than you can help. Alexander died a soldier's death, in the execution of his duty, and a more glorious death he could not have died. . . . It will be a consolation to you to know that he was buried by a clergyman of the Church of England : few have been who have perished in this country.'

The Afghan adventure was now over. As with so many dramas in real life, the curtain had risen on a comedy and descended on a tragedy. Its effect on later Indian history has been variously estimated, but there can be little doubt that it originated the war in Sind, it provoked the Sikhs to commence hostilities, and, because of the lowering of British prestige, the terrible cost in men and money and the annoyance felt by Indian soldiers at having to serve outside their country, it was the first of the causes which led to the Indian Mutiny. The campaign had a considerable effect on John Nicholson. It hardened him and made him self-reliant; it bred a deep suspicion in him of oriental peoples, especially the Afghans; it proved to him that in a crisis hesitation was fatal, that an ounce of courage was worth a pound of brains and that bluff was better than cunning; it confirmed his belief that in war safety lay in taking risks, and that audacity won more than diplomacy.

Of the four chief characters who took the stage at the opening of the comedy we already know the fate of two : Ranjit Singh died as a result of drinking to its happy conclusion, and Shah Suja was murdered because he wanted to play the leading part. The others were more fortunate: Dost Mahomed returned to Kabul and recovered his throne, while Lord Auckland, having successfully navigated the Indian ship of state on to the rocks, went home to become once more the First Lord of the Admiralty.

CHAPTER IV

Beauty and the Beast

THE English people have never been able to grasp the simple fact that what has been won in the spirit of the Old Testament cannot be held in the spirit of the New Testament. After carrying sword and fire into a country it is unreasonable to hope that the inhabitants will prove amenable to the Sermon on the Mount. But the Englishman is an optimist; having knocked a man down, he expects him to get up at once and shake hands. This attitude of mind has resulted in more rebellions and minor wars than any other nation has had to contend with, and one year's continuous peace has scarcely ever been enjoyed throughout the British Empire.

It may be that the division in spirit between the Old and New Testaments has been largely responsible for the divided nature of the Englishman who sheathes his sword in an olive branch. Or it may be that something in the climate of the British Isles makes its natives kill without animosity and expect a reciprocation of their kindly intentions. Whatever the cause, the British soldier is nearly always surprised and shocked by the hatred his actions inspire. The best expression of this unimaginative attitude is to be found in the autobiography of Lord Roberts. During the assault on Lucknow in the Mutiny about two thousand rebels were entrapped in a place from which there was no escape and all of them were shot or bayoneted: 'There they lay in a heap as high as my head, a heaving, surging mass of dead and dying inextricably entangled,' wrote Lord Roberts. '. . . The wretched, wounded men could not get clear of their dead

comrades, however great their struggles, and those near
the top of this ghastly pile of writhing humanity vented
their rage and disappointment on every British officer
who approached by showering upon him abuse of the
grossest description.' Although Lord Roberts thought it a
sickening sight, his description leaves the impression that
the writer's feelings were more outraged by the language
than harrowed by the carnage.

Nicholson was not so fastidious. His was the Old
Testament method of dealing with enemies and he did
not expect the man he was disembowelling to respect his
feelings as a gentleman. He admired the Christian
virtues, but they were foreign to his nature and
made him feel uncomfortable. 'Smite or be smitten'
was his guiding principle in life, and on leaving Kabul
he regretted that there was anything left of it to
leave.

The wars that immediately followed the Afghan
expeditions did not take him by surprise. The Amirs of
Sind, having been forced to watch in silence the spolia-
tion of their country, failed to display those signs of loyal
devotion to the East India Company which the Governor-
General expected of them. They were considered ungrateful and even disaffected, and Sir Charles Napier was
let loose in Sind to bring them to a proper frame of
mind. There was no 'Christian soldier' nonsense about
Sir Charles, who did his job thoroughly. Sind was
conquered and added to the British possessions; the
Amirs were sent to bite their nails in exile; and Lord
Ellenborough turned his attention to the Mahrattas,
who might have joined the Sikhs in an alliance against
the British and who had to be beaten as a precautionary
measure. Having taken the precaution, Ellenborough
was amazed to hear that he had been sacked by his
ungrateful employers, who were getting a little tired of
his wars and more than a little tired of his 'Victory'

speeches. He was replaced by Sir Henry Hardinge, who arrived in time for the first Sikh war.

Nicholson missed the Sind and Mahratta campaigns. He was stationed with his regiment at Meerut, still studying languages and thoroughly bored by the social life that kept his brother-officers amused in cantonments. 'I dislike India and its inhabitants more every day,' he wrote, 'and would rather go home on £200 a year than live like a prince here.' Then, not wishing to depress his mother, he added: 'At the same time I have so much reason to be thankful, that I do not grumble at my lot being cast in this country.' He was not popular with the other officers, who thought him morose and boorish; they could not get him to join in any form of pastime; he seldom opened his mouth in mess; he was on intimate terms with no one; like Cromwell 'he lived reserved and austere.' Probably because of his independence and isolation the Colonel made him Adjutant of the regiment, which in August '43 was transferred to Moradabad, and his new responsibilities helped to make a stationary life more endurable. Here he remained for over two years, performing his duties with an efficiency that must have made the soldiers wish he had been of a more gregarious nature, writing to his mother constantly, saving money to send home for the education of his brother Charles, and at last passing the language examination which qualified him for a Staff appointment. In the autumn of '45, through the influence of the military secretary to the Indian Government, who was a friend of Uncle James Hogg, Nicholson became a commissariat officer in Sir Hugh Gough's army, which was facing the Sikh force on the River Sutlej. The moment had now arrived when the last and greatest independent kingdom in India was to make its stand against the power and encroachments of the East India Company.

After the death of Ranjit Singh there had been a

succession of rulers in the Punjab, each of whom had been murdered by someone who felt he had a prior claim to govern. The old Maharajah had been too much concerned over his cash to worry about his heirs and no one was strong enough or popular enough to seize the power and maintain it. But Ranjit Singh had made one section of the community so strong that by degrees it became the chief power in the state, and within two years of its creator's death the army controlled the kingdom of the Sikhs. Not unlike the English parliamentary army under Cromwell, the forces of the "Khalsa" were run by committees and none of the many aspirants to the throne of Lahore could hope to rule unless he deferred to these democratic assemblies. The Sikh chieftains were thus placed at a serious disadvantage and at length they struck. Profiting by the general feeling against the English, whose ambitious designs had provoked the people of the Punjab and whose folly in the Afghan War had aroused their contempt, the Sikh leaders of 1845, Lal Singh and Tej Singh, encouraged the army to attack the British forces on their borders and if successful to plunder the cities beyond them. The two leaders believed that their army would be beaten and that the victors would then uphold them as ministers of a kingdom dependent upon the British power. To further their ends they decided to make all the military errors that were possible with a due regard to their own safety and at the same time to assure the British authorities of their entire goodwill. Yet in spite of their treachery the Sikh army very nearly put an end to British domination in India.

Both sides in a dispute always agree on one point: the immense superiority of the opposing force. This excuses defeat or magnifies victory. The Governor-General's assessment of the enemy's numbers showed a greater regard for glory than for truth, but the Sikh army was probably about twice as large as the British force engaged, with artillery in the same proportion.

On December 11th, 1845, the Sikhs crossed the River Sutlej and the war began. Sir Hugh Gough, the British commander, was a tough soldier of the old school. He believed in cold steel rather than hot shot and flung his troops against positions that had not been sufficiently weakened by previous artillery bombardments. The first engagement at Mudki was won by the British because Lal Singh, according to plan, took no interest in the battle after issuing the order to attack. The next engagement at Ferozshah was the bloodiest battle in British-Indian history. An hour before sunset Gough threw his men at the Sikh guns, which kept up a terrific fire and sent the attackers reeling back with great loss. The assault was repeated again and again with the same result, until the opposing forces were enveloped in darkness and mixed up so confusedly that officers could not find their men, colonels their regiments or generals their divisions, while friends and foes fired at one another indiscriminately. The next morning the armies disentangled themselves and the Sikhs were driven from their positions. No sooner was this done than a large Sikh reinforcement arrived on the scene and the English, half-dead with cold, hunger and fatigue, were faced with another struggle. But the Sikh leader, Tej Singh, was not going to risk a victory for his troops, and, having ascertained that Gough's army was at his mercy, obligingly fled. Technically, therefore, the battle was won by the British, though the Governor-General was heard to exclaim: 'Another such victory and we are undone!' The war lasted for eight weeks and was brought to an end by the encounter at Sobraon, when Gough's method of matching artillery with men once more resulted in heavy casualties and a British defeat was again turned into a victory by the convenient flight

of Tej Singh, who damaged the bridge of boats over the
Sutlej on his way and so helped to drown a large number
of his fellow-countrymen.

As the Sikh leaders, in the words of the Governor-
General, had been "as little obnoxious as possible to the
English," the peace terms were reasonable. The Punjab
was not annexed, though the chief cities were garrisoned
by British troops and Henry Lawrence as Agent for the
Governor-General became the real power in the Lahore
Durbar or Council of State, the nominal head of which
was the mother of Ranjit Singh's son, Dulip Singh, aged
eight. This woman, the Maharani Jindan, was described
by Lawrence as 'a strange blend of the prostitute, the
tigress and Machiavelli's Prince'; and since her lover,
Lal Singh, who had helped to betray the "Khalsa," was
her chief minister, and the other members of the Council
were masters of duplicity, Lawrence could not rely with
much confidence on Sikh support. He made up for the
lack of harmony at headquarters by a judicious choice
of kindred spirits to administer the districts under his
control, and one of the first men he picked for "outpost"
duty was John Nicholson.

By way of compensation for British losses in the
campaign an indemnity of one and a half million pounds
was imposed on the Sikhs, but Ranjit Singh's hoards had
been squandered in the years of misrule that followed his
death and the treasury was empty. To raise the money
the country of Kashmir was annexed and sold for a
million to Gulab Singh, a Sikh rajah who had remained
neutral during the war to see which way the wind would
blow. When it blew British he faced in the right direction and was duly rewarded with the loveliest portion of
India at an agreed price. The people of Kashmir, once
an Afghan province, were Mohammedan, and the Sikhs
had been wise enough to leave it in the hands of a Moslem
ruler. Its wholesale transference to a Hindu chieftain

was not therefore a praiseworthy act on the part of a
nation which was supposed to believe that human beings
had rights. But the rights of man are usually overlooked
when the rights of power are claimed, and Henry Lawrence, who later became the noblest ruler in the history
of British India, must take his share of blame for the
transaction.

Gulab Singh asked for the loan of several English
officers to accompany him to Kashmir and to drill his
troops. Through the influence of Lawrence two men
were chosen by the Governor-General: John Nicholson
and Captain Broome. In offering him the job Hardinge
told Nicholson that "something better" would come of
it. Nicholson accepted it gladly on condition that if he
did not like it he might return to his work in the
Commissariat.

In the spring of 1846 they set out with Maharajah
Gulab Singh for Kashmir. But they spent so many weeks
doing nothing in Gulab's own province of Jammu on the
way that Nicholson soon became restive. 'I have been
leading the most monotonous life you can well imagine,'
he wrote to his mother in May; 'I have no duties of
any kind to perform, and am quite shut out from the
civilised world. I think I mentioned to you in a former
letter that I did not believe the Maharajah was really
desirous of having our system of discipline introduced
into his army; so it has turned out he merely asked
for two European officers because he was aware of the
moral effect their presence would have at his Durbar in
showing the terms of intimacy he was on with the
British Government, and made the wish to have his
army disciplined a pretence. As it as present stands, the
appointment can't prove a permanent one, as the
Maharajah will soon become tired of paying mine and
Captain Broome's, the Artillery officer's, staff salary.
Hitherto we have both received every civility from him,

and as long as he considers it his interest to treat us well, he will doubtless do so. The Maharajah talks of going to Kashmir next month and taking me with him. I look forward with great pleasure to a trip to this beautiful valley (albeit in such company), believed by natives to have been the earthly Paradise.' June came and they remained inactive. His duties up to date had been merely nominal ones, he told his mother: 'I regret to say they still continue so, and after the busy life I have led for the last three years, and the excitement of the late campaign, my present want of employment renders my exile from the civilised world irksome to a degree; so much so that, should this state of things last much longer, I shall very likely throw the appointment up and fall back on the Commissariat, though it is not a department I am very partial to.'

Apart from his ambition to distinguish himself and his hatred of doing nothing, certain aspects of the Maharajah's personality did not appeal to him. In appearance Gulab Singh left little to be desired. He was a portly man of middle height with a superb head, long curly black hair, delicate aquiline nose, large oval black eyes and a small perfectly shaped mouth. His face was expressive, his movements were graceful, his voice was admirably modulated, his manners were extremely pleasant. Everybody was impressed by his physical beauty, his engaging address, the sincerity, simplicity and gentleness of his demeanour. Against these outward adornments must be placed certain habits which grated on European sensibilities. A contemporary remarked that the chief difference between him and his Moslem predecessor in Kashmir was that while he flayed chiefs alive, the other boiled pundits to death. When accused of indulging in this pastime Gulab Singh urged the necessity of strong measures and the ferocity of those who had to be coerced. He indignantly denounced as 'a monstrous calumny' the rumour that he had flayed twelve thousand men, asserted that he had 'only skinned three,' but added on reflection, 'hundred.' In this respect, however, he was little worse than the average Indian prince, whose normal attitude to such matters was revealed by a remark of Rhumbeer Singh, Gulab's successor in Kashmir. When the Indian Mutiny broke out Rhumbeer's brother rebelled, was caught, sentenced to death, suspended by his hair from a beam and lowered one inch into a cauldron of boiling oil; the next day two inches, the next three, and so on until he was extinct. Upon which Rhumbeer made a public announcement: 'Any one found in rebellion against me will be severely punished and not treated to the merciful death given to my brother.'

In spite of his Afghan experiences Nicholson was not yet accustomed to this sort of thing and he felt there was something hypocritical in a man who could mask so much cruelty with so much charm. As time went on the gentle speech of Gulab Singh began to jar on Nicholson's nerves; he could no longer feel the fascination of a disarming smile that frequently followed a revolting order and he summed up his general irritation by complaining of the 'many annoyances and inconveniences' to which he was subjected.

At last, in July, the Maharajah with his troops and the two British officers entered Kashmir. Nicholson was hardly in a mood to appreciate the country, the beauty of which was not then sufficiently known to the English to be in danger of destruction. The groves of walnut, apple, cherry and peach trees, the mountain tops covered in snow, the pine forests and willow-fringed lakes, the rainproof foliage of the gigantic chunar trees; even the quaint picturesqueness of Srinagar, with its floating gardens, its wooden bridges draped in creepers which at intervals for three miles crossed the river that ran through the town; all this was lost upon him. He merely observed the dilapidated houses, the horrible odours, the dirty inhabitants, the hideous old women, the army of beggars, the mangy dogs and filthy dung-hills. He was affected by the smell of the East without feeling the spell of the East.

Gulab Singh was not received with favour. The Moslem governor, according to Nicholson, 'showed an evident disinclination to surrender the government,' which was another way of saying that he brought a large force to Srinagar with the object of wiping out the invading troops and boiling his supplanter in oil. The situation of the British officers, of Gulab and his fol-lowers, was precarious. When the populace heard that the Moslem was at hand great excitement prevailed. Gulab Singh was parading the streets and a chance shot missed him by inches. In the ordinary way this would have been followed by 'red riot,' but the steadiness of Nicholson and Broome saved the Maharajah. They accompanied him into the fort and allayed suspicion by sitting in his Durbar for a while, gravely imperilling their own lives by the act. The aspect of affairs became so grave that the two British officers, having no wish to be sacrificed for loyalty to a flayer, left the country in the nick of time and saved their skins by a rapid retreat over one of the southern passes into Jammu. Gulab's troops were defeated and took refuge in a fort, while Gulab himself returned, cowed, to Jammu.

The British authorities acted promptly. Herbert Edwardes, one of Lawrence's political assistants, was sent to keep Gulab up to the mark, and in doing so he formed a friendship with John Nicholson which was to influence both their lives; a force was dispatched to maintain Gulab's prestige in Jammu; while Henry Lawrence collected an army of ten thousand Sikhs, the very men who a few months before had fought the

British, and marched into Kashmir. Lawrence was aware that the Moslem governor's rebellion had received at least the sympathy of Lal Singh at Lahore, so he instructed his brother John Lawrence to keep an eye on the chief minister. The expedition was a success; the Moslem governor capitulated and provided proofs of the conspiracy of Lal Singh, who was exiled; Henry Lawrence, supported by an army, became Resident at Lahore with full powers over the Council of Sikh leaders; Gulab Singh was reinstated in Kashmir; and John Nicholson was the only European left at Srinagar.

The combination of Kashmir and Gulab Singh had not agreed with him and for eight months he had been ill. 'I have had more sickness within this twelvemonth,' he wrote to his brother Charles, 'than in the previous six years and a half; and I sometimes fear that my constitution is going. Nothing brings *home* to a man's mind more readily in India than illness; he then thinks of the nursing and grateful acts of attention he would receive, were he among his own friends. Here I have not even the sight of a white face to cheer me. May you be never in a like predicament!' Winter arrived and he longed to leave Kashmir: 'My fingers are so cold that I can scarcely hold the pen, and glazed windows are unknown here.' His wish to go was increased by the fact that he had nothing to do while his friends were helping Lawrence to create a new state out of the chaotic jumble that was the Punjab. Herbert Edwardes was one of these friends, a genial soul who believed in converting the natives to Christianity by peaceful methods and subjecting them to British rule by war-like methods. Another recent friend was William Hodson, who had accompanied Lawrence's expedition and was later to achieve fame as the leader of Hodson's Horse. He met Nicholson in the Valley of Kashmir and they took to one another at once.

Two such remarkable men, so similar and so dissimilar, have never perhaps won distinction in the same profession, at the same time, in the same country. Both were born fighters; but though each expressed his true nature in action Nicholson fought primarily for a cause, Hodson for the joy of battle. Nicholson was of the class to which Cromwell belonged, Hodson was of the type immortalised by Shakespeare in the character of Hotspur. They were perfect representatives of the two main kinds of warrior through the ages, the heavy-hearted, purposeful, religious idealist; the light-hearted, volatile, careless opportunist. The born man of war is one who can generalise his animosity; if, like the naturally peaceful man, he could feel personal hatred, he would also be subject to the emotion of pity, which would paralyse his actions. Neither Hodson nor Nicholson hated individuals, though they inspired a good deal of hatred in others; they hated 'the enemy,' whoever he might be, but they hated him in different ways. Nicholson hated him because he was evil or rather the devil, while Hodson hated him merely because he was the enemy, someone who had to be struck down because he was there for the purpose. Nicholson was the more complex character, Hodson the more articulate; there was an unquenchable flame within the first, the second spat fire.

Their physical appearances emphasised the contrast: Nicholson was tall, massive, dark-haired, dark-eyed, dark-visaged; Hodson was of medium height, lithe, with yellow hair, a white face and bright blue eyes. Of Nicholson we shall learn more hereafter. Of Hodson it may now be said that his manner was frank, cordial and challenging. He was sarcastic and fearless, uttering things in a thoughtless way that often galled his superiors and sometimes made him life-long enemies. Usually in tearing high spirits, especially when danger threatened and other men were feeling that all was not well with their stomachs, fighting was for him the king of sports, the greatest fun in the world. Once, in a very tight corner, he described himself as 'as jolly as a bug in a rug.' Nothing could ruffle him or make him feel uncomfortable. After any number of hair-raising exploits he was as calm and cool as the average man after a Turkish bath. He could fall fast asleep on horseback and wake up in an hour as fresh as a lark. When in action his face was alight with smiles. As he pranced around his opponent, parrying terrific thrusts as if he were brushing off flies, his laughter rang between the blows and he shouted words of encouragement to the man he was about to impale: 'Try again!' 'Do you call yourself a swordsman?' 'Come along now!' 'Make me sweat for it!' 'Ha-ha!'—his sword drove home—'Too easy.' The ambition of his life, which he achieved, was to acquire such influence over the minds of his men that they would cheerfully follow him to death or glory. He thirsted for 'the maddening excitement of war, the keen contest of wits involved in dealing with wilder men, and the exercise of power over the many by force of the will of the individual.' He detested what he called the dinner-giving, dressy life of towns and expressed his heart's desire in a phrase: 'I would rather *cut* my way to a name and poverty with the sword, than *write* it to wealth with the pen.' Yet there was something about his friend John Nicholson, something alien to his own nature, something he could not fathom, a strange and incalculable force, a singleness of aim, a strength of character, a nobility of soul, a stirring of conscience, that made the brilliant, dashing Hodson admit towards the end of his life: 'After all, Nicholson is the general after my heart.'

But the generalship was more than ten years ahead, and Nicholson had a rough road to travel before he got it. While shivering in Kashmir the good news arrived that the Governor-General, at Lawrence's request, had appointed him assistant to the Resident at Lahore. His duties were henceforth to be those of a Political Officer; he was to be one of 'Lawrence's young men,' whose rule in the Punjab saved India during the Mutiny.

He left Kashmir in February, 1847, cut his way through eight and a half feet of snow that blocked one of the passes and before reaching Lahore received instructions to report on a tract of country west of the Indus. In the course of his duties there he ran across his favourite brother Charles, who had just reached India and was with his regiment in the Punjab. Charles was ten years old when John left home, so the meeting was one of amazement no less than pleasure. 'Fancy neither of us recognising the other!' John wrote to their mother. 'I actually talked to him half an hour before I could persuade myself of his identity. He is as tall, if not taller, than I am, and will, I hope, be much stouter and stronger in the course of another year or two. Our joy at meeting you will well understand, without my attempting to describe it.' Then followed a sentence which proved that John had already seen a sufficient number of those 'white faces' for which he had pined a few months before: 'You may remember my writing to you some time ago, that the want of society rendered me low-spirited. Well, I have within the last few months become so reconciled to living alone, that really, were not Charles here, I should wish myself away again in the Kashmir hills or Jammu forests.'

CHAPTER V

'Nikal Seyn'

THE month of May, 1847, was spent by Nicholson in the company of Henry Lawrence at Lahore. It was a profitable period for both of them. They sized one another up and established that affectionate intimacy between master and man which was the explanation of Lawrence's peculiar success as a ruler. Lawrence encouraged his assistants to speak their minds freely and disclosed his own thoughts with equal freedom. There was not a suggestion of diplomatic solemnity and mystery about him. Unlike most leaders of men, he had an artist's perception of character, and in choosing his subordinates he never made a mistake. He had no cut-and-dried method of dealing with every one; he quickly recognised differences in temperament and treated each man according to his nature, thus obtaining the best results from all. Having summed up a man and decided that he was worthy of trust, Lawrence trusted him completely and never let him down. He was as loyal to his assistants as they were to him and no leader in history has deserved or inspired the love and admiration of so many remarkable men.

The qualities in him that called forth the best in them were rare in a man of action. It is difficult to find a parallel, though Lincoln, to whom he also bore some physical resemblance, was more akin to him than any other notable figure. He had several faults: he was touchy and hot-tempered, sometimes inconsiderate and often intolerant of opinions that conflicted with his own. But all his shortcomings were merely the crust of his character. There was a profound spiritual quality in him, an unwearying desire to do what his instincts told him was right, an ever-present sense of the mystery of the universe and the tragedy of human creatures enveloped and bewildered by that mystery, a deep humility which engendered a passionate feeling of brotherhood, equality and sympathy with his fellow-beings, whether black or white. He was in fact a poet in action, wholly successful in his human relationships when left unfettered, certain to fail in the machinery of government when opposed by a bureaucrat. Hardinge, his chief at the period of which we are writing, gave him *carte blanche*, and all was well.

The nobility of Lawrence's character brought out the tender spots in Nicholson's. The only man for whom he ever felt an equal degree of admiration and affection was Lawrence, though later on he formed a close friendship with Herbert Edwardes, who had imbibed his humanity from the same source. By stirring all that was finest in the younger man, Lawrence captured the heart and head of Nicholson, who would have done anything and gone anywhere without question for him alone. It was perhaps Lawrence's outstanding achievement, for with others, even his best friends, Nicholson was sometimes intractable, easily offended, quick to anger, distrustful and domineering. He felt that Christianity, which as a practical creed was out of tune with his temperament, was justified in Lawrence, and he tried, not always successfully, to harmonise it with the sterner features of his own nature.

A vigilant report by Nicholson on the management of the Amritsar district gave Lawrence a good idea of what he could do and he was sent off to take control over a large tract of country between the Rivers Indus and Jhelum known as the Sind Sagar Doab. Lawrence's directions to an assistant who was about to govern a

district as large as Wales were not concealed in the
phraseology used by most high officials. 'Settle the
country: make the people happy: take care there are no
rows,' was all he said. And if pressed for more detailed
instructions he would add: 'Act on your own judgment: do what you think right.' But with his knowledge of Nicholson's imperious nature he went a little
further and advised him to treat the Sikh governors with
cordiality, to support their authority and attend to
'their moderate wishes and even whims,' and not to
forget 'those small courtesies that natives look to, even
more than they do to more important matters.' Nicholson's chief duty was to protect the people from the
oppressions of the revenue officers. Then, without unduly
harassing the troops, he was to maintain a thoroughly
efficient force. 'I insist upon insubordination and
plunder being promptly punished,' concluded Lawrence;
'and bring to my notice any particular instances of good
conduct. Avoid as far as possible any military movement during the next three months; but should serious
disturbance arise, act energetically.'

There was no need to tell Nicholson to act energetically. The difficulty was to make him stop once he had
started. Within a couple of months he had tamed the
troops, curbed the greed of the tax-gatherers, suppressed
lawlessness, introduced justice and thoroughly cleaned
the district up. At the request of James Abbott, who
supervised the hilly country of Hazara, he helped to
quell a rebellion beyond his northern borders. Towards
the close of '47 he was able to report that his district,
"hitherto more or less disturbed," was perfectly quiet, and
that the revenue officers, "for the first time for years,"
were able to move about without guards. He was in the
saddle all day, and the busy open-air life suited him, in
spite of dust-storms that filled his mouth, eyes and ears
with grit, powdered his food and thickened his coffee,

in spite too of hot winds that reminded him of the rush of air from a furnace and played over his face and limbs like an invisible colourless flame, that choked, scorched and seemed to shrivel him, making his hair and skin crackle and stiffen.

The Punjab appeared to be settling down under British rule, and except for the occasional clashes between Moslems and Hindus at Lahore there was peace throughout the land. Not even Lawrence could put an end to these quarrels, because the Moslem butchers openly slaughtered cattle and sold beef, and as cattle were sacred to the Hindus the two sects had many bloody disagreements which were regarded as "sporting events" by British onlookers, who called them "cow-rows." The last obstacle to peace was removed by Lawrence a few months before he went home on sick-leave. The exile of her lover, Lal Singh, had vexed the Maharani Jindan, who became a centre of intrigue against the government established by the British. She was not a lady with many interests in life, and when not employed in seducing young men, or pushing her slave-girls into a pond for the fun of ducking them and watching their struggles to get out, her sole hobby was the planning of assassination. Her connection with a plot to murder the Resident was sufficient reason to get rid of her, and she was sent into "honourable restraint" at a safe distance, threatening vengeance on those who removed her and doing her best to scratch their eyes out as a hint of her future intentions.

In January, '48, Lawrence sailed for England in the company of Hardinge, the retiring Governor-General. He had, as he thought, pacified a province and he looked forward to many years of steady constructive work on his return. But he reckoned without the new Governor-General, Lord Dalhousie, and he little realised that the Sikh chieftains to whom he had been so kind might forget the Christian spirit in which he had ruled and remember only the fire and sword with which they had been subdued. His place at Lahore was temporarily filled by Sir Frederick Currie, and early in the New Year John Nicholson was sent as chief assistant to Henry's brother George Lawrence at Peshawar, where he was stationed when the bolt fell at Multan.

The second Sikh war was the outcome of official tardiness and incompetence and it would never have been fought if Henry Lawrence had been at his post in the Punjab. It started with an unfortunate accident. Mulraj, the governor of Multan, a strong fortress in the southwest of the Punjab, was the son of the man to whom Ranjit Singh had given command of the place. At his father's death Mulraj had not paid the succession-duty demanded of him by the court at Lahore. There was some dispute and much negotiation concerning the payment, but when at last the amount was fixed Mulraj resigned his post in a fit of petulance. Greatly to his chagrin he was taken at his word and a new governor was appointed. In April '48 Currie, the temporary Resident, sent a civilian, Vans Agnew, and an officer, Lieut. Anderson, to effect the exchange. Without the least notion that there would be trouble they made no arrangements to meet it and were caught off their guard by a band of fanatics as they rode through the gateway of the city by the side of Mulraj. They were fiercely attacked and the greater part of their Sikh escort deserted them. Badly wounded, they took refuge in a ruined mosque, which they defended with the few Sikhs who remained loyal. Although aware that their lives could not be saved, Lahore being 200 miles away, the nearest military post 80 miles and a mob of blood-thirsty fanatics surrounding them, they managed to dispatch two urgent appeals for help. Mulraj, who may not have been privy to the attack, made the best of it and called on the inhabitants of the Punjab to rise against the white men in their midst who were usurping the government. The authorities did nothing. Currie asked Lord Gough, the Commander-in-Chief, to send troops. But Gough was enjoying life at Simla under the deodars and did not wish to expose British troops to a summer campaign. When at last the authorities acted the hot season was over, but by that time the entire country was in open revolt and the Sikh guns made it a great deal hotter for the troops than a little energy at the right moment under a burning sun would have done.

Though Lawrence was away in England his "young men" were busy in the Punjab, and while political chiefs gasped under punkahs and military chiefs basked in the cooler climate of the hills, Herbert Edwardes, James Abbott, George Lawrence, John Nicholson and others were trying to persuade the Sikhs that the hot weather kept them cool. Vans Agnew, Anderson and their faithful bodyguard were murdered, but a few hurried lines scrawled by Agnew just before his death reached Herbert Edwardes in his tent beyond the Indus. He acted without a moment's hesitation, as Lawrence would have done and as Nicholson did. Turning to advantage the racial and religious differences of the Punjab people, he raised a troop of raw Mahommedan levies, mostly Pathans, and with about 3,000 of these "bold villains ready to risk their own throats and cut those of any one else" he rushed at Mulraj, who had taken the field with 4,000 Sikh warriors and eight guns, thrashed him in two pitched battles, drove him back into the fortress, and, feeling "like a terrier barking at a tiger," commenced a siege of Multan. But he could not work miracles. He could not get the Commander-in-Chief at Simla, the Resident at Lahore or the Governor-General at Calcutta to exert themselves until the cold season. 'As if rebellion could be put off, like a champagne tiffin, with a three-

cornered note to Mulraj to name a more agreeable date!'
he exploded in a letter to William Hodson. Their supine-
ness in the emergency was incomprehensible to Nicholson, whose habitual gravity was almost upset when he
heard that Sir Frederick Currie was claiming credit for
what Edwardes had done. 'This is remotely verging
upon the extreme confines of coolness!' he remarked.

The revolt spread quickly. The Sikh nobility had
resented the presence in their districts of young British
"politicals" who told them how to behave, and now that
there was no longer a large "Khalsa" army to be feared
they wished to avenge their defeat and regain their
independence. While Edwardes was battering the walls
of Multan in the south and Dalhousie was wondering
what to do in Calcutta and Gough was meditating a
winter campaign in Simla and Currie was giving and
receiving orders in Lahore, a great Sikh chieftain in the
north named Chatar Singh was becoming the focus of
rebellion, and at Peshawar George Lawrence and John
Nicholson were rapidly raising a corps of Pathans,
quelling minor disturbances and preparing for the major
outbreak which they knew would result from the procrastination of their Government.

In August '48 serious news came to Peshawar from
James Abbott, who had been keeping his eye on Chatar
Singh and had armed the Mohammedan peasantry of the
Hazara hills to deal with the Sikh forces the moment
their leader threw off the mask. Abbott now reported
that the Sikhs were rallying to Chatar Singh, who
intended to march on Lahore, to restore the Maharani
Jindan and to expel the British from the Punjab. The
old soldiers of the "Khalsa" were gathering to his
banner to fight once more for freedom, and those Sikh
officers who were loyal to the Company were being cut
down. It was therefore of the utmost importance that
such forts as were garrisoned by Sikhs should be

re-garrisoned by troops that could be trusted; and
George Lawrence, who realised the immense strategic
importance of Attock on the Indus, the loss of which
would isolate Peshawar and encourage Dost Mahomed
to join the Sikhs, hurried off to break the news to
Nicholson, finding him in bed with a high fever. Nicholson listened carefully to Lawrence's survey of the
situation and then asked: 'What do you wish done?'
Lawrence replied: 'Had you been fit I should have
wished to send you to secure Attock, but that is out of
the question. Someone else must go.' Nicholson rose
from his bed saying, 'I will start to-night.'

Although in the grip of fever, he calmly set about
making arrangements with a clear sense of what was
required. Within a few hours he was in the saddle at the
head of sixty Pathan horsemen, and off they went into
the night followed by 150 raw Mohammedan levies on
foot. It was fifty miles to Attock, the month was August
and Nicholson had a high temperature, but he outrode
his escort and arrived in the early morning at the Indus
with less than thirty of his horsemen and the infantry
sixteen hours' march behind him. Crossing the river, he
galloped up to the gate of the fortress and dashed through
it just before the Sikhs within had tumbled to what was
happening. His authoritative language and commanding
manner quickly brought the majority of the garrison to
their senses, and when a company of men at one of the
gates displayed hostility he walked right in amongst
them, dared them to touch him and ordered them to
arrest their leaders, which they did. The mutinous Sikhs
were soon marched out of the fort and Nicholson began
at once to collect supplies, to get in touch with Abbott,
to reconnoitre the district and to prepare the fort for
a siege.

The infantry turned up at midnight; he made the
necessary dispositions; and on the following day,

leaving a loyal commander in charge of the fortress, he
rode eastwards with his sixty Pathans to Hasan Abdal,
where over a hundred Sikh horsemen had got rid of their
leader because he refused to join Chatar Singh. This
time Nicholson's force was only outnumbered by two to
one, but he dealt leniently with the offenders. 'I paraded
the party and dismissed and confined the ringleaders on
the spot,' he reported to Currie. 'The remainder begged
forgiveness, and having some reason to believe them
sincere, and wishing to show that I was not entirely
without confidence in Sikhs, I granted it. I shall, of
course, keep a sharp look-out on them in future. . . . I
am raising a militia for the protection of this district.
A regular soldier of any kind I have not with me, and
of the small party I brought with me from Peshawar,
there are but three men whom I ever saw till I started.
. . . Everything, if I may offer an opinion, depends on
promptly sending up troops.'

Within an hour of dispatching this letter Nicholson
heard that a mutinous regiment with two guns had just
arrived at Rawal Pindi on its way to join Chatar Singh.
Half-way between Hasan Abdal and Rawal Pindi the
road cuts through a rough ridge of hills at a place called
Margalla. Nicholson determined to concentrate his
levies at this pass and oppose the march of the mutineers.
His followers were not very warlike, but on no account
could the regiment be allowed to swell the ranks of
Chatar Singh, and if reason failed he would have to match
his raw recruits not only with the veteran soldiers and
artillery in front of him but with a Sikh force that was
marching from the north to join hands with them.
Hiding his levies in a bit of jungle, he rode out to see
what bluff could do. His harangued the officers and men
of the offending regiment, advised them to return to
their allegiance and warned them that if they did not
follow his advice he would treat them as mutineers and

punish them accordingly. Taking out his watch, he gave
them half an hour in which to make up their minds.
There was a noisy debate, but the sight of Nicholson
sitting grimly on his horse with a watch in his hand had
a sobering effect on the men and before the time was up
they begged pardon for past transgressions and promised
future obedience. Nicholson ordered them back to
Rawal Pindi and took their salute as they marched away.

And now for days on end Nicholson was in the saddle,
fourteen to sixteen hours at a stretch, keeping in touch
with Abbott's force, thrusting between bodies of Sikh
troops that were trying to join one another, suppressing
risings in various parts of the country, stopping Chatar
Singh's supplies, cutting his communications and
harassing his camp, rushing to Attock whenever it was
threatened and leaving it at a moment's notice when his
presence was required elsewhere. Although his Mohammedan followers were observing the feast of Ramadan,
when for a month they were forced to abstain from food
and drink between sunrise and sunset, they followed him
wherever he led them and however long the march they
had to make. Again and again he begged the Resident
at Lahore to send troops. The arrival of a single brigade,
he declared, would induce half the Sikh army to join him
and keep his levies staunch. But if no troops were sent
he prophesied that the whole country between the Indus
and the Jhelum would declare for Chatar Singh and
probably the still loyal Sikh force at Peshawar as well.
A hint of the restless life he was leading at this time was
given in a note he sent to James Abbott: 'I intended
writing you . . . but sleep overpowered me before the
writing materials came. My fine chestnut died during
the night of the effect of a gallop to Margalla and
back again.'

By the end of August Chatar Singh had come out into
the open and was marching south to Hasan Abdal.

Nicholson hung on his flanks, watching his movements and hoping for the best. It was impossible to oppose eight regiments of regular troops and sixteen guns with his three hundred horse and seven hundred foot, semi-trained and without artillery, and Chatar Singh reached his destination unopposed. In the middle of September one of the Sikh leader's sons, who had recruited a force at Rawal Pindi, started to join his father at Hasan Abdal. Nicholson hoped to forestall the juncture by capturing a tower which commanded the Margalla Pass. A few good marksmen in the tower could hold up a large body of troops, so Nicholson took some of his men to wrest it from the Sikh garrison. Having quietly gained a spot within easy reach of the building, he gave the order to charge and led the way, followed by a dozen Pathan chiefs. A furious fire burst from the stronghold and several of his followers fell. He reached the tower untouched, only to find that its entrance was twelve feet above the ground and that the occupants had the ladder inside. He also found that his levies had funked the ordeal of a charge across open country under fire and not one of them was to be seen. The explanation that they had stayed behind because 'he being ahead could not see who misbehaved' enraged him. He began to pull the wall down stone by stone and would no doubt have torn an opening in it for himself and his few followers if the besieged party had not started to hurl masonry at them, one large portion of which hit him squarely in the face. Even then he was only forced to retire because a body of Sikhs was seen approaching, and he had so thoroughly scared the men in the tower that they let him depart without firing a shot.

A Pathan chief who was killed that day left a small son, to whom Nicholson became a second father. One day this lad, aged seven, asked Nicholson to grant him a special favour.

'Tell me first what you want,' said his guardian.

'Only your permission, sahib, to go and kill my cousins, the children of your deadly enemy, Fathi Khan.'

'To kill your cousins?'

'Yes, sahib, to kill all the boys while they are young; it is quite easy now.'

'You little monster! would you murder your own cousins?'

'Yes, sahib; for if I don't, they will murder me.'

Though very fond of the boy, Nicholson refused to grant him the special favour.

Writing to his mother shortly after the affair at Margalla Tower,* Nicholson said: 'I received a slight hurt from a stone in a skirmish in the hills a week or two ago. I have often had a worse one, however, when a boy at school, and I only mention this because a friend wrote me from Lahore that it was reported I had been seriously hurt, and I fear lest the rumour should reach and cause you anxiety.'

Nicholson gradually gained an extraordinary ascendancy over his Pathans. His unflinching courage, his powers of endurance, his alertness, forethought and physical skill in battle, won their amazed admiration and later their awed worship. His effect on the enemy was almost as great and in time attained superhuman proportions. Unfortunately his influence depended entirely on his presence, and though as a rule he was at the head of his men in the hottest part of the fighting, there were occasions when, unable to be in two places at the same moment, a detachment was left to hold a position while he was doing the dirty work elsewhere. Though it was a risk he had to take, he soon realised that it was no longer a sporting risk but a moral certainty that if he remained away for any length of time his men would desert the post he had ordered them to

* A memorial to Nicholson now stands where the tower did.

hold and seek him out. On one occasion, leaving a
number of his levies on a hill to check the enemy, he
galloped off to bring up reinforcements. The mere
sight of him quitting a place of danger completely
demoralised his followers, who did not appreciate the
reason for his retirement, and the whole of his force
fled in dismay.

Towards the end of September it was learnt at
Peshawar that the Sikh army which had been sent by the
Resident to reduce Multan and which was commanded
by Chatar Singh's son, Sher Singh, had revolted and was
on its way to join the old Sikh chieftain in the north.
This meant that all the troops of the "Khalsa" except
those at Peshawar were now in arms against the Company. George Lawrence immediately dispatched his wife
and children from Peshawar to Lahore under the escort
of Dost Mahomed's brother, who owed his life and lands
to Henry Lawrence and could therefore be trusted to
protect George's family. But Dost Mahomed's brother
was after all an Afghan and before long Mrs. George
Lawrence and her children were prisoners in his castle
beyond the Indus. Nicholson got to hear of their plight
and tried without success to save them. By October the
whole country from the Indus to the Jhelum was in a
state of insurrection; the Sikhs at Peshawar at last
joined their co-religionists; George Lawrence became
a prisoner; Dost Mahomed, still tingling from past
insults and promised his old province of Peshawar as the
price of his alliance, joined the Sikhs; and Nicholson
dashed from place to place, marching by night and day,
in a valiant but futile effort to extinguish the flames of
rebellion. But it was now a bonfire and all he could do
was to stamp on the sparks.

The cool season having arrived, the British authorities
began to warm up, Lord Dalhousie helping to raise the
temperature at a military ball: 'Unwarned by precedent,

uninfluenced by example,' he bellowed, 'the Sikhs have called for war; and on my word, sirs, they shall have it with a vengeance!' Lord Gough quitted the shade of the deodars and prepared to slaughter the thousands whose lives would have been spared if he had responded to the calls of men like Edwardes and Nicholson six months earlier. And so the second Sikh war commenced.

Chatar Singh's army lay in the Margalla Pass between Nicholson's force and the capital. Early one morning Nicholson galloped his eighty Pathans clean through the Sikhs, whose astonishment was so great that the action was unopposed, and reached Lahore by forced marches. Nicholson, now a Captain, served under Gough as a political officer, as a commissariat officer, as a transport officer, as an intelligence officer, as an aide-de-camp, and in any other capacity required at the moment. His comments on the tactics and strategy of the campaign made him unpopular with the senior officers and the fact that what he said was true did not make his remarks any the less irritating or his company any the more welcome. Good ground for criticism was supplied him in November when Gough sent his cavalry across a dry but treacherous river bed two miles in width against a shattering cannonade. Further ground for complaint was provided early in December when eight thousand troops were sent under the command of Sir Joseph Thackwell to "turn" the enemy. Nicholson and his Pathans collected boats with which the force could cross the River Chinab, guarded a ford twelve miles higher up in order to hold the enemy on the other side, obtained supplies and kept Thackwell fully informed of the movements of the Sikhs. But when, after the crossing, Thackwell encountered some artillery fire from an invisible battery in a village he ought to have occupied he halted for a day and a night, missing a first-rate opportunity to take the enemy by surprise. By the next morning the force in front of him had decamped and the main body under Sher Singh had vanished into the blue. Gough described this as a victory.

In January came the ghastly fiasco of Chilianwala. The British and Sikh armies were again facing one another and a battle was necessary because Attock had just been taken by Chatar Singh and it was essential that Gough should beat Sher Singh before his father's force could join him. Both armies were in position by two o'clock in the afternoon of January 13th. Gough had been warned not to repeat his error at Ferozshah and start a battle late in the day. He had promised to commence operations the following morning, but the Sikhs had not been consulted and tactlessly opened fire on the afternoon of the 13th. This was too much. 'The impudent rascals fired on me!' he afterwards explained. 'They put my Irish blood up, and I attacked them.' One cannot resist feeling that if only someone staying at Simla the previous summer had playfully pulled Gough by the nose or blown rice in his face through a tube he might have lost his temper and helped Nicholson to save the Punjab without a war.

At any rate the inconsiderate behaviour of the Sikhs empurpled his neck and he ordered the infantry to advance against an enemy twice their strength protected by sixty-two guns and screened by a jungle of thorn and mimosa scrub about a mile in depth. He was begged by his Political Officer to use artillery and warned that the Indian soldiers dreaded the jungle, the nature and depth of which was unknown. 'I am C.-in-C. of this army,' said Gough, 'and I desire you to be silent.' The British guns could not fire because they were in the rear, and the British troops went forward against a hail of bullets and grapeshot from an unseen enemy into a dense growth that tore the flesh and spurted death. The cavalry got entangled in the thickets, the horses were ripped by thorns that pierced like swords, and the men, only too willing to mistake a word of command for an order to retreat, galloped backwards, careered madly through their own artillery, rushed into their own field hospital, knocked over the surgeons who were busy amputating limbs, and only pulled up when the chaplain appeared with a cocked pistol in his hand. By nightfall the British had taken the jungle and forty guns at a cost of 2,446 lives. Gough claimed a victory and fell back on the village of Chilianwala, leaving many of his wounded to be murdered by the Sikhs, who crept back in the dark and recaptured twenty-eight guns.

Nicholson did duty as aide-de-camp during the action, taking orders from Gough to divisional and brigade commanders and keeping headquarters informed of the progress of events. Someone happened to observe him at a moment when his nature was expressing itself more fully than his duties as an aide-de-camp permitted. An English officer was hanging back before a withering fire. Nicholson caught him by the shoulders and kicked him into action. Both in word and deed he was violent throughout the campaign, but as most of the senior officers were decrepit his energy was not misplaced. William Hodson agreed with him about many of the British commanders who fought against the Sikhs: 'At the age at which officers become colonels and majors, not one in fifty is able to stand the wear and tear of Indian service. They become still more worn in mind than in body. All elasticity is gone; all energy and enterprise worn out; they become, after a fortnight's campaign, a burden to themselves, an annoyance to those under them, and a terror to every one but the enemy. The officer who commanded the cavalry brigade which so disgraced the service at Chilianwala was not able to mount a horse without the assistance of two men. A brigadier of infantry, under whom I served during the three most critical days of the late war, could not see his regiment when I led his horse by the bridle until its nose touched the bayonets; and even then he said faintly, "Pray, which way are the men facing, Mr. Hodson?" This is no exaggeration, I assure you. Can you wonder that our troops have to recover by desperate fighting, and with heavy loss, the advantage thrown away by the want of heads and eyes to lead them?'

Gough's "victory" aroused little enthusiasm in England and it was decided to give the Indian command to Sir Charles Napier, aged nearly seventy, as the only alternative to the Duke of Wellington, aged eighty. But for once in a way Gough took time by the forelock. Greatly assisted by the troops that had been released by the fall of Multan, he opposed the sixty thousand Sikhs under Sher Singh and Chatar Singh with his twenty-five thousand men on February 21st, 1849, at Gujarat. The Sikhs had sixty guns, but Gough had ninety and this time he determined to use them. Hitherto he had regarded a cannonade as a sort of fireworks display introducing the serious business of the bayonet, the "hors d'œuvre" before the "roast," but the repeated comments of onlookers that tons of lead dropped in the enemy's lines before infantry action had a depressing effect on the foe nerved him to give the guns a chance. He was delighted with the result and exclaimed, like a child who has just discovered the possibilities of a new toy, that the bombardment was the most magnificent and the most terrible he had ever witnessed. He described the battle with truth as his last and his best. He commenced it in the morning instead of the afternoon and following two or three hours of artillery fire the Sikh guns were silenced, the British troops swept forward, the enemy's lines were broken, and by one o'clock in the afternoon the victory had become a rout, the British casualties being less than a third of the losses at Chilianwala.

Sir Henry Lawrence, knighted at Hardinge's request during his stay in England, had quickly returned to India when the Sikh war broke out and saw something of Nicholson during the later stages of the campaign. The plundering of villages by Indian troops and camp-followers infuriated Nicholson, who spoke of 'the moral wrong of plundering like so many bandits' and wrote to Lawrence: 'Unless I am vested with sufficient power to check this, and protect the people whom it is my special duty to protect, I would rather not be with the army.' He declared that the mischief could not be stopped by flogging and applied for the full powers of a provost-marshal. 'If I get them, rely on my bringing the army to its senses within two days,' he told Lawrence. But he did not get them and he criticised the authorities openly and unsparingly. Lawrence got to hear of the personal dislike his opinions aroused and wrote a friendly remonstrance:

'MY DEAR NICHOLSON. . . . Let me advise you, as a friend, to curb your temper, and bear and forbear with natives and Europeans, and you will be as distinguished as a Civilian as you are as a Soldier. Don't think it is necessary to say all you think to every one. The world would be one mass of tumult if we all gave *candid* opinions of each other. I admire your sincerity as much as any man can do, but say thus much as a general warning. Don't think I allude to any specific act; on the contrary, from what I saw in camp, I think you have done much towards conquering yourself; and I hope to see the conquest completed.'

Nicholson replied:

'MY DEAR COLONEL,—*Very many* thanks for yours of the 7th, and the friendly advice which it contains. I am

not ignorant of the faults of my temper, and you are
right in supposing that I do endeavour to overcome
them—I hope with increasing success. On one point,
however, I still think I am excusable for the plain
speaking which, I am aware, made me very unpopular
with a large portion of the officers of the Army of the
Punjab. I mean with reference to the plundering of the
unfortunate people of the country, which generally
prevailed throughout the campaign, and which was, for
the most part, winked at, if not absolutely sanctioned,
by the great majority of officers. I knew from the first
that I was giving great offence by speaking my mind
strongly on this subject; but I felt that I should be
greatly wanting in my duty, both to the people and the
army, if I did not, to the best of my ability, raise my
voice against so crying an evil. For the rest, I readily
admit that my temper is a very excitable one, and wants
a good deal of curbing. A knowledge of the disease is
said to be half the cure, and I trust the remaining half
will not be long before it is effected.'

He was able to work off some of his indignation in
the days that followed the battle of Gujarat. With his
Pathan irregulars he headed Sir Walter Gilbert's flying
column which pursued the Sikhs until they had all
surrendered, and flung their Afghan allies back into the
Khyber hills. He brought in guns, rounded up
marauders, foraged for the column, and volunteered
three times to push on to the rescue of George Lawrence's family, but his offers were not accepted. Early in
March the Sikh leaders gave themselves up, the Sikh
guns were handed over to Gilbert and the Sikh infantry
laid down their arms. It was a doleful ceremony, for
many of the vanquished army would have liked yet
another fight, knowing that their surrender meant the end
of Sikh rule in the Punjab. 'To-day Ranjit Singh is
dead!' mourned one old warrior as he saluted the pile of

arms. Nicholson, who witnessed the scene and had an un-
canny memory for faces, recognised a veteran about to
deliver up his sword: 'How is this, friend? Did you not
say you would drive us all into the sea?' he asked. 'Your
guru should have advised you better.' 'Ah, sahib, there's
no striving against Fate. There's no fighting upon a diet
of cabbage. Try it yourself, sahib.'

Peshawar was retaken, the Lawrences were handed
over, the Punjab was annexed, and John Nicholson sent
in his bill: 'I suppose compensation will be allowed me
for my property lost at Peshawar, Attock and Hasan
Abdal. I estimate it at one thousand rupees. I also rode a
horse worth four hundred rupees to death on Government service—not running away.'

Decorations were of course showered on those who
had helped to make the war, on those who had managed
to prolong it, and on those who had done their best to
lose it. But Nicholson received a distinction which his
sovereign had not the power to confer: the unique
distinction of deification by his enemies. His bravery
and ubiquity had so deeply impressed the Sikhs that they
endowed him with supernatural faculties; and when
after the battle of Gujarat he released all the prisoners
on his own responsibility, telling them to go home
quietly, the combination of mercy and courage in him
quite subdued them and they came to believe he was
another incarnation of their god. They said that if he
would openly profess the Sikh religion they would raise
a Taj for him far more wonderful than the Golden Taj at
their holy city Amritsar. What he said in reply was not
reported. But his fame among them increased, his deeds
became fabulous, and they were convinced that he alone
had conquered them; for whenever an old Sikh warrior
was prevailed upon to show visitors over the great
battlefields of those wars, he would pause reverently at
certain places and say: 'There Nikal Seyn stood.'

CHAPTER VI

Recreation

LORD DALHOUSIE was an efficient administrator with a mean nature. He was quite incapable of appreciating the finer qualities of Henry Lawrence and quickly made up his mind to curb the power of a man who placed the happiness of a people before the interests of his employers. Lawrence was entirely opposed to the annexation of the Punjab, feeling so strongly on the point that he sent his brother John to discuss details with Dalhousie. John Lawrence had the typical civil servant's outlook; he thought in terms of revenue and chiefly for that reason favoured annexation. Naturally enough, Dalhousie took to him at once and John made the most of the time he spent with the Governor-General.

Henry Lawrence felt Dalhousie's antagonism and proffered his resignation. But Dalhousie was no fool; he knew perfectly well that the Sikhs loved and trusted Henry, the only man in the country, therefore, who could effect the annexation without incurring trouble from the people who were to be dispossessed. So Dalhousie cunningly suggested that Henry's resignation would be injurious to the Sikhs, for was he not their friend and counsellor and would he not with his well-known moderation help them through a difficult period? Henry could not resist such an appeal, as Dalhousie knew quite well before he made it, and a Board of Administration was set up to govern the Punjab with Henry Lawrence as President, his power shorn by the appointment of his brother John and another civilian C. G. Mansell as coadjutors on the Board. John Lawrence was to be responsible for finance, Mansell for the magistracy, and Henry Lawrence for military, political and diplomatic affairs.

One of Henry's famous assistants, Herbert Edwardes, remained with him at Lahore; the rest became his Deputy Commissioners, brother George in Peshawar, James Abbott in Hazara, Reynell Taylor in Bannu and John Nicholson in Rawal Pindi. The functions of a district Deputy-Commissioner were manifold. He had to carry out the judicial, fiscal and governmental duties which are undertaken by the various departments of state in a western country; he had to collect revenue, to act as judge and jury, to control the police and hunt down criminals, to supervise the gaols, the excise, stamps, taxes, roads, bridges, ferries, woods and forests; and sometimes he had to do the work of recruiting sergeant and chaplain.

Nicholson's protection of the poor from the ruthlessness of tax-collectors and the depredations of soldiers had made him extremely popular in the district of Rawal Pindi, and the contrast between his justice and the exactions they had so long endured soon made him the idol of the peasantry. With the disappearance of the revenue officers who had robbed and bullied them to enrich the Sikh chieftains their sole enemies were professional marauders, but Nicholson's way of dealing with these men quickly reduced their formidability. One famous freebooter managed to keep out of his reach for some time and he offered a reward for the man's capture. The headmen of the villages dared not stir because the criminal had surrounded himself with friends. Sitting in his office one day, Nicholson asked whether the fellow had yet been caght.

'No, not yet,' he was informed.

'Double the reward at once, then,' said Nicholson.

Four hours later he asked the same question, received

the same answer, and was told that a strong force of police would be required to get the man, who was a desperado and lived amongst his own kinsmen.

'Saddle my horse,' said Nicholson.

He rode off alone to the village of the robber, who by a curious coincidence was the first person he met. Upon being ordered to surrender the man rushed at Nicholson, who ran him through, rode back and had the body brought to him. Cutting the head off, he placed it beside him in the office and contemptuously asked every village headman who entered whether he recognised to whom it belonged.

Most of Nicholson's energy was absorbed by his work, but very rarely he would relax and take a day off for recreation. In tiger-hunting he discovered a respite from bandit-hunting, and he became expert in a method of approaching his game that has never much appealed to English sportsmen. Having found a tiger, he put his horse to a gallop and rode round and round the beast at a terrific speed, never slackening for a second and gradually contracting the circle. The tiger crouched ready to spring and waiting for an opportunity, but Nicholson never gave it one; his horse went whirling round, getting nearer the tiger with every circle it made, until the hunted animal, revolving faster and faster as the horse got closer and closer, became utterly stupefied by the strange manœuvre and Nicholson's sword settled the contest. It was a ticklish business, for if the horseman had got too near the beast to strike effectively, or not near enough, and if the blow had been delivered with insufficient strength and skill, it would have been the tiger's turn.

This was not perhaps the average Deputy-Commissioner's idea of an agreeable afternoon's entertainment free from the cares of office, but Nicholson was not an average Deputy-Commissioner. He was, among other things, a god, and one of his sacred duties, following the most approved models, was to chasten his worshippers. This year, 1849, saw the birth of a new creed instituted by a devout Hindu, who declared that the great hero Nikal Seyn was the reincarnation of Brahma. The annunciation took place at Hasan Abdal and a brotherhood or sect of Nikalseynites was soon flourishing. It was an extreme form of the Sikh worship already alluded to; but whereas the Sikhs were never able to reconcile Nicholson's religion with their own, which prevented their absolute recognition of his godhead, the Nikal-Seyn fakirs did not bother much about his beliefs, contenting themselves with a belief in him.

A young engineer named Alex Taylor,* who was working on the extension of the Grand Trunk Road from Lahore to Peshawar, received a strange party of visitors one day. He was sitting in his small bungalow at Hasan Abdal when twenty helmeted men, dressed very quaintly, entered in single file, saluted courteously, and squatted in a row before him without speaking a word. He was at a loss to account for this strange proceeding and his surprise changed to disquietude through a long silence, during which he looked wonderingly at them and they gazed thoughtfully at him. At last their leader spoke: 'We are Nikal Seyn's fakirs. You are a white sahib. We are come to pay our respects to you as one of Nikal Seyn's race.' A brief conversation ensued and he heard of the new faith for the first time; then he dismissed them and they passed on southward towards the object of their adoration. But their god was a stern god and when they bowed to the ground before him and chanted pæans in his honour he drove them from his presence with blows and maledictions. 'He is a just god,' they said, 'and punishes us for our own good.' They returned and he ordered them to be flogged; this too they appre-

* Later to become General Sir Alexander Taylor.

ciated, coming back at intervals for further instalments
of their god's righteous chastisement. He was troubled
with their attentions for the rest of his life, and though
he told them about the god he worshipped and had
them flogged or imprisoned whenever they attempted to
worship him, their adoration of Nikal Seyn never
wavered and they testified to their belief in him up and
down the country.

Whenever he was able to do so Nicholson spent the
summer days of 1849 in the valley of Hasan Abdal,
where the great Mogul emperor Akbar had built himself
a palace in lovely surroundings. Nicholson's residence
was on a less ambitious scale; it consisted of a tent
pitched on a wooden platform over a stream, and here, to
the sound of running water, he brooded upon the Scriptures, upon salvation, predestination, free will and such-
like questions. He accepted the puritanical creed in which
he had been brought up, yet he could not help wondering
whether all the natives in India were condemned to
eternal death merely because they had not been converted to Christianity. The whole question of Biblical inspiration was a very difficult one; even a deeply sincere
and brilliantly clever fellow like Henry Lawrence thought
"God's dealings with the Jews very mysterious," so how
could he, plain John Nicholson, be expected to solve
such complicated problems? Nevertheless, he continued
to ponder them.

He was beginning to feel the need of a change. He
had been in India for ten years and was entitled to go
home on furlough. No more wars were in prospect; the
Punjab was tranquil, no district more so than his own;
and he longed to see his mother again. She too was in
need of him, for she had just lost another son in India.
William Nicholson had joined the Bombay Army as a
cadet in '47 and though he had not met his elder brother
he had been able to write long letters home about

John's growing fame. Then William died, suddenly and mysteriously, on June 1, 1849. One morning he was not present on parade and was found in bed, bruised from head to foot, with two broken ribs. He was almost unconscious and could only murmur something about having dreamt of a fall from a great height. It was thought that he had been walking in his sleep, had fallen down a cliff from the verandah, and had somehow got back to bed; but his bungalow remained untenanted for years and was called by the natives "Murder House." This tragedy strengthened John Nicholson's desire to go home and comfort his mother. His departure would result in the loss of his appointment, but he hoped his chief would find him another on his return. Henry Lawrence was not slow to reassure him, writing: 'One line to say how sorry I am to have missed you. To-morrow we shall be at Damtur, the scene of your gallant attempt to help Abbott. But what corner of the Punjab is not witness to your gallantry? Get married, and come back soon; and if I am alive and in office, it shall not be my fault if you do not find employment here.'

The summer passed by and still he could not leave his post. India, he said, 'is like a rat-trap, easier to get into than out of.' At last someone was found to take his place and he arrived at Lahore in December, to find that Herbert Edwardes was also going to England, taking John Lawrence's two little daughters with him. The friends decided to make the journey together as far as Egypt, after which Nicholson intended to do a little sight-seeing. They travelled by river to Karachi; every night their boatmen drew in to the bank and while the evening meal was being cooked they took Lawrence's children for an excursion, showing them the footprints of a tiger on the shore and telling them stories of elephants or the other monstrosities that inhabit jungles and are only romantic in stories.

The friendship between Edwardes and Nicholson was cemented on the journey. They had one emotion in common, a love and veneration for Henry Lawrence, and two characteristics in common, courage and quickness in action. But they were unlike in every other respect. Nicholson was a solitary man, Edwardes a social one. Nicholson sometimes doubted whether he was doing right and had a gloomy temperament. Edwardes never had a shadow of doubt about himself and his outlook was cheerful; he possessed enormous self-confidence, a clear intellect, a sound judgment; he was a convinced Christian, never at a loss to explain the meaning of a text or to reconcile apparent contradictions in sacred writ. He could persuade any one that black was white and no one could corner him in argument. He had an expansive nature, expressing himself as well on paper as in conversation, in light verse as in dialectics. He was in brief an eminently adaptable and resilient personage. Nicholson admired his sureness, his joviality, his versatility, and felt life would be much easier if he himself had been born with a similar range of faculties. 'You must not compare me with Herbert Edwardes,' he said to someone in a burst of humility, and indeed no one who knew the two men at all well would have dreamt of doing so.

On their way down the river they talked of the incompetence of the military and civil authorities in India, or rather Edwardes talked while Nicholson agreed with him, and prophesied trouble in the future due to misgovernment, foreseeing the Mutiny as clearly as their master Lawrence did. They reached Bombay in January, '50, and had Lord Gough as a fellow-passenger on their steamer, Charles Napier having superseded him as Commander-in-Chief. They felt safer with Gough at sea than they had felt with him on land, and the voyage passed without trepidation. Gough asked Nicholson to accompany him to Dublin and share in the civic reception that was to be accorded the victor at Gujarat, but Nicholson declined the honour. He parted from Edwardes at Cairo and after seeing the Pyramids and the ruins of Thebes, which he called 'the oldest and greatest of cities,' he went on to Constantinople, where he stayed three weeks, behaving on two occasions in a manner which explained his posthumous popularity with Victorian schoolboys.

Kossuth, the famous Hungarian patriot, had announced the independence of his country in '48, and about a year later he was forced to flee from Austrian tyranny, taking refuge in Turkey. The latter country was asked to hand him over, but with the sympathetic backing of England refused, and Kossuth remained in honourable arrest at a Turkish fort. He went for a ride every day, accompanied by an armed escort, and certain English and American admirers planned to rescue him during one of these excursions and put him on board an American vessel. Nicholson was asked to give a hand and promptly gave it. The date was fixed; the direction of the ride was ascertained; the best spot for taking the guard by surprise was chosen; and the rescue party was on the point of setting out when news arrived that the plot had been discovered and Kossuth was off in a different direction under an alert and reinforced escort. It turned out that one of the American rescuers had told his wife of the plan in the closest confidence; she had passed it on to a friend in the strictest secrecy; the friend had revealed it to an intimate acquaintance in the utmost privacy; and somehow the Austrian embassy had got to hear of it. Kossuth was eventually released and lived for a while in England.

Nicholson's second adventure was more successful. General Guyon, an Englishman, had obtained a commission in the Austro-Hungarian army, had married the

daughter of a Hungarian nobleman, and had fought for
Hungary when Kossuth rallied the country against
Austria. After the war he too found an asylum in
Turkey, but his wife had been imprisoned in an Austrian
fortress and each was entirely ignorant of the other's
condition. His wife did not even know whether he was
alive and he was unable to enlighten her, for had he
shown himself in Austria he would have been shot. He
asked Nicholson to take a letter to her and he did not
have to ask twice. Nicholson crossed the border and soon
found himself in front of a massive structure which
could only be entered with the help of heavy artillery.
Realising at a glance that "there was no getting in
without leave," he marched straight up to the gate and
informed the guard that he wished to see the officer on
duty, to whom he was instantly taken.

'I am an English officer,' he said, 'and would be very
much obliged for your permission to see Madame Guyon.'

The request was highly irregular and the Austrian
officer was taken aback. But there was something about
Nicholson that persuaded people to grant his requests,
and after a brief hesitation the officer ordered that he
should be given five minutes alone with Madame Guyon.
The cell-door closed behind him and having apologised
for his behaviour he pulled off a boot, extracted the
letter and handed it to her with the words:

'You have just five minutes to read it and give me
any message for your husband.'

She read as fast and said as much as she could in
the time, and Nicholson departed, gravely thanking the
Austrian officer, who, unable to account for his impulse,
must have done his best to forget the incident.

Nicholson left Constantinople on March 15th in a
French steamer which owing to a snowstorm ran
aground the next morning in the Dardanelles, the
passengers being taken off in a British boat. He spent

a week at Athens and reached England by way of Vienna and Berlin at the end of April. His mother was staying at the house of her brother Sir James Hogg in Grosvenor Square, and he made that his home whenever he was in London. Although he wandered about the metropolis with Herbert Edwardes, seeing the sights and looking at the horses and carriages in Hyde Park and Piccadilly, he felt out of place on the London pavements. The bustle of "the season" did not appeal to him and he wondered how people could find pleasure in doing nothing with so much energy. He was depressed by a debate in the House of Commons and bored by a dinner at the Mansion House, at which the Duke of Wellington was present and Herbert Edwardes, replying to the toast of the Indian Army, turned towards Nicholson and declared: 'Here, gentlemen, here is the real author of half the exploits which the world has been so ready to attribute to me.' He went to the Italian Opera at Covent Garden and remarked of the ballet, 'We have nothing so bad in India.' It struck him that there was more poverty and vice in London than in the Punjab and he failed to appreciate "the blessings" of progress and civilisation.

He revisited Ireland, staying at Lisburn and going about the country with his two sisters, one of whom was married and lived at Barnsley, where he also spent a short holiday, testing the courage of his nephew, aged four, by making him sit on the top of a door and by holding him over the banisters. 'He used to chaff me,' wrote this nephew many years later, 'for liking sweet things and assured me that if I would come to Bannu with him I should have butter on one side of my bread and sugar on the other, which was the way they always lived there. I meekly remonstrated that I shouldn't like to go there, because there were sure to be lions and tigers. To which he replied that he would write to Uncle Charles to have them all killed.'

Edwardes was married in the summer of '50 at Petersham, near Richmond, Nicholson acting as "best man," and on the eve of his departure for India with his wife he wrote a word of advice to John: 'If your heart meets one worthy of it, *return not alone.* I cannot tell you how good it is for our best purposes to be *helped* by a noble wife who loves you better than all men or women, but God better than you.' It is the natural desire of every married man to see his friends in a similar state of happiness or servitude, and everybody except Nicholson felt that he ought to marry. When his mother discussed the question with him he replied that he could not bear the thought either of taking a wife with him across the Indus or leaving her behind. But the real reason that he did not marry was that he did not wish to marry. His heart and soul were in his work and he had no emotion to spare for a woman. Whatever sexual desire he may have felt was controlled by his puritanism and released into his outdoor activities, which dissipated or absorbed it.

Women admired him greatly and his physical appearance was sufficiently striking. He made the most of his six feet two inches, carrying his head as if he scorned the earth. He was very strongly built, broad-shouldered and deep-chested. His facial resemblance to the leader of the Opposition, Disraeli, was noticed by many people during his visit to England, a resemblance chiefly marked in the eye and the contour of the face. His eyes were dark-grey, with black pupils which dilated under excitement like a tiger's, very penetrating in their effect and causing acute discomfort to any one who received his hostile regard. His countenance was colourless, anger giving it a cloudy look. While in England he was clean-shaven, though on his return to India he grew whiskers and a large black beard that matched the hair on his head. He never smiled, was laconic in speech and had a

cold, abrupt, haughty manner which antagonised many
people. His aloof bearing, said his friends, concealed a
tender nature, and he was certainly capable of deep
feeling, but people could scarcely be blamed for super-
ficial judgments when they were only permitted to see
the surface.

The combination of strength, reserve, pride, will-
power, imperiousness and implacable resolution in him
may or may not have inspired Tennyson's "One still
strong man in a blatant land," but among all the great
soldiers in history he was assuredly the only "strong
silent man." Most men of action are extremely talkative.
Cæsar overflowed with conversation, Cromwell was
hysterically communicative, Napoleon chattered cease-
lessly and even talked in his sleep; while those sup-
posedly iron characters who have a great reputation for
silence are usually as garrulous as old women: Kitchener, for example, whose volubility was such that
George V. "could never get in a word edgeways" and was
"reduced to silence." Nicholson never talked much, even
with his intimate friends, and his speech was always
clipped into terse phrases that seldom comprised paren-
theses. He was a great fighter and leader of men, expressing himself in action as fully and freely as Keats
expressed himself in poetry or Mozart in music. This
does not mean that he was merely a great soldier. Born
fighters and leaders are as rare in the military profession
as born barristers in the legal profession or born any one
in anything. Most men choose their professions either
because one form of life is less obnoxious to them than
another or because circumstances favour their choice.
The born fighter and leader is seldom to be found in the
army until a crisis precipitates him into it; or, if he is in
the army, he remains a nobody until a crisis makes him
somebody. There were lots of things about the army that
Nicholson disliked: promotion by seniority instead of

merit, refusal to adopt new inventions in arms and general hostility to fresh ideas. Hodson noted another absurdity. 'There are, I doubt not, many clever and able men who would in a year put any boy with tolerable abilities into a state of intellectual coma which would enable him to write out examination papers by the dozen, and pass a triumphant examination in paper-military affairs. I am not called upon to state how much of it would avail in the hour of strife and danger.'

Although their criticisms of the army were identical, Hodson and Nicholson had nothing except fighting ability in common. Spiritually they were poles apart. Hodson revelled in Shakespeare, Nicholson read scriptural tracts; Hodson would have gone home on leave to have a good time, Nicholson went home on leave to see his mother; Hodson, the sportsman, damned the sins he had no mind to, Nicholson, the puritan, damned the sins he had a mind to. There is a revealing passage in a letter Nicholson wrote to his mother just before going home: 'What you say about our prosperous days being those of the greatest temptation, is quite true. I have long felt it so, and prayed for grace to resist the temptation. I also fully agree in all you say about earthly distinctions. Believe me, I estimate them at their proper value.' His ambition was to win high place and fame in the world, but he condemned it as vain and sinful and cloaked it with duty and service. There was no hypocrisy in this. One side of his nature really did despise ambition, and duty was its watchword. He believed in the British Empire, in England's right to rule the heathen for their own good. It would not have occurred to him that any one could question the morality of such a dispensation. Thus his duty as a Briton served his desire for distinction as a human being, though he did not see it in that light.

The greater part of his furlough was spent in attention to duty; the duty he owed to his mother, whom he loved, and the duty he owed to his calling, which he loved. He visited the Prince Consort's great Exhibition of 1851 in Hyde Park, but it was the display of foreign firearms that interested him more than anything else in Paxton's Crystal Palace. He studied the military systems on the Continent, attended big reviews of troops in Paris, St. Petersburg, Vienna and Berlin, and was much impressed by the way in which Tsar Nicholas personally manœuvred twelve thousand men on parade, saluting them on his appearance with a loud 'Good-morning,' and receiving the reply 'Good-morning' from twelve thousand throats in unison. He returned from these trips convinced that the British Army was hopelessly out of date and that there would be a serious administrative collapse in the event of war. The collapse occurred in the Crimea a few years after his prophecy. From Berlin he brought back one of the new needle-guns which fifteen years later enabled the Prussians to beat the Austrians at Sadowa and shifted the balance of power in Europe. He did his utmost to make the War Office scrap the old heavy smooth-bore "Brown Bess" for a light quick-firing breechloader that could kill at five hundred yards; but the War Office was at peace with itself and did not want to kill anything at five hundred yards.

Nicholson's last thought before leaving England was for his mother, who had often asked him to have his photograph taken. He would rather no doubt have faced a tiger than a camera, but one morning in Regent Street he entered a studio, and the resultant daguerreotype faithfully pictured him at the age of twenty-nine.

CHAPTER VII

Justice in Shirtsleeves

PASSING through Italy on his way back to India, Nicholson was disgusted by what he saw and heard of Bourbon rule, and, moved to indignation by King "Bomba's" treatment of political opponents, he called on the British ambassador at Naples, intending to acquaint that functionary with his views and to offer his services in any liberating movement that would overthrow the reigning dynasty. It is not, however, the custom of British ambassadors to foment rebellions against the courts to which they have been appointed, and this particular diplomat courageously declined to see him. Nicholson exercised a manly restraint. Instead of fighting his way into the presence of his Excellency or tearing the embassy down with his hands, he carried his indignation to India, exploding at intervals on the way.

In those days the journey from the Mediterranean Sea to the Gulf of Suez was tedious and uncomfortable. Travellers went by canal from Alexandria to Atfih, then down the Nile to Cairo by steamer, then across seventy miles of uneven desert to Suez by a mule-drawn two-wheeled van, which frequently stuck in the sand and jolted so abominably that passengers forgot all their troubles in their concentrated efforts to prevent their insides from coming outside. But the journey did not make Nicholson think kindly of Bourbon rule in Italy, because when he got to Lahore he was still boiling with wrath, and, sitting one day on the verandah of a bunga-low, he unburdened himself to his friend Neville

Chamberlain, who had just become Military Secretary to the Punjab Board of Administration. Feeling all the better for a full recital of his political opinions, he struck a softer note and 'descanted lovingly' on the merits of the needle-musket he had brought with him from Berlin, stressing the urgent need for it in the British Army.

The Punjab, when Nicholson returned to it in the spring of 1852, was in a flourishing condition. The Board had administered it well, the coffers of the East India Company had benefited by over a million pounds in three years, and the directors were happy. Having sacrificed his political appointment by going home, Nicholson would have been posted as a Captain to some regiment if Lawrence had been unable to secure another job for him. Fortunately Reynell Taylor was about to leave on furlough and Nicholson took his place as Deputy-Commissioner for Bannu, a district of some 6,500 square miles lying south-west of Peshawar between the border of Afghanistan and the River Indus.

Ranjit Singh had taken the country from the Afghans, and occasionally during his reign a Sikh army had arrived to collect revenue, which it did with so much looting, burning and murdering that the inhabitants came to regard with disfavour the appearance of an alien force in their midst. In 1847 Henry Lawrence sent Herbert Edwardes to make a report of the country and to offer good government to the natives in return for their co-operation. Edwardes thought the Bannuchis 'the most ignorant, depraved and bloodthirsty' people in the Punjab. They refused his offers and he threatened a speedy return with an army, when he would disarm them, take their country and level their forts. Later the same year he reappeared and proceeded to fulfil his promise. Without firing a shot he forced the wild Waziris in the hills to pay tribute and the people in the valleys to destroy their forts. He constructed a military road, founded a new town, irrigated large tracts of country, disarmed the natives and introduced a legal system. Edwardes was followed by Reynell Taylor, a conscientious man of a gentle chivalrous nature, who performed many feats of valour in the second Sikh war and afterwards governed Bannu justly but too mildly. Taking advantage of his amiable disposition, the Waziri hillmen not only refused to pay tribute, but frequently descended upon the husbandmen in the valleys, killing and pillaging. Taylor treated them with systematic forbearance in the belief that they could be tamed by kindness, with the result that the border country had been in a ferment for about three years when John Nicholson arrived in May, 1852.

Taylor's assistant, a young lieutenant named Richard Pollock, was not at all agreeably impressed by the new Deputy-Commissioner. He loved Taylor, whom he thought 'a saint on earth,' and he resented the self-confident tone of Nicholson, who scarcely troubled to listen to Taylor's explanations of the work he had tried to do, but stated brusquely what he himself intended to do. While Pollock felt resentment, the native officials and people of Bannu experienced emotions of a more irruptive order. Taylor had been long-suffering, painstaking, sympathetic. Nicholson was abrupt, stern, forbidding, and the Bannuchis at first regarded him as a hard-hearted, self-willed tyrant whom they dreaded and detested. He was unapproachable; he would not listen to their grievances; he had no understanding of their weaknesses, no appreciation of their wants; he gave orders and insisted on immediate unquestioning obedience. A devil, it seemed to them, had displaced an angel. But a satan of some sort was needed to cast out satan, and Nicholson had not been in the country for many months before the more law-abiding members of the community became aware that a strange transformation was taking place. Men and women found that justice, though stern, was swift and sure, that they could till the fields in security and move about freely by day and night without risk of losing their lives.

The new ruler was a terrific worker. From early morning till late at night he never spared a moment for leisure; and he was quite tireless, riding thirty miles before breakfast to decide some question of landownership and then working in court through a long day with a temperature of over ninety degrees. He went everywhere investigating things for himself. He personally visited scenes of crime or disputation, giving an ear to the people as well as the police and satisfying himself of the rights and wrongs of cases. He never wasted time in his court: trials were brief, appeals were promptly dealt with. He did not believe in sending criminals to prison, which only confirmed them in crime, but had them flogged instead. His punishments were meted out with deliberation; he repeatedly warned before he struck, and was always ready to give offenders "another chance"; but persistent troublers of the peace were shown no mercy.

Some years later his successor was trying a case and wondering which of the disputants was the bigger liar when one of them said to the other: 'Turn your back to the sahib and he will see it still waled from the whipping which Nikal Seyn gave you.' But the other had a good memory too and replied: 'You need not talk, for your back is also well scored.'

Nicholson was skilful in the judgment of character and could be very patient with fools and criminals when he thought that patience would pay. 'Never remove a native official unless you know that you can replace him by a better one,' he said to Pollock; 'otherwise you will get an equally stupid or corrupt man, minus the experi-

ence of his predecessor.' One of his chief difficulties was
the suppression of corruption among the officials, but
in time the law-officers became as law-abiding as those
over whom they were set in authority.

As Henry Lawrence realised, the Punjab could only
be well governed by men like Nicholson and Edwardes,
men who would not spare themselves and who would
do 'prompt justice in their shirtsleeves.' In this respect
Edwardes himself gave the palm to Nicholson: 'I only
knocked down the walls of the Bannu forts,' he said;
'John Nicholson has since reduced the *people* ... to such
a state of good order and respect for the laws, that in
the last year of his charge not only was there no murder,
burglary or highway robbery, but not an *attempt* at any
of these crimes. The Bannuchis, reflecting on their own
metamorphosis in the village gatherings under the vines,
by the streams they once delighted so to fight for, have
come to the conclusion that the good Mohammedans of
historic ages must have been just like Nikal Seyn.
They emphatically approve him as every inch a Ruler.'
Nicholson was the first man to cow the north-west
frontier of India into good behaviour, and he was also
the last. But it took him three years of incessant toil
to work the miracle.

He began with the hill tribes. Armed Waziris used
to come from the border and raid the towns. At night-
time they crept up the dry beds of irrigation channels,
attacked houses, killed the inhabitants and made off with
their plunder. Nicholson secreted police in the channels
and soon made a useful discovery. The leader of one
armed party was a village headman, a landowner, who
lived as a respectable farmer by day and as a murderous bandit by night. In a skirmish with the police he
was killed, and Nicholson had his body strung up in the
market-place like a crow or weasel to frighten his kind.
These Waziris were outlaws, living in the border hills.

inaccessible, safe from attack; they could plunder and cut throats with impunity, being subject to no law but their own. Nicholson decided to teach them a lesson and to prove that they were accessible by him. Putting himself at the head of fifteen hundred mounted police, he penetrated their mountains, destroyed their villages and established a blockade. They could teach him nothing in the science of mountain warfare, and when they realised that he had not come solely to enjoy the scenery they sued for peace. He wasted no words: 'Pay a rupee a head and behave well in future.' They paid and behaved.

It was characteristic of Nicholson that after this success he should have proposed to deal with another peccant hill tribe by personally leading a body of frontier troops against them, entirely overlooking the fact that their commanding officer ought to have been consulted. He was with difficulty persuaded to leave the matter in the hands of the proper military authority. Red-tape always made him see red. 'This is the way I treat these things,' he said to a friend as he kicked a bundle of government regulations across the floor. It has already been remarked that Nicholson was not merely a great soldier, one whose nature can best be expressed within the framework of his profession, whose achievements are made possible by certain limitations imposed from without. In a sense it might even be said that Nicholson was not a soldier at all. He rebelled against all authority, was intolerant of reasonable restraint, disregarded rules, derided "schools" of tactics and strategy, and always acted on instinct. He belonged to that small class of inspired leaders which included Cromwell and Clive, leaders who could make human beings do apparently superhuman things, whose personal bravery and tireless fortitude infected their followers and whose handling of every situation, however unexpected, was so masterly that their officers and men lost all sense of criticism and followed them blindly. 'I know that Nicholson is a first-rate guerrilla leader, but we don't want a guerrilla policy,' grumbled Lord Dalhousie. Yet all inspired leaders are guerrilla leaders; that is to say, they adapt themselves to the exigency of the moment and never have a settled policy. The real soldier, the born professional, could not get along without a settled policy. He is amenable to discipline, to rules of warfare, to 'terms of reference,' to orthodox methods of organisation; and within such limits, which do not exclude the exercise of genius, he can attain his full stature. The great professional soldier is to the inspired leader what the great scholar is to the inspired artist, and to mention Wolfe, Moore, Wellington and Kitchener is to show that men of very rare abilities have been able to give of their best because of their temperamental need of conditions that would have galled and cramped Nicholson and his like.

Force and fearlessness of character are perhaps the two qualities most easily appreciated by a barbarous people, and very soon after Nicholson's arrival in Bannu he gave evidence of them. One day he met a deputation of native chiefs from the border. They had become accustomed to a weak ruler on the frontier and treated the new Deputy-Commissioner with hauteur, one of them showing his disdain in a marked manner by hawking and spitting on the ground between Nicholson and himself. He was totally unprepared for what followed. 'Orderly!' said Nicholson, 'make that man lick up his spittle and kick him out of the camp.' The orderly grasped the fellow by the scruff of the neck, held his nose to the ground until he had licked it clean, and then completed the rest of the order. On another occasion Nicholson was passing through a village with his mounted escort. Every man in the street saluted him except a Moslem priest who was

sitting before the mosque and gave him a look of hatred.
Nicholson asked an orderly if he had noticed the priest's
scowl. 'Yes, sahib,' said the orderly. 'Then go and
bring him to my camp,' commanded Nicholson, who
also sent for the village barber. The priest's replies to
Nicholson's questions were sufficient to prove him guilty
of insolence to a British officer and the barber was
ordered to shave the man's beard, a fearful affliction to
a Mohammedan. The sight of a beardless priest caused
endless discussion throughout the countryside and
thereafter, we must presume, scowling was carried on in
secret.

Having paralysed the people with force, he placated
them with justice. For example, it came to his notice
that a man named Alladad Khan, who was guardian of a
nephew's estate, had dispossessed the lad and forced him
to leave the neighbourhood. The man was powerful in
his village and Nicholson could find no one with sufficient courage to swear that the land was not his. One
morning a labourer discovered Nicholson's white mare
feeding in a meadow on this estate. He rushed away and
reported the occurrence to Alladad, who was thoroughly
scared and ordered that the animal should be driven off
his land, as he might be accused of trying to steal it.
By this time the entire village had collected to gaze at
the mare, and suddenly someone espied Nicholson himself tied to a tree a little distance off. The sight terrified
the villagers, who were about to bolt when Nicholson
stopped them with a shout. A few of the braver spirits
advanced to release him, but he ordered them to stand
off and demanded in an angry voice: 'Who is the owner
of this land?' All of them pointed at Alladad, who went
forward tremblingly and declared that the land was not
his but his nephew's. Nicholson made him repeat his
statement and swear that it was true. After the man's
oath had been given *coram populo* Nicholson allowed

himself to be released. The case was settled in court next
day, the nephew returned to his inheritance, and the
uncle, unable to bear the grins in his locality, went on
a pilgrimage to Mecca.

In a letter to Edwardes the governor of Bannu gave a
remarkable picture of everyday life in his province. He
was not by inclination a writer of letters, telling his
mother in a postscript that his sister would not hear
from him for another month, as he was unable to 'fill
up two overland letters at once,' and informing his
sister that a certain epistle was brief because he 'had no
news to communicate, and I always find great difficulty
in filling up a letter unless I have.' But while he was
at Bannu he wrote several letters to Edwardes which were
probably the greatest literary feats of his career. One of
them, dated June 21, 1854, ran as follows:

'If there are any humming-tops, Jew's-harps, or other
toys, at Peshawar, which would take with Waziri children, I should be much obliged if you would send me
a few. I don't ask for peg-tops, as I suppose I should
have to teach how to use them, which would be an
undignified proceeding on the part of a district officer.
Fancy a wretched little Waziri child, who had been put
up to poison food, on my asking him if he knew it was
wrong to kill people, saying he knew it was wrong to
kill with a knife or a sword. I asked him why, and he
said *because the blood left marks.*' It ended in my ordering him to be taken away from his own relatives (who
ill-used him as much as they ill-taught him) and made
over to some respectable man who would engage to treat
and bring him up well. The little chap heard the order
given, and called out, 'Oh, there's *such* a good man in
the Miri Tappahs, please send me to him.' I asked him
how he knew the man he named was good? and he said
'He never gives any one bread without butter on it.'
I found out, on inquiry, that the man in question was

a good man in other respects, and he agreeing, I made the little fellow over to him; and I have seldom seen anything more touching than their mutual adoption of each other as father and son, the child clasping the man's beard, and the man with his hands on the child's head. Well, this is a long story for me, and all grown out of a humming-top! Before I close this I must tell you of the last Bannuchi murder, it is so horribly characteristic of the blood-thirstiness and bigotry of their dispositions. The murderer killed his brother near Goriwala, and was brought in to me on a frightfully hot evening, looking dreadfully parched and exhausted. "Why," said I, "is it possible you have walked in, fasting, on a day like this?" "Thank God," said he, "I am a regular faster." "Why have you killed your brother?" "I saw a fowl killed last night, and the sight of the blood put the devil into me." He had chopped up his brother, stood a long chase, and been marched in here, *but he was keeping the fast!*'

Edwardes started a Christian mission at Peshawar, and though Nicholson made it clear that he felt no inner urge to support it, he sent a subscription: 'I wish your mission at Peshawar every success, but you require skilful and practical men as well as good men. . . .I will send you five hundred rupees (£50), and as I don't want to get credit from you for better motives than really actuate me, I will tell you the truth, that I give it because I know it will gratify my mother to see my name in the subscription list. . . . On second thoughts, I won't have my name in the Mission subscription list. Write me down "Anonymous." I can tell my mother it is I.' Two months later he let his mother know what he had done, and in the same letter proved that he did not lack the instincts of a Christian: 'If you have not yet received any rent from the C——s, I would ask you not to take any. It would seem to be inconsistent with the friendly relations which I believe exist between you, to take rent for accommodation which one friend should be happy to have an opportunity of affording another.'

Like all men who are not essentially mean-natured, Nicholson took no interest in money-making; he spent little on himself and gave generously. He provided his mother with every comfort she required and insisted that she should take long holidays at the seaside, which she enjoyed. He helped the poor in his district and was especially liberal where children were concerned, often pensioning from his own purse those whose fathers had fought with him and fallen. And he was not only generous with money : he would add to his own labours in order to benefit a man who had served him well. Pollock, whose feeling for him began with resentment and ended with reverence, was abruptly advised one day to go for a holiday to Kashmir, and though he pointed out that it would be difficult to get a *locum tenens* Nicholson merely said that he would not ask for one. Before leaving Nicholson handed him a letter of introduction to Gulab Singh and favoured him with a specimen of that ruler's table-talk :

'Alas !' said Gulab Singh, 'one of my best cooks tried to poison me.'

'And what did you do?' asked Nicholson.

'I had him brought before me,' explained the Maharajah gently, 'and I ordered my people to separate the skin of the head from the neck behind to the throat, then to flay the head, and then to put up the skin over the skull.'

'Did he die?'

'Oh dear no! he lived for weeks.'

At regular intervals during the four years Nicholson spent in Bannu the fakirs who believed in his divinity turned up and went through the grovelling process proper to deities. On each occasion they were well whipped for their pains, though at their last appearance

Nicholson relented, saying that if they would go back
to Hazara and worship the Deputy-Commissioner there
he would let them off. They duly called on that official,
but apparently he did not come up to standard, for when
they returned to their monastery they preached the
gospel of "Nikal Seyn" and continued to do so until they
heard that he was dead, when the two leaders of the sect
cut their throats and were buried in the graves they had
made before committing suicide. The next in command
took a different line: 'Nikal Seyn always said that he
was a man such as we are, and that he worshipped a god
we could not see but who was always near us. Let us
then learn to worship Nikal Seyn's god.' The rest of the
brotherhood agreed, travelled to Peshawar, placed themselves under Christian teachers, and were baptized to
a man.

Nicholson was also troubled by two other matters
during his Deputy-Commissionership: the assessment
of rent and the reclamation of waste land. He could
not work up any interest in figures or routine and would
far rather have left the natives to enjoy the full fruits
of their cultivation than be bothered with the collection
of revenue. However, these were jobs that had to be
undertaken and two years after his arrival they were
completed.

While he was in Bannu the feeling of the inhabitants
was accurately summed up by a border chief: 'Nikal
Seyn! he *is* a man. There is not one in the hills who
does not shiver in his pyjamas when he hears his name
mentioned.' But when he left the country his successor
told a different tale, which Nicholson related in a note
to Edwardes: 'Old Coke writes me that the Bannuchis,
well tamed as they have been, speak kindly and gratefully
of me. I would rather have heard this than got a present
of £1,000, for there could be no stronger testimony of my
having done my duty among them. I hear that in an

assembly the other day it was allowed "that I resembled a good Mohammedan of the kind told of in old books, but not to be met with nowadays." I wish with all my heart it were more true; but I can't help a feeling of pride, that a savage people whom I was obliged to deal with so sternly, should appreciate and give me credit for good intentions.'

CHAPTER VIII

Quarrels

IN the spring of 1852 Henry Lawrence made his last tour of inspection through the Punjab and while in Bannu read the Church of England service one Sunday to a congregation of eleven which included Nicholson. Immediately after the ceremony a report arrived that a raid of bandits had taken place in the district, and Nicholson made one of those sudden sorties from Bible-meeting to battle-ground that were common in the lives of the first British rulers in the Punjab. Fortified by the Word, he wielded the sword to such effect that the bandits regretted their ill-timed raid.

Though he could not have guessed it, he was never to see Henry Lawrence again. Ever since the arrival of Dalhousie, the annexation of the Punjab and the appointment of the Board of Administration, there had been serious friction at Lahore between the two brothers, John and Henry Lawrence. The root cause of the trouble lay in their dissimilar temperaments, but the situation was made unbearable by the character of the Governor-General.

Dalhousie made up for his physical insignificance by his dictatorial manners. He was a proud ambitious man, despotic and imperious in his bearing and behaviour, an egotist who resented opposition and crushed any one who attempted to thwart him, stern and severe in his treatment of those who disagreed with him. Charles Napier described him in an acute phrase as 'vain as a pretty woman or an ugly man.' Entirely lacking in imagination, he was never able to understand the Indians, their love of old traditions, their veneration of ancient dynasties, the fact that they preferred their own habits and customs however imperfect, to those of their white rulers, however perfect. He believed in Progress, which he thought was synonymous with British forms of government, and in that belief he wished to paint the map of India red. Progress was also another term for financial success; and since the destruction of dynasties and the paring of pensions to Indian rulers helped to swell the Company's profits, he was able to satisfy his ambition while increasing the pleasure of his employers. Like so many forceful and unimaginative people, he worked like a steam-engine, was prompt in action, thorough in method, and had that ability to absorb facts, figures and so on which is a leading feature in such characters.

Naturally a man like this could have no use for a Henry Lawrence. Everything that Dalhousie was Lawrence was not. Lawrence understood and sympathised with the Indians as no man before had done, as no man since has done. He was neither proud nor dictatorial. He did not believe that British government was the last word in human progress; indeed he was not at all sure that it was better for India than government by Indians; in many respects he thought it worse. He was gentle and considerate with every one, irrespective of pigmentation, whether they agreed with him or not. He was sensitive and imaginative and he gauged success, not by a favourable balance sheet, but by the happiness of the people. He had no head for figures and cared so little for money that he got annoyed when people talked of it as a ruling element in human affairs, his irritation being due partly to a conviction that it was not so with him and partly no doubt to an uncomfortable feeling that it was so with others. Someone who knew the two Lawrence brothers said: 'Henry would have had a contented people and an empty treasury, John a full revenue and a mutinous population.'

From the start, therefore, it was John Lawrence who gained the confidence and evoked the friendship of the Governor-General. John was full of zeal, a man of method, strong, honest, frank, definite, efficient; there was no mystery about John, who substituted reason for sentiment in the affairs of state, who understood the intricacies of finance, who never acted on impulse as his brother Henry did, who was not the victim of moods, now melancholy, now vivacious, as Henry was, who worked systematically, not spasmodically like Henry. Someone called John "a civilian Ironside" and it would be true to say that while Henry was a great public servant, John was a great civil servant. Like his master Dalhousie he was a glutton for work: duty was his delight. Born without an atom of romance in his nature, all his actions were the result of careful deliberation and the realistic weighing of pros and cons. He was free from what were called "moral infirmities" and had no understanding of human frailty, being an iron-cast Christian without sympathies, without weaknesses, as hard as nails. He seldom praised men for good work, frequently blamed them for errors, and so while he earned their respect he never gained their love. Perhaps the only man in India who felt real affection for him was Dalhousie, whose willing tool he was and who at length wrote him letters which began: "My dear Old Boy."

John Lawrence was greatly admired by Victorian writers, for he eventually became Viceroy of India, but to the impartial student of character who is not impressed by titles or human machines his most pleasing quality was a carelessness about things that most men covet. After the second Sikh war the crown jewels so greatly prized by Ranjit Singh came into the possession of the East India Company, among them the famous

Koh-i-noor diamond, which was wrapped up in numerous folds of cloth and handed in a little box to John Lawrence to take care of. He shoved it into his waistcoat pocket, went on working, forgot all about it, and when changing for dinner that night flung his waistcoat to one side without remembering what was in it. Six weeks later Dalhousie wrote that Queen Victoria wanted the jewel immediately. Henry Lawrence mentioned this at a meeting of the Board, and John said, 'Send for it at once.'

'But *you've* got it,' Henry reminded him.

John recalled in a flash where he had put it, but gave no sign of confusion or anxiety. 'Ah, yes, of course; I forgot about it,' he said, and calmly went on with the business of the meeting. At the first opportunity he slipped away and sent for his personal servant.

'Have you got a small box which was in my waistcoat pocket some time ago?'

'Yes, sahib. I found it and put it in one of your boxes.'

'Bring it here.' An old battered tin trunk was produced. 'Open it and see what is inside.'

The servant did so, undoing all the folds of cloth with great care while John Lawrence held his breath in suspense.

'There is nothing here, sahib, but a bit of glass.'

The bit of glass is now in the imperial crown of England.

Neither Queen Victoria nor Dalhousie would have thought this incident funny; though the latter would have excused John on the ground of his absorption in public affairs, whereas if it had been Henry he would have blamed him for indifference to public affairs. He was jealous of Henry and disliked him before meeting him. Henry was the acknowledged ruler of the Punjab, beloved by the natives as no Englishman was ever loved, and Dalhousie had no intention of playing second fiddle.

'Lawrence,' he wrote to a friend, 'has been greatly praised and rewarded and petted, and no doubt naturally supposes himself a King of the Punjab; but as I don't take the Brentford dynasty as a pattern, I object to sharing the chairs, and think it best to come to an understanding as to relative positions at once.'

Henry started badly by criticising the Governor-General's slackness in the opening stages of the second Sikh war. Dalhousie was furious in his glacial way and hit back by informing Henry, whose sympathy with the Sikhs was notorious, that he intended 'the utter destruction and prostration of the Sikh power, the subversion of its dynasty, and the subjection of its people.' When Henry, a little later, drew up a generous proclamation to the Sikhs, Dalhousie wrote a stinging comment: 'It is objectionable in manner because . . . its whole tone substitutes you personally, as the Resident at Lahore, for the Government which you represent. It is calculated to raise the inference that . . . you come as a peacemaker for the Sikhs, as standing between them and the Government. This cannot be.' Against Henry's advice the annexation was effected, the Board was set up and his own hands were tied.

Dalhousie never allowed Henry to forget who was master. A passage in one of the Governor-General's letters reveals the essential vulgarity of his nature and portrays in miniature a cad in office. They had been arguing points at issue and Dalhousie told a friend how he had treated Henry Lawrence: 'I tipped him a little of the "grand seigneur," which I had not given him before, and the storm sank into a whisper in a second.' Lawrence, being a gentleman, never in his life tipped any one 'a little of the grand seigneur,' and it is not surprising that he should have complained to his brother that Dalhousie 'vents his impertinence on us in a way that would be unbecoming if we were his servants.' But his brother John did not feel about it in quite the same way. In fact brother John was beginning to see so nearly eye to eye with the Governor-General that it is permissible to wonder whether he hankered after Henry's place. He had frequently taken that place in the past, for whenever Henry had been absent from Lahore he had begged Hardinge to let John act for him, and in those days the brothers had agreed. But now, conveniently, John's policy was the same as Dalhousie's and the brothers disagreed. In effect their disagreement amounted to this: Henry did not wish to hit the Sikhs when they were down, while John felt no compunction and only thought of making the country a paying concern. The Governor-General, of course, backed John.

In addition to their political cleavage their dissimilar temperaments clashed for the first time when John was placed on an equal footing with his brother, a point that has been ignored by biographers, all of whom have insisted upon the love they bore one another. That Henry loved John is proved by what Henry did for John: he helped him and advanced him at every stage in his career. That John loved Henry is disproved by what John did to Henry; and the still-accepted view of John as a noble, great-hearted brother torn between love and duty is not supported by the facts and is flatly contradicted by our knowledge of his character. Very soon after the creation of the Board he wrote to Dalhousie complaining of his disagreements with Henry, of the consequent difficulties of his office, and throwing out a hint that he would be glad to go elsewhere; and though he paid handsome compliments to his brother, he knew perfectly well where Dalhousie's sympathies lay. Again, when Henry begged him with good reason to modify a report he had made on the conduct of Gulab Singh, he doubled his strictures and forwarded them to the Government. 'I have seldom, if ever, made a proposal that he has not opposed it,' said Henry to Robert Montgomery, who had taken Mansell's place on the Board and who acted as a sort of buffer between the brothers, describing himself as 'a tame elephant between two wild oxen.' Yet again, when Henry suggested that he and his brother should each do his own work and not encroach upon the other's province, sadly contrasting their past amity with their present disharmony, John would not meet him half-way, but continued to thwart him whenever he displayed sympathy with the fallen Sikh chieftains.

John, whose driving force and executive ability had settled the whole question of land revenue in the Punjab, was angry because Henry neglected the office work and went for long tours through the province; he even began to say that no one but himself did any serious work at all; but all this was merely the vexation of a man conscious of his own powers, confined to one sphere of activity, and keenly aware of the popularity of another whose genius rebuked his.

The situation got worse and worse. They could not discuss business together without losing their tempers. Henry was the more explosive of the two; he realised this and spent his life in trying to check the surge of feeling that spent itself in a deluge of words. John's anger was to be seen in his clenched jaw, in a greater emphasis of speech and wider spacing of words, in a more determined manner and intransigent attitude. Sometimes Montgomery, the buffer, feared that words would end in blows; the scenes between them were terrible and the Board meetings frequently ended with Henry, his eyes aflame, stamping out of the room, and John, his face aglow, mopping his forehead. ·

The time at last arrived when they would not meet, and they communicated through Montgomery, who took messages from one to the other, messages that were fortunately toned down in transit, or letters that had

H.D.—5

been rewritten on the bearer's advice. Henry Lawrence summed up the whole wretched period when he confessed there was 'scarcely a month of the four years, since annexation passed, that I did not suffer more annoyances than in any year of my previous career,' and again: 'A Board is not a bed of roses; my berth was one of thorns.' Hodson described him as 'utterly broken up, body and mind'; his physical appearance and mental demeanour changed; his hair whitened, his body shrank, he seldom smiled, the lines on his face became grooves, his cheeks hollowed, he grew gloomy, less sociable, and he was haunted with a sense of failure. When things were at their worst he wrote a prayer in which he asked God to make him 'humble, reasonable and contented, thankful, just and considerate. Restrain my tongue and my thoughts. . . . It is not in me to be regular. Let me be so, as much as I can. Let me do to-day's work to-day, not postponing; so living in humility, thankfulness, contentment.' His repeated wish for thankfulness and contentment indicated his chief need at that time, and his second reference to humility showed how John's behaviour had soured him and turned his modesty to arrogance.

In December, '52, Henry Lawrence, worn out by the constant bickerings with John, made up his mind to leave India and go to New Zealand 'with a view of spying out the land and settling there.' But hearing that a new Resident was about to be appointed to Hyderabad, he decided to end an impossible position with a letter to the Governor-General. Before sending it, however, he wrote to tell John of his decision. John had already written to Dalhousie's secretary, 'I care not how much work I have, or how great my responsibilities, if I have simply to depend on myself, but it is killing work always pulling against wind and tide,' and had suggested that he should be transferred to another post.

He knew that he was the favourite, that with every compliment he paid his brother and with every complaint he made, the Governor-General's dislike of Henry would be deepened, his opinion of him lowered. Iago's praise of Cassio, whose place he coveted, had a similar effect on Othello. Thus Henry's note was a godsend to John and, having dispatched it to Dalhousie without Henry's permission, he let the knowledge of his action trickle through the usual channel. Henry, when he got to hear of it, at once wrote to Dalhousie:

'There is so much that is unpleasant in my position, in reference to my brother, that I would willingly make way for him, should your Lordship be disposed to appoint me to Hyderabad. I would do much to preserve amity with my brother, with whom I never disagreed until we came together on this Board. . . . Could I see him provided for to his satisfaction, and be myself entrusted with the sole executive responsibility on this frontier, as Chief Commissioner on my present salary, I would have nothing to desire for the short remainder of my Indian career.'

Needless to say, Dalhousie jumped at the opportunity of getting rid of the man who 'supposes himself a King of the Punjab,' and of promoting his 'dear Old Boy.' The pacification of the Sikhs had been easily accomplished by Henry's presence on the Board; he was no longer needed in the Punjab; and he was a thorn in the Governor-General's side. Dalhousie plucked out the thorn. A new Resident had already been appointed to Hyderabad, but Rajputana required an Agent, and Henry was offered the post. The blow, though partly expected, was not the less shattering when it descended. He never properly recovered from it, and four years later wrote to Lord Canning, who succeeded Dalhousie: 'Ever since I was so cavalierly elbowed out of the Punjab, I have fretted even to the injury of my health.' He felt it bitterly and deeply, admitting that it had aroused his "worst passions." The brother who "loved" him, and who was generally supposed to be suffering agonies of distress, bravely shouldered his cross and became Chief Commissioner of the Punjab; while the noblest ruler England ever sent abroad was kicked out of the kingdom he had created and paid, in his own words, '£6,000 a year to watch the wayward fancies of a score of effete princes.'

The Sikhs heard the news with dismay; Henry's lieutenants heard it with grief, indignation and disgust. Nicholson wrote to him on January 4th, 1853: 'I have just got your express of the 1st, and am very sorry for the country's sake to hear you are going, and also not a little selfishly sorry on my own account; for I don't know how I shall ever get on when you are gone. If there is any work in Rajputana I am fit for, I wish you would take me with you. I certainly won't stay on the border in your absence. If you can't take me away, I shall apply for some quiet internal district like Shahpur.'

John Lawrence was well aware that his appointment would not be popular with Henry's "young men," and the first letter he wrote as Chief Commissioner was addressed to Nicholson: 'You have lost a good friend in my brother, but I hope to prove just as staunch a one to you. I set a great value on your zeal, energy, and administrative powers, though I may sometimes think you have a good deal to learn. You may rest assured of my support and good-will in all your labours. . . .' Nicholson merely acknowledged receipt of this letter and promptly wrote again to Henry on January 30th:

'I only got yours of the 19th yesterday. . . . The same date brought me a letter from your brother, in which he said that he hoped to prove as staunch a friend to me as you had ever been. I cannot but feel obliged to him; but I know that, as a considerate and kind patron, you are not to be replaced. I would, indeed, gladly go with you, even on reduced allowances. I feel that I am little fit for regulation work, and I can never sacrifice common sense and justice, or the interests of a people or country, to red-tape. A clever fellow like old Edwardes can manage both; but it is beyond me. It would do your heart good to hear the Sikhs in the posts along the border talk of you. Surely, in their gratitude and esteem "you have your reward." '

Henry, returning good for evil, strongly advised Nicholson to stay where he was and help John. Edwardes also, though he wept when he heard that Henry Lawrence was going and said that the Punjab would never again be the same place for those "who had caught from him their inspiration," dissuaded Nicholson from acting impulsively. 'Old Edwardes' was, as Nicholson perceived, 'a clever fellow' and had not the smallest intention of leaving a good job and following his master. But Nicholson was inconsolable and wrote again to Henry with a hint of deep feeling rare in him: 'Certainly if good wishes are of any use, the sun of your prosperity will not cease to shine. I don't know how to say all I would, but I hope you will be able to imagine it.'

Before he left the Punjab for ever, Henry wrote a letter to John: 'If you preserve the peace of the country and make the people happy, high and low, I shall have no regrets that I vacated the field for you. . . . I think we are doubly bound to treat them kindly *because they are down*. . . . I would simply do to them as I would be done by. . . .' John replied: 'I will give every man a fair hearing, and will endeavour to give every man his due. More than this no one should expect.' The appeal and the answer reveal the two brothers. Henry might have retorted in Hamlet's words: 'Use every man after his desert, and who shall 'scape whipping? Use them after your own honour and dignity; the less they deserve, the more merit is in your bounty.' The chief objection to acting fairly instead of generously is that man's sense of justice is fallible. Henry knew his own weaknesses, John did not. This was the chief difference between them, as it was between, say, Jesus Christ and Augustus Cæsar.

Surrounded by many Sikh chieftains and followed by a weeping concourse of people, Henry and his wife Honoria set out for Rajputana, the first part of their journey being described as "a long, living funeral procession from Lahore nearly to Amritsar"; and honest John became sole ruler of the Punjab, the Board disappearing with Henry.

As an autocrat of the Bismarckian type John Lawrence was, with a single exception, completely successful. He governed the province with masterful ease, but he failed to govern John Nicholson, who had been like a child in the hands of Henry. Do what he could, say what he might, John Lawrence was quite unable to control the Deputy-Commissioner of Bannu, whose innate haughtiness and wilfulness gained him a title by which he was known to every official on the frontier: "The Autocrat of All the Russias." Nicholson was aware of the general feeling about himself, for he once admitted: 'There is one thing in life I have failed in, and which I wished to attain; that is, to be popular with my brother-officers. I know I am not.'

No one so clearly appreciated the value of Nicholson as John Lawrence, who described him to Dalhousie as 'the best district officer on the frontier. He possesses great courage, much force of character, and is at the same time shrewd and intelligent. He is well worth the wing of a regiment on the border, as his *prestige* with the people, both on the hills and plains, is very great. He is also a very fair civil officer, and has done a good deal to put things straight in his district.' John Lawrence could not say more than 'very fair,' for Nicholson disregarded his instructions, refused to send in reports and did not even acknowledge his letters. 'Report officially all incursions,' urged the Chief Commissioner: 'I shall get into trouble if you don't. The Governor-General insists on knowing all that goes on, and not unreasonably; but I can't tell him this if I don't hear details.' Again, when Nicholson dispatched criminals to Lahore with some such statement as: 'Herewith two men to be hanged,' Lawrence begged him to be more explicit: 'Don't send up any more men to be hanged direct, unless the case is very urgent; and when you do, send an abstract of the evidence in English, and send it through the Commissioner.'

On a tour of inspection through the Punjab Lawrence visited Nicholson, who was especially nice to Mrs. Lawrence and her child; but the effort of being polite to John Lawrence exhausted him and his irritation broke out in a curious way. He discovered that a native officer in the Chief Commissioner's service was making money on the sale of supplies brought into camp with the retinue. 'I am going to flog him,' shouted Nicholson angrily; 'you have no objection, have you?' Lawrence could not think of one on the spur of the moment and the officer, gaudy in gold lace and scarlet coat, duly suffered, partly perhaps for the sins of his master. In reflecting upon the consideration he had received, Nicholson wrote to Henry Lawrence that 'John has been very forbearing, and I am sure puts up with much from me on your account.'

In the latter part of '53 Edwardes was given the chief frontier post, becoming Commissioner of Peshawar, which for a time reconciled Nicholson to his job; he could thenceforward enjoy occasional talks with his friend, riding the 120 miles from Bannu to Peshawar at a stretch because Edwardes sent remounts for him to the half-way post, and always spending a week at Christ-

mas with Edwardes and his wife, who had a number of
frontier officers staying with them on those occasions.
Nicholson was never at his best in a social gathering;
the presence of three or more people made him shy and
uncomfortable; he hardly ever spoke; and if he was out
of sympathy with a single member of the party, or
disliked the look of a stranger, he withdrew completely
into himself, making other people equally uncomfortable
whenever his watchful eye rested upon them. He was
quite at ease with Henry Lawrence, Herbert Edwardes
and their respective wives, but with others, even his
friends, he was never wholly in tune.

Henry and Honoria Lawrence returned his affection,
and when in the autumn of '53 Honoria was dying
Nicholson received a letter from Henry:

'I write now by my wife's bedside to give you a
message she has just sent you. "Tell him I love him
dearly as if he were my son. I know that he is noble
and pure to his fellow-men; that he thinks not of himself; but tell him he is a sinner; that he will one day be
as weak and as near death as I am. Ask him to read but
a few verses of the Bible daily, and to say that collect,
*Blessed Lord who hast caused all holy Scriptures to be
written for our learning, grant that we may in such wise
hear them, read, mark, learn,* etc., etc." (Collect for
Second Sunday in Advent.) I have just told her I had
written to you as she had bidden me—(she has often, in
a general way, done so the last month); she replied,
"May God bless what you have said to him! I love him
very much." '

Honoria died early the following year and Henry
sent Nicholson her copy of the New Testament, writing
on the fly-leaf, 'John Nicholson: In memory of his
friend and warm well-wisher, Honoria Lawrence, who
was this day laid in her grave: January 17, 1854.'

Not all those who called him a friend could also call

him a sinner, or resent being called one by him, without
risk of a rupture. Even his oldest friend in India, Neville
Chamberlain, was not exempt from the risk. Towards
the end of '54 Nicholson applied for the command of the
Punjab Frontier Force, one of the plums of the Indian
Army, but the moment he heard that it had been offered
to Chamberlain he withdrew the application and wrote
to congratulate his friend, assuring him that he was all
round the better man. Chamberlain did not receive the
letter and was very much surprised when Nicholson
avoided meeting him after he had become Brigadier of
the Frontier Force. Nicholson, of course, having had no
acknowledgment of his letter, was feeling a little sore.

Early in '55 an event occurred which, on account of
the preceding coolness between the disputants, resulted
in more heat than it would normally have generated.
A body of Mahsud Wazirs raided a border district and
killed Zeman Khan, one of Nicholson's most valued
lieutenants, who was well to the rear of the frontier post
in that district. Nicholson reported the incident to the
Chief Commissioner, stated that the troops at the post
had been warned to expect trouble, made a general complaint of the negligence of the Frontier Force, and
asserted that the detachments at the outposts did not
effectually guard the border.

An expurgated version of this criticism was forwarded
to Neville Chamberlain, a hot-tempered and extremely
efficient officer, who defended his force with such
warmth that John Lawrence at once tried to calm him
down, writing: 'There is no man in the Bengal Army
whom I would so gladly see at the head of the Punjab
Force as yourself, and few for whom I have a greater
regard and respect. It is my sincere desire to consider
your views and feelings in all matters connected with
your command. If Nicholson had said more than the
case warranted he must make the amende. I am sure he-

is too honest a fellow not to do so.' Lawrence then told Chamberlain that Nicholson had asked for the command of the Frontier Force, but had cancelled his request the instant he had heard that Chamberlain was in the running for it, on the ground that he was far less fitted for the post. 'Now I think,' added Lawrence, 'that a man who wrote and thought of you in this way would be the last to mean to asperse the force under your orders.' Lawrence did not tell Chamberlain one-tenth of what Nicholson had said, which was perhaps as well, for even with the aid of the synopsis he had received Chamberlain could not get rid of the notion that in accusing his people of palpable negligence and patent incompetence Nicholson had "aspersed the force under his orders."

Following a strained correspondence with the Brigadier, John Lawrence was forced to appeal to Nicholson: 'Chamberlain is very sore and scruples not to say that he will resign unless the amende is made. I think he is somewhat unreasonable. Nevertheless his resignation would be a public loss and bring much obloquy. I hope, therefore, that you will write and express your regret at having led me to conclude that the detachment in the post had received notice of the affair. I have written to you two or three times officially to send me the precise facts and dates of the four raids to which you alluded in reporting Zeman Khan's death. Pray send this without further delay, and in it express your regret for the mistake which occurred.'

Nicholson sent a few details and made some attempt at an apology; but though Lawrence wrote a long explanatory justification of his Deputy-Commissioner's attitude and tried to make his apology appear more sincere than it really was, Chamberlain refused to be placated and entrenched himself behind a questionnaire. 'I have got an official letter from Chamberlain,' Law-

rence informed a friend, 'putting twenty queries on each
of the four raids to Nicholson! Now if anything will
bring Nick to his senses it will be these queries. He will
polish off a tribe in the most difficult fortress, or ride
the border like "belted Will" of former days; but one
query in writing is often a stumper for a month. The
pen-and-ink work, as he calls it, does not suit him.'

Yet not even the eighty queries brought "Nick" to
his senses, and the controversy raged on for months,
Chamberlain bombarding Lawrence with questions,
Lawrence begging Nicholson for details, and Nicholson
refusing to withdraw what he had said and occasionally
adding something he had forgotten to say.

John Lawrence endured the campaign with praiseworthy equanimity; he never once lost control of himself;
he even had the hardihood to suggest to Nicholson at
the height of the quarrel that he should co-operate with
Chamberlain against some troublesome border tribe.
Nicholson of course exploded and promptly announced
his intention of leaving the Punjab for good. He wrote to
Lord Hardinge asking for a job in the Crimea, where the
War had just broken out. He wrote to Henry Lawrence,
saying that he longed to serve under him at whatever
loss in position and money to himself, and he confessed
to Henry what he would never have hinted to John: that
he had been in the wrong, not Chamberlain, who was
superior to him in every way. In reply Henry urged him
not to act rashly and strongly advised against the
Crimean project, reminding him of the annoyance and
opposition he would encounter there and of the prospects he would abandon if he left India. John also had
a few words to say concerning the Crimea: 'You are
much more useful with us. . . . I hope to see Ross* made
a Bishop or a Commander-in-Chief in the Crimea, and
so his post will fall naturally to you. . . . I look on the

* The feeble Commissioner of Leia in the Punjab.

way things are managed in the Crimea as perfectly distressing; and setting aside my desire to retain your services, I should be sorry, on your own account, to see you in the Crimea.' Nicholson then asked to be sent to Peshawar as Deputy-Commissioner under Edwardes, but John would not hear of having 'two top-sawyers in one place." Nicholson kept Edwardes abreast of what was going on and explained why he wanted to go to the Crimea: 'I trust to have an opportunity of doing the State some service, the feeling of which will compensate me for the worldly advantages which I forego.'

Calm was at length restored by a letter from John Lawrence to Nicholson: 'Two such soldiers ought not to be in a state of antagonism. I think he is wrong in taking exception to your remarks on the post system, and I defend your views both privately and officially to him. Still, the fact that he does not feel convinced by your arguments, and would not concur in our conclusions, is no reason why we should not be friends.' Lawrence then quoted a letter he had received from Chamberlain, which ran: 'I never considered the question personal, and even the official discussion was buried when I last addressed you on the subject. If I am correct he feels cool towards me. But I shall be happy to receive him with the same feeling of respect and admiration which I have all along borne towards him. He has only to come within reach of me to extend both hands towards him, and in doing so I shall be doubly glad, for I shall know that the Government, of which we are the common servants, will be the gainer.'

This was after all as much as one wronged gentleman could expect from another who thought he had been wronged, and Nicholson asked Chamberlain to be his guest at Kohat, an invitation which Chamberlain gladly accepted. Explanations were given and received. Nicholson was greatly perturbed to learn that Chamberlain had not received his letter of congratulation, the non-acknowledgment of which had been at the bottom of all the trouble; indeed he was so deeply humiliated by the discovery of the injustice he had done Chamberlain from the start that in his agitation he picked up an ivory paper-knife and bit it in two. From that moment the friends were reunited.

Throughout this protracted quarrel John Lawrence had displayed a patience that Job might have envied, yet he failed to arouse a spark of gratitude in the breast of Nicholson, who still wanted to serve under Henry and continued to vex the Chief Commissioner with his laconic notes. 'As to Nicholson,' wrote John Lawrence to Edwardes, 'I will never help him to leave the Punjab, though I will never oppose his going. I feel very sore about him. You might as well run rusty as he should. By the bye, he shot a man the other day who went at him with a drawn sword.' John must have heard about the drawn sword from the bearer of the message, for this was Nicholson's official report of the incident:

'SIR,—I have the honour to inform you that I have just shot a man who came to kill me. Your obedient servant, JOHN NICHOLSON.'

In a letter to Edwardes, dated January 21st, 1856, Nicholson expanded this statement in another of his rare literary exploits:

'MY DEAR EDWARDES,—I take up my pen to give you an account of a narrow escape I had from assassination the day before yesterday. I was standing at the gate of my garden at noon, with Sladen and Cadell, and four or five chuprassies, when a man with a sword rushed suddenly up and called out for me. I had on a long fur pelisse of native make, which I fancy prevented his recognising me at first. This gave time for the only chuprassie who had a sword to get between us, to whom he called out contemptuously to stand aside, saying he had come to kill me, and did not want to hurt a common soldier. The relief sentry for the one in front of my house happening to pass opportunely behind me at this time, I snatched his musket, and, presenting it at the would-be assassin, told him I would fire if he did not put down his sword and surrender. He replied that either he or I must die; so I had no alternative, and shot him through the heart, the ball passing through a religious book which he had tied on his chest, apparently as a charm. The poor wretch turns out to be a Marwutee, who has been religiously mad for some time. He disposed of all his property in charity the day before he set out for Bannu. I am sorry to say that his spiritual instructor has disappeared mysteriously, and, I am afraid, got into the hills. I believe I owe my safety to the fur chogah, for I should have been helpless had he rushed straight on.

'The chuprassie (an orderly from my police battalion) replied to his cry for my blood, "All our names are Nikal Seyn here," and, I think, would very likely have got the better of him, had not I interfered, but I should not have been justified in allowing the man to risk his life, when I had such a sure weapon as a loaded musket and bayonet in my hand. I am very sorry for this occurrence, but it was quite an exceptional one, and has not at all altered my opinion of the settled peaceful state of this portion of the district. Making out the criminal returns for 1855 the other day, I found that we had not had a single murder or highway robbery, or attempt at either, in Bannu throughout the year. The crime has all gone down to the southern end of the district, where I am not allowed to interfere.

'Yours affectionately,
'J. NICHOLSON.'

In the spring of '56 Nicholson, still restless, got the

temporary job of "officer on special duty" in Kashmir.
For six months of the year Kashmir had become a
health resort for the British in India; but the Englishman, so well behaved in the world of regulations and
respectability with which he is familiar, is liable to
become a nuisance when freed from all restraint, and
Gulab Singh had complained to the Indian Government
that his European visitors were misconducting themselves. To quote an authority, they 'indulged in larking,
often of a most immoral kind. . . , English ladies were
scandalised by the scenes on the river and in the gardens
and orchards about Srinagar, in which foolish young
officers and the native women of the town played the
chief part.' Furthermore the delinquents frequently took
things from the natives without paying for them and
generally speaking behaved with a freedom that offended
the Maharajah's delicate sense of propriety. The Indian
Government determined to send an officer every year to
keep the visitors in order, and the first to be appointed
was Nicholson, who cleaned the place up so effectively
that his successors "found the moral atmosphere much
purified by his vigorous and timely action."

While checking the misdemeanours of English
subalterns in Kashmir he continued to worry John
Lawrence. A Persian army was again before Herat and
he volunteered to go and settle the matter once for all,
writing to Edwardes: 'Five thousand picked men, with
picked officers, and armed with the best description of
weapon (such as the revolving rifle, with which the
Yankees overthrew the Mexicans) would roll up the
Persians like a carpet back from Herat, and do more for
the maintenance of our influence and reputation than a
year's revenue of India spent upon treaties and subsidies.' Several notes in an abusive strain made John
Lawrence feel that he had had about as much as he
could stomach; so he asked Lord Canning, who suc-

ceeded Dalhousie as Governor-General in '56, to transfer Nicholson to Bhurtpore where he would again be with Henry Lawrence. But before the appointment could be made the Deputy-Commissionership of Peshawar fell vacant and John Lawrence made one more effort to appease Nicholson by offering him the post. As Edwardes would be his direct chief, with whom he could work happily, he accepted it.

But even under the friendly eye and skilful handling of Edwardes he contrived to give John Lawrence another severe jolt. A treaty had been made with Dost Mahomed in March, '55. Edwardes had decided that the peace and safety of the Indian frontier was dependent upon good relations with the Amir of Afghanistan, and against the advice of nearly every one, including John Lawrence, he had negotiated with the Dost. Nicholson, too, had strongly opposed it, warning him: 'In dealing with the Afghans, I hope you will never forget that their *name* is *faithlessness*, even among themselves; what, then, can strangers expect? I have always hopes of a people, however barbarous in their hospitality, who appreciate and practise good faith among themselves— the Waziris, for instance—but in Afghanistan son betrays father, and brother brother, without remorse. I would not take the trouble to tell you all this, which you no doubt know already, but I cannot help remembering how even the most experienced and astute of our political officers, in Afghanistan, were deceived by that winning and imposing frankness of manner which it has pleased Providence to give the Afghans, as it did to the first serpent, for its own purposes.' But Edwardes had persevered, with the concurrence of Dalhousie, and eventually the treaty had been signed. Not content with that, Edwardes then proposed a still closer alliance and arranged several meetings near the mouth of the Khyber Pass between John Lawrence and Dost Mahomed in

January, '57. As Deputy-Commissioner of the district Nicholson should have been present; but he flatly declined to have anything to do with the business. He detested the Afghans so heartily that he could not trust himself in their neighbourhood, fearing lest he might be 'tempted to shoot one.' Having informed Lawrence of his decision, he put fifty miles between himself and the conference at the Khyber Pass, returning after the departure of the Afghans when he could breathe freely. As the treaty had the effect of keeping the Amir friendly with the British during the Indian Mutiny, Edwardes deserved high praise for his prevision; but John Lawrence, who had been hostile to the negotiations, took all the credit for their successful conclusion.

Within a few months Nicholson had very nearly, as Edwardes said, 'brought the Peshawar district, as he had before brought Bannu, to the minimum of crime and its every official to the maximum of exertion.' What the natives felt about him was expressed by one of them: 'You could hear the ring of his horse's hoofs from Attock to the Khyber.' What his fellow-countrymen felt about him was expressed by a young officer named Frederick Roberts, who was later to become Field-Marshal Earl Roberts, the last Commander-in-Chief of the British Army, but who in April '57 was a subaltern in the Quartermaster's Department, engaged in drawing up a report on the suitability of Cherat as a sanatorium for British soldiers in the Peshawar district. Each night he returned to his tent in the plain and on one occasion was surprised to find that a camp had sprung up in his absence. It belonged to Nicholson, who was on a tour of inspection. He invited Roberts to dine with him:

'John Nicholson was a name to conjure with in the Punjab,' wrote Roberts forty years later. 'I had heard it mentioned with an amount of respect—indeed, awe—which no other name could excite, and I was all curiosity to see the man whose influence on the frontier was so great that his word was law to the refractory tribes amongst whom he lived. . . . Nicholson impressed me more profoundly than any man I had ever met before, or have ever met since. I have never seen any one like him. He was the beau-ideal of a soldier and a gentleman. His appearance was distinguished and commanding, with a sense of power about him which to my mind was the result of his having passed so much of his life amongst the wild and lawless tribesmen, with whom his authority was supreme. Intercourse with this man amongst men made me more eager than ever to remain on the frontier, and I was seized with ambition to follow in his footsteps. Had I never seen Nicholson again, I might have thought that the feelings with which he inspired me were to some extent the result of my imagination, excited by the astonishing stories I had heard of his power and influence; my admiration, however, for him was immeasurably strengthened when, a few weeks later, I served as his staff officer, and had opportunities of observing more closely his splendid, soldierly qualities and the workings of his grand, simple mind.'

When Roberts first met him Nicholson was in sole charge of the Peshawar district, Edwardes having gone to Calcutta to see his wife off to England. While still at the capital he received a wire from Nicholson: 'I wish to leave the Punjab. My reasons hereafter by letter.' Nicholson had at length decided that he could no longer serve under John Lawrence, who, he was convinced, did not appreciate his services. He wished for complete independence or at least complete confidence and he knew he would never achieve either under a man who fussed about details which he considered unimportant. It was a constant source of irritation for an out-and-out individualist to be reined in by a bureaucrat whenever he started to gallop, and Nicholson foresaw a moment when he would be unable to restrain himself from personally assaulting Lawrence. The born fighter who is also a born rebel may be tamed by a Christ, but his gorge rises against a Cæsar. Moreover the knowledge that John had jockeyed Henry out of the Punjab never ceased to rankle within Nicholson; so he determined to go while the going was good. 'I feel very sorry indeed to have been obliged to come to the conclusion that it is better for me to leave the Punjab at once while I can do so quietly. . . . If you got my telegraphic message before leaving Calcutta, I think you will probably have spoken to Lord Canning. As I said before, I am not ambitious, and shall be glad to take any equivalent to a first-class Deputy-Commissionership. I should like to go to Oudh if Sir Henry would like to have me. It would be a pleasure to me to try and assist him, but if he would rather not bring in Punjabees, do not press it on him. What I should like best of all would be, if we could get away together, or anywhere out of this.'

Edwardes spoke to Canning, giving him a piece of advice which the new Governor-General never forgot: 'You may rely upon this, my Lord, that if ever there is a desperate deed to be done in India, John Nicholson is the man to do it.' While Canning was still considering the matter events were occurring in India which settled the question of Nicholson's future employment. Edwardes returned to Peshawar, where on the night of May 11th, 1857, he and Nicholson read a wire containing the last message that was flashed from Delhi:

'The sepoys have come in from Meerut and are burning everything—Mr. Todd is dead and we hear several Europeans—we must shut up.'

CHAPTER IX

Making ' Pandies '

'NEITHER greased cartridges, the annexation of
Oudh, nor the paucity of European officers were the
causes. For years I have watched the army and felt
sure they only wanted their opportunity to try their
strength with us.'

Such was Nicholson's explanation of the origin of the
Indian Mutiny, but it was a better explanation of
Nicholson than of the origin of the Indian Mutiny. In one
sense, however, he was right. Until the disasters of the
Afghan War the native soldiers had felt that the English
were invincible; after the retreat from Kabul in '42
British prestige slumped and the native soldiers* began
to think that they could easily rid their country of rulers
who had given so many lamentable exhibitions of
feebleness and incompetence. Following the Afghan
War the sepoys had been encouraged to think still less
of their British leaders by the appointment of successive
Commanders-in-Chief who curtailed the powers of regimental officers, favoured appeals to army headquarters,
insisted on the promotion of native officers by seniority
instead of merit, introduced red-tape into every department and believed that the War Office was the repository
of all wisdom. As the wisdom of the War Office had
recently been manifested by the conception of a uniform
so tight that if a soldier dropped his rifle he could not
stoop to pick it up, it will be guessed that the Com-

---

* Called "sipahis" by correct historians, "sepoys" by several
generations of Englishmen and, therefore, by the present writer.

manders-in-Chief sent out to India were not of a highly imaginative cast.

But the Afghan War and the weakening of regimental discipline only encouraged rebellion without provoking it. As with all wars and revolutions, the Indian Mutiny was caused by greed and superstition, or, in more imposing terms, by statecraft and priestcraft.

The landowners in the various states annexed by the East India Company had in many cases acquired their possessions by force and maintained them by fraud; that is, they had taken the property of their weaker neighbours and evaded taxation by making incorrect returns of their holdings. The Company employed officers to survey and assess all the newly-acquired territories and to examine the rights of ownership. A rigid system of land-tenure was introduced, valuations were made and revenue was regulated. Thus the spoliators were themselves spoliated and they did not like it. The wealthy classes were still further incensed by the enforcement of a law which provided for the lapse of property and pensions whenever there were no direct or collateral heirs, the Indian Government of course benefiting by these lapses.

Such modern changes, unsuitable to native habits, were resented by the poorer classes as well as the rich, for the poor of all countries prefer the rapacity of their own people to that of foreigners. What brought their grievances to a head was the annexation of Oudh in 1856. For more than half a century the Governor-Generals of India had strongly urged the transference of that kingdom to the Company on the ground that it was in a state of absolute anarchy. The King had been repeatedly advised to improve both his government and his personal conduct, but he had disregarded the warnings and at length he was removed. 'Let Oudh be at last governed, not for one man, the King, but for the

King and his people,' wrote Henry Lawrence. 'Let the administration of the country be Native; let not one rupee come into the Company's coffers.' His humane advice was ignored, the country was formally annexed, quite a number of rupees came into the Company's coffers, and the universal unpopularity of the act resulted in the emergence of the ex-King's adviser Ahmad Ullah, known as the "Moulvi of Faizabad," who by degrees converted the prevailing discontent into active rebellion. More than any single act the dethronement of the King of Oudh aroused the hostility of the native princes to British rule. They wondered when their turn would come.

But there were other causes of disaffection. The royal family of Delhi was threatened. The descendant of the Mogul emperors was eighty years old, and it had been decided that at his death the title of "King" should be dropped and his family removed from Delhi. This humiliation of a once-mighty dynasty was felt keenly by all Mohammedans and even by the dissatisfied Hindus. Among the latter was Dandu Pant, who later achieved infamy as the Nana Sahib. He was the adopted son and heir of the last of the Peshwas, the overlord of the Mahratta confederacy, and although the inheritor of a large fortune he claimed a continuance of his foster-father's pension, which had lapsed on the death of the Peshwa in '51. Failing to get his claim allowed in India, he sent a Mohammedan named Azimulla Khan to plead his cause in England. Azimulla discovered, as so many of his race had done, that a dark skin was an asset in a white community. Many fashionable ladies pirouetted round him and with him; one of them wrote letters to him beginning 'My dear Eastern Son'; others granted him favours of a more intimate nature; he became engaged to a pretty girl, who promised to marry him in India; in fact he found life in Mayfair very sweet, and though he failed to get a pension for the Nana he

was able to report the good news that the British Army
was about to be annihilated in the Crimea and that the
princes and people of India would have little difficulty
in driving the English out of the country.

Two more influential rulers had grounds for complaint: a Rajput landowner named Kunwar Singh, who
had watched his estates being swallowed up by the
Board of Revenue; and the Rani of Jhansi, who had
claimed the right under Hindu law to adopt an heir to
her husband on his death in '54, but whose claim had
been disallowed by Dalhousie, with the result that Jhansi
came into possession of the Company.

Yet the Indian Mutiny did not break out solely on
account of the greed of the dispossessed or the greed of
the dispossessors. Superstition had a lot to do with it,
and the rebels* had to use superstition to gain their ends.
The British had prohibited infanticide, the indiscriminate slaughter of female babies, and suttee, the
practice of burning widows with the corpses of their
husbands; they had permitted the execution of Brahmins
for capital offences; they had abolished every legal
obstacle to the remarriage of widows; they had brought
in female education; they had encouraged Christian
missionaries and protected Indian converts; they had
introduced railways, in which people of every caste
were forced to travel together, and the electric telegraph,
which suggested to the natives that the ruling race was
able to work miracles; they had dared to irrigate the
country from the sacrosanct Ganges. None of these
novelties found favour with the high-caste Hindus, whose
social privileges were dependent upon the Brahminical
religion, and all of them endangered the power and
prestige of the priesthood, whether Hindu or Moham-

---

* Or "nationalists" if the reader prefers to call them so. The
biographer is not a partisan, but "rebels" is a simpler and a
nobler term, and on that account will be used throughout.

medan. Thus every consideration of cash and creed inspired the chief malcontents to work upon the gullibility of the peasants and the loyalty of the native army with the object of subverting British rule, which had already lasted a century and yearly increased in presumption.

The chief difficulty was the army; but here the seditionists were in luck. The demoralisation which had resulted from the Afghan War was increased by the treatment of the sepoys in the Sind campaign. Until then it had been the rule that extra allowances should be given native soldiers in the Bengal Army for service beyond the frontier. Prior to its conquest Sind was of course a trans-frontier state and service in that parched region was extremely displeasing to Bengal troops, who were promised a large addition to their pay while fighting there. But the moment the country was annexed the Indian Government, with a stupidity that was only matched by its cupidity, announced that the troops still busy "pacifying" the country were no longer on foreign soil and cancelled their special allowances. Four regiments detailed for duty in Sind refused to march and the Government got out of the difficulty by dispatching native troops from Bombay. One of the intractable regiments was disbanded, selected sepoys in the others were punished, and the Government believed that the matter had been settled; but this shifty proceeding had a widespread effect on the native army and the confidence of the sepoys in the justice and honesty of their white masters was permanently undermined.

Something more serious was to follow. In 1852 Dalhousie wished to send a native regiment to fight in Burma. The entire Bengal Army, excepting six regiments, was enlisted for Indian duty only; overseas service was absolutely barred. Dalhousie therefore had the option: he could either send one of the six regiments unaffected by this rule or call for volunteers. He did not avail himself of the option. Instead he ordered to Burma a regiment that had been enlisted solely for service in India. The regiment flatly declined to embark, Dalhousie was forced to give way, and the sepoys concerned were acclaimed as heroes by their fellow-soldiers throughout the Bengal Army, the discipline of which sharply deteriorated.

Error followed on error, imbecility on imbecility. A great number of sepoys in the Bengal Army and a fair portion of the Bombay Army came from Oudh, where the act of enlistment carried with it the right to petition the British Resident at Lucknow on every matter affecting the personal interest of the soldier and of his family in that kingdom. This meant, in effect, that the Resident became the sepoy's advocate in the courts of justice, the advantage of which was so great that hardly a family was unrepresented in the army, and Oudh became the most fruitful recruiting ground in India. But when the state was annexed the native judges were displaced by English officials, the sepoy's right to petition was abolished, the main inducement to enlist was removed, and a privilege that had been exercised by generations of fighting men disappeared. At a stroke the larger part of the Company's force became hostile to their employers.

Finally, in 1856, an Act was passed in which it was set down that "no Native recruit shall be accepted who does not at the time of his enlistment undertake to serve beyond the sea, whether within the territories of the Company or beyond them." This was the last straw, for although it did not affect sepoys already enlisted the conspirators were able to insinuate that it was part of a sinister scheme by the British Government to make the Hindus lose caste and in self-defence become Christians.

Thus the train had already been carefully laid by the British and it only remained for the disaffected Indians to light it. The two most energetic rebels were the lean, expressive Ahmad Ullah and the fat, impassive Nana Sahib. While the latter was busy fomenting trouble among the leading landowners of Oudh, the former was circulating seditious papers about the country and devising his famous "chapati scheme," whereby the rural population were to be warned by the distribution of chapatis (cakes of unleavened bread) that a simultaneous rising of soldiers and peasants was about to take place. These two men and their adherents had little difficulty in persuading the average villager that the object of the British was to destroy his religion: they had merely to point out that in the prisons a communal system of messing had been instituted which prevented each inmate from cooking his own food, and they untruthfully asserted that in order to defile and degrade the prisoners the food was prepared by men of an inferior caste. But in spite of the mutinous spirit already prevalent in the army the soldiers could not be induced to shoot their officers merely on account of communal feeding in gaols or communal travelling in trains or the education of women or the application of an equitable land-tax or even of their own grievances. Something more was required before they could be incited to general mutiny; and the British authorities, always ready to oblige, provided more than was required.

One day in the middle of January, 1857, a low-caste lascar employed in the Government factory at Dum-Dum, near Calcutta, asked a high-caste sepoy for a drink of water from his pot. The sepoy objected that he would be unable to drink from it again if it had been defiled by a low-caste lascar. 'You will all soon be biting cartridges smeared with beef-fat and hog's lard,' replied the lascar with a pitying grin, and went on to explain that the cartridges then being made for the new Enfield rifle would shortly be distributed to the sepoys, who would lose caste the moment they touched the degrading substance. As the cow was sacred to the Hindus and the pig unclean to the Moslems, this item of news interested the entire army, and it travelled from one station to another with that seemingly miraculous speed which should have made the introduction of the electric telegraph quite unimpressive to the native mind. Here at last was tangible proof that the British Government intended to destroy the native religions and to convert the army to Christianity. At least that was how the sepoys saw it, though in reality the Government had no such intention. The Government was far more concerned with making money than with saving souls, and it was quite ignorant of what was taking place. With a disregard of religious feeling among the soldiers that might be described as incredible if it had not been typical, the new cartridges were being prepared with a lubricating mixture composed of the obnoxious ingredients mentioned by the lascar at Dum-Dum. True, these new cartridges had not yet been issued to the troops, only a few of whom were being instructed in the use of the Enfield rifle, but the sepoys had heard enough to believe anything. The mere thought that they would have to bite off the paper ends of cartridges which had been greased with the fat of the sacred cow and the unclean pig sent a thrill of horror through the Hindus and Moslems, and from the moment the news was "in the air" it may appropriately be said that the fat was in the fire.

When the Government had been fully advised of the situation everything possible was done to allay the fears of the sepoys. Orders were telegraphed to various depots that no greased cartridges were to be issued. Wherever signs of obduracy were manifested the whole situation was carefully explained to the men, who were granted every facility to inquire into the nature of the cartridges issued and told that they could pinch the ends off with their fingers instead of biting them off. With regard to the rumour that the British were planning to make them lose caste, the divisional commander at Barrackpore, General Hearsey, informed his troops that not only was there no intention of compelling them to become Christians, but that even if they desired conversion they could not be baptized until they were convinced of the truth of Christianity. But it was too late; the conspirators had done their work thoroughly; the official explanations had been anticipated and answered by the simple statement that the word of the British could not be trusted, for had not Oudh been annexed? had not home-service soldiers been ordered abroad? had not their allowances on foreign service been curtailed? and so on. The work of sedition went on under the very noses of the army authorities: nocturnal meetings, when men with muffled faces went from tent to tent and from hut to hut; mysterious fires, when burning arrows were hurled at the thatched roofs of officers' bungalows; secret letters, posted in Calcutta and Barrackpore, urging the soldiers at all the chief stations of the Bengal Army to resist by force the intended evil.

The first attempt at organised resistance took place at Berhampore, 120 miles north of Calcutta, where detachments of men had arrived from headquarters at Barrackpore and told their fellow-soldiers all about the greased cartridges. One evening late in February the commanding officer at Berhampore, Colonel Mitchell, was informed that the men were in a state of great excitement over the blank ammunition that had been issued for the next morning's parade. Irritated by their stupidity, for they had used similar cartridges for years without a breath of complaint, Mitchell galloped down to the lines, sent for the native officers and expressed himself forcefully on the behaviour of the men. Having explained that the cartridges were at least a year old, he

said that if the men persisted in their refusal to take the
ammunition they would get into serious trouble. He
then mounted and rode off. His manner had not been
conciliatory and the native officers, feeling that his
irritation was a proof of guilt, were unable to reassure
the men. Late that night Mitchell heard a confused
uproar and the beating of drums. He bounded out of
bed, sent for the cavalry and artillery, hurriedly dressed
himself and went down to the parade ground, where he
found the infantry drawn up in line, armed and in a
state of panic. Again he sent for the native officers and
again he spoke harshly. They reasoned with him,
begging him to keep calm and explaining that the men,
ignorant and superstitious, believed the cartridges would
defile them. They promised the Colonel that if he would
order the withdrawal of the guns and mounted men the
infantry would lay down their arms and return to duty.
As Mitchell could not be sure that the native cavalry
and artillery would kill their comrades if he gave the
command, he decided after some hesitation to send them
away. The submission of the sepoys followed their
disappearance and next morning the men fell in on
parade as if nothing out of the ordinary had happened
during the night. But a Court of Inquiry went into the
matter, and after sifting all the evidence decreed the
disbandment of the offending regiment.

The decree was soon being discussed by the sepoys at
Barrackpore, the great military station on the banks of
the Hooghli sixteen miles above Calcutta, and coupled
with the news that a British regiment had suddenly
arrived from Rangoon it made a deep impression. One
young man in the 34th Native Infantry named Manghal
Pandi, whose naturally excitable disposition had not
been improved by doses of bhang, felt that the moment
for action had arrived. On Sunday afternoon, March
29th, he donned his uniform, took his musket and sallied

forth, calling on his comrades to join him as the only alternative to biting greased cartridges. Taking up a position in front of the quarter-guard, he ordered a bugler to sound the assembly. He was not disheartened by the refusal of the bugler to act on his instructions, but strode up and down in a state of great excitement, threatening to shoot any Europeans on sight, a threat he did his best to carry out when the English sergeant-major came to inquire the reason for the disturbance. Whether the sergeant-major ducked at the right moment or Pandi fired wide is not known, but the shot missed its object and the sergeant-major did not stay to prosecute his inquiries.

Meanwhile the native officer (a jemidar) and twenty men of the guard looked on with interest but did not appear to think their interference necessary, and it was left to a native corporal to report the occurrence to the Adjutant, Lieut. Baugh, who instantly seized his sword, loaded his pistols, got on his horse and made for the quarter-guard. Spotting him from afar, Pandi skipped behind the station gun, whence he fired at the Adjutant, missed the rider but hit the horse, bringing both to the ground. Baugh got free of his charger and had a shot at Pandi, failed to hit him and went at him sword in hand. Pandi drew his tulwar and they closed. There was a brisk encounter, the odds being against the Hindu because the sergeant-major, perceiving that the situation had improved, reappeared and joined in the fray. But Pandi, influenced by religious enthusiasm and bhang, was a desperate fighter and delivered such furious blows that before long the Adjutant and the sergeant-major were temporarily knocked out. The native guard continued to treat the incident as one that did not concern them and the two Englishmen would undoubtedly have been polished off if a Mohammedan soldier named Sheikh Paltu had not rushed to their rescue and held Pandi at bay while they lay wounded on the ground.

The sound of strife had brought a crowd of sepoys to the spot. What they saw was novel enough to provoke controversy among them, but they did not interfere and Sheikh Paltu's cries for assistance met with no response until certain members of the guard, feeling no doubt a little shamefaced over their inaction, stepped forward and struck the fallen officers with the butt-ends of their muskets. Convinced that an appeal to their better natures would be ill-timed, the officers took advantage of Sheikh Paltu's protection and got clear as quickly as their wounds would let them.

The first report of the occurrence to reach the veteran divisional commander, General Hearsey, was exaggerated. An orderly dashed into his house and said that the Brigade had mutinied. After dispatching notes for assistance to officers commanding European regiments, Hearsey and his two sons ordered their horses, put on their uniforms and were about to leave for the scene of action when a more accurate report arrived. The General could hardly believe his ears. A single sepoy defying the whole army! Why had no one shot the lunatic? Followed by his sons he galloped down to the parade ground, and having reached it he could hardly believe his eyes.

Still master of the situation, Pandi was walking about, daring any European to approach him, urging his comrades to fight for their religion or rounding on them for cowardice, for having promised their support and deserted him at the hour of danger. The comrades were not equal to the occasion and moved about uncertainly wondering what to do, until their minds were made up for them by the appearance of the General, who went straight for the quarter-guard. Someone shouted a warning that Pandi's musket was loaded. 'Damn his musket!' replied the General, pulling out his revolver and commanding the guard to seize Pandi or take the consequences of disobedience. His sons drew their revolvers too and the guard was faced by three stern gentlemen who had every intention of seeing that orders were obeyed with alacrity. The guard fell in behind the General, who then advanced upon Pandi. Suddenly one of his sons called out, 'Father, he is taking aim at you.' The General replied: 'If I fall, John, rush upon him and put him to death.' But Pandi thought better of it. He turned the musket on himself, pressed the trigger with his foot and fell wounded to the ground. Hearsey addressed the onlookers:

'Why did you not arrest this murderous rebel?'

They answered that he was mad and under the influence of bhang.

'Then why did you not shoot him as you would have shot a mad dog?'

Someone replied that he was armed with a loaded musket.

'What! are you afraid of a loaded musket?'

They were silent.

The 34th Native Infantry were disbanded, after Manghal Pandi, whose wound was a slight one, had been tried by court-martial, condemned to death and hanged in the presence of the regiment. The jemidar in charge of the guard, whose name was also Pandi, suffered a similar fate and almost achieved a similar fame, for in the minds of the British in India the word "Pandi" symbolised the Mutiny and henceforth all the mutineers were to be called "Pandies."

Incendiarism soon became a feature of every-day life in many parts of the country, and barracks, store-houses, huts, hospitals, telegraph offices, bungalows 'burst out into mysterious conflagration.' Rumours of all sorts flew from mouth to mouth, rumours which proved that a reign of mental terror had commenced and that people would believe anything they heard. It was whispered in the bazaars that the flour sold to the natives was mixed with the powder of ground bones, that the butter was adulterated with animal fat, that the sugar was tainted with burnt bones, that the wells had been polluted by the flesh of pigs and cows. The distribution of chapatis came to the notice of the authorities and the notion that a chapati could be used as a fiery cross was laughed to scorn by the Government officials in Calcutta. But chapatis were not the only messengers of ill-omen. The disbanded soldiery were returning to their homes and most of their homes were in the centre of disaffection: Oudh, the cradle of the Bengal Army.

The Chief Commissioner of Oudh was Sir Henry Lawrence. He had been offered the post in January, '57, by Lord Canning, who thus tried to right the wrong done him by Dalhousie. Lawrence's time had been wasted in Rajputana; and continual fretting over his uselessness there, combined with the injury he had received at the hands of his brother and the blow he had sustained by the death of his wife, had wrecked his health. He was on the point of leaving for England when Canning begged him to postpone the journey and go to Oudh, which was being governed in a very unsatisfactory manner by Coverley Jackson. Lawrence arrived at Lucknow in March and found that the annexation of the province had produced the worst effects: the native landowners hated British rule and the innumerable families that had previously benefited by having a relative in the army were in a condition of incipient revolt. Lawrence had always opposed the Company's annexation and the sudden introduction of occidental forms of government to a country unprepared for them. If his advice had been taken, his warnings attended to, there would have been no Indian Mutiny. His essays in the *Calcutta Review* had foretold it, had even specified

H.D.—6

the centres of danger, Delhi and Meerut. *'Come it will, unless anticipated,'* he had printed in italics: 'A Clive may not be then at hand.' Fortunately for the English in India a Clive was at hand, his name being John Nicholson.

When Henry Lawrence reached Lucknow the harm had already been done, and he reported the substance of an hour's conversation he had had with a jemidar of the Oudh Artillery, a Brahman of excellent character who had been in the army for twenty years and who firmly believed that the Government had been trying for a long period to convert the natives to Christianity either by force or deceit. He argued that as the British had won India by fraud they were not above mixing bone-dust with the grain sold to Hindus. When Lawrence expatiated on the power of England, which could raise any quantity of troops and did not depend on the Indians, the jemidar replied:

'I know you have plenty of men and much money, but Europeans are expensive and therefore you wish to take Hindus to sea and conquer the world for you.'

Lawrence reminded him that the sepoy, though a good soldier on shore, was a bad one at sea because of his poor food.

'That is just it,' answered the Brahman. 'You want us all to eat what you like, that we may be stronger and go everywhere. I tell you what everybody says.'

'Fools and traitors may say so, but honest and sensible men cannot think so.'

The Brahman refused to say whether he believed the common stories, but as for most of the sepoys 'I tell you they are like sheep; the leading one tumbles down, and all the rest roll over him.'

Not long after the disbanded regiments from Berhampore and Barrackpore had scattered themselves over the province of Oudh, Henry Lawrence discovered treasonable correspondence between the units in and

about Lucknow. He kept a watchful eye on their
behaviour but did not act until he heard that the sepoys
of one regiment were making no secret of their intention to murder their English officers. Then he moved
so quickly that the mutineers were ignorant of his plans
until they found themselves facing his artillery and were
forced to lay down their arms. The immediate effect of
his action was salutary, but in a few days the feelings
of the sepoys were being expressed in the usual way,
mysterious fires occurring in military quarters.

And so the danger to the English grew, while the
rumours circulated by the conspirators were turning the
superstitious fears in the minds of the sepoys to panic,
until at last their madness burst forth in open mutiny
and cold-blooded murder. It happened at Meerut.

Situated about thirty-six miles from the imperial city
of Delhi, the important military station of Meerut was
a centre of intrigue and excitement. The bone-dust
rumour had been set afoot there and was implicitly
believed by the sepoys, who were circumspect in their
purchase of food, much given to incendiarism and
insolent to their officers. Towards the end of April '57
the 3rd Native Light Cavalry refused to receive the
cartridges issued to them on parade; and although their
commanding officer explained that the same ammunition had been in use for over thirty years, and that it
was free from grease, they remained obdurate. Their
behaviour could not be overlooked; eighty-five of them
were tried by a court-martial composed entirely of native
officers and were sentenced to imprisonment with hard
labour for ten years. General Hewitt, in command of
the Meerut division, remitted one-half of the sentence in
the case of eleven young troopers who might have been
misled by their seniors. On the morning of May 9th, in
the presence of the other regiments, the eighty-five men
were stripped of their uniforms, fettered and marched off

to gaol, some two miles from the cantonment.

The English officers at Meerut were easy in their minds that night and the English residents had no inkling of the wild reports spreading through the bazaars and among the sepoys that the whole native army would soon be shackled and the population massacred by the white soldiers. On Sunday morning, May 10th, many native servants absented themselves from the barracks of the English soldiers and the bungalows of the English officers. No one thought much of it and the church-going portion of the white community attended morning service. The afternoon was passed in repose by the Christians, in preparation by the Hindus and Mohammedans. The hour for evening service approached, but not until the bell began to toll did the gathering congregation realise that trouble was afoot. The notes of a bugle were heard, mingled with the sharp rattle of musketry. Parties of armed men appeared and disappeared. Clouds of smoke were seen rising from the bungalows of civilians and officers. The screams of women cut through the sultry air. Then, for the first time, it dawned upon the English stationed at Meerut that the situation was serious, that they no longer had to grapple with the problem of greased cartridges and bone-dust but to face the certainty of cut throats and brute force. Some faced it bravely. Colonel Finnis rode down to calm the sepoys of his regiment, was unseated by a ball in the back, and while he lay stretched on the ground the men of another regiment plugged him with bullets. Many more officers fell while trying to discharge their duty. But the indecision and stupidity of the divisional commander, General Hewitt, and the station commander, Colonel Archdale Wilson, were calamitous.

A crowd of mutinous troopers made for the gaol and released the eighty-five men who had been committed thereto the day before; the entire native force revolted and commenced an indiscriminate slaughter of every white man, woman and child they could lay their hands on; the dwellings of British civilians and soldiers were fired and their possessions stolen or destroyed; and then under cover of night the rebels started for Delhi. That night was one of horror. What the sepoys had started the inhabitants of Meerut completed. A horde of criminals, and not a few normally law-abiding citizens eager for booty, descended upon the residences of the white community, destroying, killing and plundering. The roar of the flames, the yells of the victims, the shrill cries of horses being burnt to death in their stables, the crash of falling timber, the shouts of the murderers and looters, combined to make a din that should have aroused even a staff-officer. It failed to animate General Hewitt and Colonel Archdale Wilson, who were paralysed by the shock of the outbreak. They were after all Regular Army officers, accustomed to official routine, and they could not believe that such a thing had happened, or that, having happened, anything could be done about it.

'Mutiny is like small-pox,' said John Nicholson; 'it spreads quickly and must be crushed as soon as possible.' Apparently Hewitt and Wilson looked upon it as a rash which would quickly disappear if left alone. At any rate they did nothing and at a later period each blamed the other for not having done something. After considerable delay Hewitt ordered some troops to proceed to the gaol; they lost their way in the dark, but long before they could have reached it the prisoners had been released. Then Hewitt and Wilson with some British infantry and artillery went to look for the mutinous sepoys, but they had departed and no one knew where they had gone. Then Hewitt and Wilson returned to protect the barracks, and having posted a few pickets they bivouacked for the night on the parade ground, where the officers and men of two English regiments and two batteries of artillery slept out the bloody drama being enacted in the European quarters. When he awoke next morning it suddenly occurred to the General that the rebellious sepoys *might* have gone towards Delhi. He sent out some troops to reconnoitre the road, but the mutineers had spent the night in motion and could not be seen. Seemingly this effort exhausted General Hewitt, for after issuing an order that the mutilated remains of all the Europeans should be collected and placed in the theatre he sat down and, continuing the policy he had pursued before getting up, did nothing. Archdale Wilson followed suit, blissfully unconscious that he would one day be forced to reverse this policy at the command of an insubordinate junior called John Nicholson.

Delhi was within the divisional command of Hewitt, and apart from the fact that it contained one of the largest stores of arms and ammunition in the country, its possession was vital to the conquerors of India, for the descendant of the Moguls lived there and the strongly fortified capital of that ancient dynasty might easily become the centre of a successful rebellion. The royal family at Delhi were ill-disposed towards the British, who had left them merely the apparel of monarchy and intended to remove the last wrapping of royalty at the death of the present King, now an old man. It has already been said that if Henry Lawrence had been able to influence the Government of India the Mutiny would not have broken out. It may further be said that if John Nicholson had been in command at Meerut when the Mutiny did break out it would have been nipped in the bud. Ordinary soldiers, like ordinary politicians, are useless in a crisis; they lose their heads; they are alternately swayed by panic and spasms of futile bravery; they dare not act on their own initiative because their lives have been hedged round with orders, habits, red-tape; routine has been the death of them as individuals; and so in a crisis an intelligent community should instantly scrap its professional leaders, both military and civilian. The Indian Mutiny was provoked by the bureaucratic politicians and prolonged by the bureaucratic soldiers, whose ages, owing to promotion by seniority, averaged: generals, 70, colonels, 60, captains, 50.

While the English regiments were sleeping beneath the moon, the native regiments were travelling to Delhi by its light, and in the early morning of May 11th the cavalry crossed the Jumna by the bridge of boats, sabred the toll-keeper, set alight the toll-house, killed an Englishman who was strolling on the bridge, and arrived under the Palace windows, where they shouted for admission. The King sent for the Palace Commandant, Captain Douglas, who said he would descend and speak to the men. The old monarch begged him not to go down, so he addressed them from a balcony, telling them to depart, as the King did not desire their presence. The rebels had not murdered their officers and journeyed to Delhi in order to obey the first white man who enjoined them to good behaviour. They entered the city, took possession of it without opposition, and began to search for Europeans. The sepoy guards sided with the Meerut troops, and when it became clear that no English regiment was coming to the rescue the townsmen joined in the hue and cry. A few English people, Captain Douglas, the chaplain, his daughter, another lady, the Commissioner, the Collector, were in the Palace when the mutineers forced a way in and dispatched them. The Delhi bank was attacked, its employees killed, and though the manager and his family put up a stout defence on the roof they were ultimately overcome and cut down. The staff of the *Delhi Gazette* were butchered, and the white inmates of every European dwelling met the same fate, though a few escaped to the main-guard and a few were captured and taken to the Palace.

The native brigade stationed at Delhi occupied cantonments on the ridge that was to become so famous, about two miles out. The English officers believed in the loyalty of their men and when the news came that mutineers had reached the city from Meerut they marched some infantry and artillery down to the Kashmir Gate, on the other side of which was the main-guard. But the men at the main-guard and their own followers revolted almost simultaneously and five British officers lay dead on the ground. The artillery coming up, the mutineers were dispersed and the main-guard was occupied. More troops came in obediently from the cantonments and for several hours the post was held in the hope that the British regiments at Meerut were on their way to Delhi. It was a desperate situation. The few English officers at the main-guard were uncertain of their men, European fugitives came in at intervals with blood-curdling accounts of incidents in the city, and the sounds of tumult seemed to increase in volume as the day wore on. At about four in the afternoon a terrific explosion was heard and not long after two British subalterns, their faces so blackened by smoke that they were scarcely recognisable, came running into the main-guard. They had a strange tale to tell.

One of them, Lieut. George Willoughby of the Bengal Artillery, had been in charge of the great Delhi Magazine. The other, Lieut. Forrest of the Ordnance Department, had been with him. These two officers, a third named Raynor and six N.C.O.'s were the only Europeans in the establishment, the remainder being Indians. When they heard that the city was in the hands of the Meerut troops they realised that on account of its huge stock of war material the Magazine would speedily be attacked. They also perceived that the natives with them could not be trusted; but they felt sure that the British regiments at Meerut would soon be on the track of the mutineers, and they determined to defend the Magazine until succour should arrive, failing which they were prepared to blow it up and themselves with it. So they shut and barricaded the outer gates, placed and loaded the guns, laid a train from the powder-magazine which was to be ignited at a signal from Willoughby, and waited. An order to surrender in the name of the King soon arrived. They did not answer it. Messenger after messenger appeared with orders that became more peremptory in tone. The nine Europeans still waited; and at last the attack commenced. Scaling-ladders were placed against the walls and the enemy swarmed up them. The moment they appeared on the walls all the native gunners and artificers in the Magazine climbed some sheds and joined their comrades outside. Then, as the attackers poured over the walls, the grapeshot began to fly. On they came in an endless stream and the ammunition of the defenders was soon running out, for not a man at the guns could be spared to fetch more shot. Two of their number were wounded and the guns were being loaded for the last time when Willoughby gave the fatal signal. In a few seconds there was an ear-splitting detonation; the Magazine went upwards with several hundred mutineers, and by some extraordinary stroke of luck four out of the nine Britishers escaped with their lives, two of whom got to the main-guard, two eventually to Meerut.

The failure of the British regiments at Meerut to come to the relief of their comrades at Delhi had momentous and disastrous results. The King was encouraged to believe that the days of British rule were numbered and allowed himself to be nominated as the leader of a great national uprising to expel the detested foreigner, when Hindus and Mohammedans would again possess their country and the Mogul dynasty would be restored.

Such sepoys as had not already mutinied when the Magazine was destroyed hesitated no longer, and from that moment the life of every English man or woman in the main-guard and cantonments was in jeopardy. The sepoys near the main-guard fired a volley into the group of officers within a few yards of them. Three fell dead. The rest made a rope of their belts, lowered the women who had managed to escape from the city through an opening at the rear of the building into a ditch thirty feet below, dropped down after them, and somehow contrived, after many slips back into the ditch, to get the women and themselves to the top of the opposite bank, whence they made their way through some jungle towards the cantonments.

Here they found that the remaining sepoys had turned upon their officers and were in possession of the guns. The mutineers, however, were good enough to let the British depart; and so for days the white men and women endured all the hardships of an escape under a blazing sun through a country already hostile. Some were killed, others died on the way, several were abandoned because they could go no farther, many were stripped and robbed, most were starving. The lucky ones received help here and there from the people in rural districts, but the best policy was to hide in the day-time and travel by night. Wretched though their plight was, they were all more fortunate than their fellow-countrymen left behind in Delhi, about fifty of whom, mostly women and children, had been captured and lodged in a dungeon beneath the Palace. After four or five days of intense suffering they were tied together, taken out and butchered before large crowds of jeering, jubilant people.

India had now risen against her rulers, and a British force of 36,000 men was opposed by 257,000 sepoys and an unspecified number of native inhabitants. In the fighting that followed no quarter was given.

CHAPTER X
Smiting the Amalekites

THE news of the Meerut and Delhi outrages was received by the white population of Calcutta with a storm of indignation and dismay. The rich people in the capital were in danger of losing their money and were naturally more upset than those in distant posts who were only in danger of losing their lives; in fact they gave way to panic, and if the power had lain with them they would have denuded the country of soldiers and ringed Calcutta with bayonets. Fortunately Lord Canning was less concerned over his salary and skin. He realised at once that the fate of the country depended on the recapture of Delhi, the possession of which by the mutineers had given a national and political significance to what would otherwise had been a local military revolt, and he wrote, 'Delhi once crushed . . . we shall have no more difficulties.' After dispatching urgent messages for British troops to be sent him from Rangoon, Ceylon, Bombay and Madras, and having arranged that regiments destined for China should take India on their way, he made himself extremely unpopular with the wealthy residents of Calcutta by ordering every available man up-country to the points of danger.

The safety of the Punjab was vital to the safety of India, and the Governor-General was much worried by the thought that the Sikhs, who had only been conquered eight years before, might wish to pay off old scores and side with the mutineers. With the Punjab in an uproar India was lost, for many of the British troops in that province would be required to retake Delhi, and although

a treaty had been made with Dost Mahomed it would
undoubtedly be broken if the English were too closely
pressed elsewhere and the wily Amir saw a chance of
realising the dream of his life by seizing Peshawar.

But the Punjab was in good hands. At this juncture
John Lawrence was the right man in the right place.
If his brother Henry was born to prevent insurrection,
John was born to quell it. Henry believed in conciliating
people, John in curbing them. The hour for John had
struck.

The Chief Commissioner was absent from the capital
when the Delhi telegram was placed in his hands; he was
travelling to the hills for the sake of his health, but the
bad news held him at Rawal Pindi. His substitute at
Lahore was Robert Montgomery, the Judicial Commissioner, who lost no time in testing the temper of the
sepoys stationed at Mian Mir, the chief military station
in the province. He discovered that they were ripe for
revolt—'up to the throat in sedition,' a Brahman
loyalist reported—and in conjunction with the military
commandant he acted with boldness and promptitude.
A general parade was ordered for the morning of May
13th, but to allay suspicion a ball that had been arranged
for the officers of the station for the night of the 12th
was allowed to take place. It was important that the
English should appear careless and unconcerned, and as
very few officers could be trusted not to over-act their
parts, had they been conscious of playing them, scarcely
anyone was let into the secret. 'On with the dance!
let joy be unconfined,' wrote a poet of another ball held
on the eve of a military crisis; but the joy at Mian Mir
was partly confined by the knowledge that there was a
parade the following morning, and between dances the
officers cursed their Brigadier's lack of consideration.
'Damme! has the man no heart?' However, they were
not going to spoil the fun for the sake of a good night's

sleep, and when the sepoy guards saw the officers escorting wives and daughters home in the early hours they must have felt that their plans had not miscarried. But their feelings were different on parade a few hours later, when they were ordered to 'Pile Arms!' and a white regiment that had been facing them quickly stepped back, disclosing the artillery and gunners ready for action. They sullenly piled arms.

The real danger-point not only for the Punjab but for India was Peshawar, the capture of which either by the Afghans or by the tribes on the north-west frontier would have caused the whole of India to rise in revolt. Its peculiar importance was perceived by the leading Sikhs, one of whom, in conversation with an English official, dismissed the reports from Delhi as of little significance. 'What news from Peshawar?' he asked. 'Excellent; all quiet there,' he was informed. 'That is the best news you can give me,' he said. 'Why do you always ask so anxiously about Peshawar?' the English official wanted to know. The Sikh chieftain took the lower end of his scarf with his finger and thumb and rolled it up from bottom to top, saying. 'If Peshawar goes, the whole Punjab will be rolled up in rebellion like this.'

It so happened that the one man in India who could prevent such a process, who was quite capable of rolling back and flattening out any rebellion that started, was at Peshawar. Within a few minutes of reading the Delhi telegram John Nicholson, whose brain worked with amazing rapidity and lucidity in circumstances that numbed the intelligences of men who thought him dull and slow-witted in social intercourse, had sketched out a plan that was to save the Punjab and break the back of the Indian Mutiny. He suggested to Edwardes that a Movable Column should at once be formed, its object being to go from one place of danger to another throughout the province, to strike here, there, everywhere, giving the mutinous units no chance to join one another and co-operate. Next he proposed that a strong levy of Multani horse should be raised in southern Punjab, to be commanded by himself. He could depend on their fighting qualities, on his personal popularity with them, above all on their loyalty if they were promised loot. Edwardes jumped at both suggestions and telegraphed for John Lawrence's permission to carry them out, which was soon obtained. Nicholson also advised Brigadier Sydney Cotton, who commanded the troops at Peshawar, to remove a suspected sepoy regiment from cantonments to some frontier forts, the pretence being that an attack was anticipated in that quarter.

On the morning of May 13th there was a Council of War at the house of General Reed, the senior officer in the Punjab. In addition to Reed there were present Brigadier Cotton, Edwardes, Nicholson, Neville Chamberlain, Captain Wright and young Frederick Roberts, who was "greatly impressed with the calm and comprehensive view of the situation taken by Edwardes and Nicholson.' In spite of the presence of the leading military authority Edwardes and Nicholson had it all their own way, every suggestion they made being adopted: the formation of the Movable Column, the raising of Punjab levies, the substitution of Punjabis for Hindustanis at the important fort of Attock, the scattering of native units along the frontier where they could not conspire with one another, and even the removal of General Reed himself to Rawal Pindi. This last was a ticklish theme to broach and both Nicholson and Edwardes amused themselves in devising the surest way of making an ancient divisional commander clear out and leave the field for them to bustle in. They hit on a certain way. They declared that as head of the army in the province his place was near the Chief Commissioner at Rawal Pindi or Lahore or wherever the local government was situated, so that the civil authority could consult him on every matter of importance. They knew well enough that John Lawrence would be the real ruler of the Punjab, but that Reed would think himself so if flattered by constant consultation. Pleased with the picture they painted of him as a military dictator, Reed consented to go, and concealing their delight at the prospect of their freedom from red-tape at Peshawar Edwardes and Nicholson quickly went on to the next item on the agenda.

Who was to command the Movable Column? Of course Nicholson wanted to. So did Edwardes. So did Chamberlain. So also did Cotton. They wired to John Lawrence, who replied that neither Edwardes nor Nicholson could be spared from Peshawar. Eventually the Commander-in-Chief, no doubt guided by Lawrence's objection to Cotton as too old for the job, gave the command to Chamberlain. As a matter of fact Cotton was an admirable soldier, and for a General could be counted a chicken, being only sixty-five.

At the conclusion of the meeting Roberts was ordered to take all the messages which he and Wright had written out to the telegraph office. One of these messages was from General Reed to John Lawrence; it summarised the decisions of the Council of War, and was repeated to the commanding officers of stations throughout the Punjab. Roberts was told that he must see the wires dispatched personally, as it would not do to let them be read by the native clerks. He carried out his instructions and returned to his bungalow 'in a not unpleasant frame of mind,' for the trust reposed in him was most gratifying, chances of promotion were in the offing and he was very young.

But a few hours later his dreams of glory were dispelled by the arrival of Nicholson in a more than usually sombre mood. The proceedings at the meeting that morning had 'in some unaccountable manner' become known, said Nicholson, adding that Roberts himself had perhaps been guilty of divulging them. Roberts was extremely angry and indignantly rebutted what he considered a monstrous accusation. Nicholson made no comment, but quietly proposed that they should visit the telegraph office together and make inquiries.

They must have made a curious pair as they marched along side by side : the tall man with brooding eyes and solemn set face, provokingly silent; the tiny man, trying to keep in step with his companion, spluttering incoherent phrases of disgust, his eyes glancing sharply to right and left as if in hope of spotting the real criminal. It was an uncomfortable walk for the youngster and by the time they got to the telegraph office Nicholson seemed to have added several feet to his height and to have achieved a closer resemblance to granite. 'The signaller was a mere boy,' wrote the future Lord Roberts, 'and Nicholson's imposing presence and austere manner were quite too much for him; he was completely cowed, and, after a few hesitating denials, he admitted having satisfied the curiosity of a friend who had inquired of him how the authorities intended to deal with the crisis. This was enough, and I was cleared. The result to me of this unpleasant incident was a delightful increase of intimacy with the man for whom above all others I had the greatest admiration and most profound respect. As if to make up for his momentary injustice, Nicholson was kinder to me than ever, and I felt I had gained in him a firm and constant friend. So ended that eventful day.'

The telegraph service did not provide the only means of leakage and Nicholson made a raid on the regimental correspondence. He seized the mail at Attock, had all the letters for native troops copied before the originals were sent on to Peshawar, seized the mail at Peshawar, had all the letters copied before they were sent on to Attock, and though the style in most of them was of a figurative and allusive nature they revealed the important if unpleasant fact that the majority of sepoys were deep in treasonable correspondence, or, as the writers would have preferred to call it, religious correspondence. Precautions were taken; the treasure was moved from cantonments to the fort which contained the arms and ammunition and which was thereafter guarded by Europeans; Cotton left the cantonments and established his headquarters at the old Residency; as far as possible the sepoys were distributed at various posts and watched; while Edwardes went off to discuss matters with John Lawrence at Rawal Pindi, leaving Nicholson in charge at Peshawar.

On May 16th Nicholson wrote to his mother that all was quiet in the Punjab and that he hoped she was enjoying herself 'at some sea-bathing place.' But it was the last "all quiet" report he was ever to make. Three days later the native cavalry at an outlying fort betrayed symptoms of disaffection, the Persian editor of a native newspaper published a statement that sepoys had killed their officers at a frontier post, and a fakir was caught in possession of a letter which incited the Mohammedan sepoys at the outposts 'to come in with a few officers' heads and join in a rising on May 26th.' The Persian editor was imprisoned, the fakir was hanged, and Nicholson asked the chiefs in the Peshawar valley for men who could be trusted to stand by the British in the event of a sepoy revolt. But the chiefs were waiting to see what would happen; they had heard that the British had lost Delhi; they remembered Kabul; and one of them even told Nicholson that it was a crisis in which the sahibs would have to look after themselves.

The outlook was grim when Edwardes returned to

Peshawar on May 21st. Mutiny was spreading throughout India and no native regiment could be relied upon;
the very atmosphere seemed heavy with foreboding. All
through the day Nicholson and Edwardes were busy
trying to influence the village chiefs to raise men, but
their efforts were unsuccessful. With a strong sense of
coming danger they slept in their clothes that night and
at twelve o'clock were awakened with the news that the
sepoys had mutinied at Naushera, some thirty miles east
of Peshawar. They held anxious counsel, deciding
quickly that they could not at the moment weaken the
British garrison at Peshawar because the native troops
there would certainly revolt when they heard of their
comrades' action at Naushera. There was only one thing
to be done. They went straight to Cotton and asked him
to disarm the native garrison at daylight.

The average General of sixty-five would have resented
the intrusion of two political officers at the dead of
night, especially if told by them that he had to disarm
his troops. Cotton, however, was above the average and,
although he realised that such an action would gravely
imperil the frontier by encouraging the Afghans to
strike a blow for Peshawar, he did not hesitate. Sending
for the British commanders of the native regiments, he
informed them of his decision. 'A most painful scene
ensued,' wrote Edwardes: 'The commandants of those
regiments which were to be disarmed unanimously and
violently declared their implicit confidence in their men.
One advised conciliation and another threatened us that
his men would resist and take the guns.' They felt,
naturally, that the disgrace of their regiments reflected
upon themselves, and the intransigent attitude of the
two "politicals" did not sweeten their lot. After the
colonels had vigorously testified to the loyalty of their
men, Nicholson rose and handed each of them a packet
of papers with the words 'Perhaps these letters will

interest you.' The proof of treason in the private correspondence of their men aroused more anger than interest in the colonels, their rage no doubt chiefly inspired by the meddlesome efficiency of Nicholson, and they continued to assert that their sepoys could be trusted. At last Edwardes, seeing that precious time was being wasted, broke into the controversy: 'The matter, gentlemen, rests entirely with Brigadier Cotton.' He was promptly supported by the Brigadier: 'No more discussion, gentlemen! The troops will be disarmed. Those are my orders, and I must have them obeyed.' It was now six in the morning; an hour later the men were paraded.

Two British regiments with the artillery were posted at the two ends of the cantonment, ready for trouble if it should occur, but not too near the native regiments to provoke them. Edwardes and Cotton then rode down the lines from one end, Nicholson and the second-in-command from the other; they were escorted by a body of shaggy ruffians recruited from the hill-tribes and a troop of Multani horse. The command rang out: 'Pile arms!' It was followed by a few moments of intense nervous strain for the British officers. But the sepoys were taken completely by surprise and after the first shock of astonishment began automatically to lay down their arms. 'It was a painful and affecting thing to see them putting their own firelocks into the artillery waggons—weapons which they had used honourably for years,' reported Edwardes. 'The officers of a cavalry regiment, a very fine set of fellows, threw in their own swords with those of their men, and even tore off their spurs. It was impossible not to feel for and with them. . . .'

Rapid and courageous action has never been so quickly and completely justified. The air, said Edwardes, was cleared as if by a thunderstorm. 'As we rode down to the disarming, a very few chiefs and yeomen of the country attended us, and I remember, judging from their faces, that they came to see which way the tide would turn.' On their way back from the parade hundreds of petty chieftains who had held aloof until that moment came pouring in with offers of service. Friends were suddenly 'as thick as summer flies.' Levies arrived by the score from districts that had but recently been subdued. Towns that had buzzed with rebellion and bristled with armed men became 'as quiet as a Bayswater tea-garden.'

But the sepoy mutineers at Naushera had still to be dealt with; they had marched off to join the main body of their regiment, the 55th, at the fort of Mardan, where Colonel Henry Spottiswoode was in command. Like so many officers in the Bengal Army, Spottiswoode firmly believed in the loyalty of his troops and when the Sikhs in his regiment warned him that the Hindustanis were not to be trusted he shook his head, saying he would stake his life on their staunchness; which was precisely what he did, for when he heard that Cotton had sent out a force to disarm his men he yielded to despair and blew out his brains.

The force from Peshawar was commanded by Colonel Chute, who was accompanied by Nicholson as political officer. At daybreak on May 25th its approach was perceived from the walls of the fort. The mutineers at once seized all the money and ammunition they could carry and taking their regimental colours with them made off for the hills of Swat. It was a blazing hot day and the troops under Chute were tired after their march and not too anxious to do their duty. Also the mutineers had gained a long start and the ground was bad for the movement of artillery. Chute soon gave up the chase, but his political officer was not so easily satisfied.

With a handful of mounted police and a squadron of Multani horse John Nicholson started off in pursuit of the sepoys. In the words of Edwardes, he 'hurled himself like a thunderbolt on the route of a thousand mutineers.' He was in his element; the man of action, who had for so long been cramped by official duties, could at last express his personality with absolute abandon. It was a mode of self-revelation which could only be enjoyed by those who witnessed it from the rear. At the head of his small force, mounted on a big grey charger, he fell upon the main body of sepoys, who turned to receive him, broke under the shock and scattered in every direction. He hunted them out of villages, grappled with them in ravines, chased them over hills. He seemed to multiply himself many times over as he rode hither and thither; now he was seen, his sword flashing, on the bare outline of a ridge, and now emerging, his sword dripping, from a dark gully. All day long, beneath a relentless sun, the pursuit went on, the hunted sepoys fighting desperately, 'as men always do who have no chance of escape but by their own exertions,' said Nicholson. For twenty hours he was in the saddle, covering more than seventy miles in that time and killing many of the 150 dead sepoys that were counted and of the others that were not counted. As the sun sank the pursuit ceased and Nicholson returned to Mardan with 120 prisoners and the regimental colours.

All the prisoners were sentenced to death. Nicholson felt that some discrimination should be made and wrote to Edwardes: 'I must say a few words for some of the 55th prisoners. The officers of that regiment all concur in stating that the Sikhs were on their side to the last. I would, therefore, temper stern justice with mercy, and spare the Sikhs and young recruits. Blow away all the rest by all means, but spare boys scarcely out of their childhood, and men who were really loyal and respectful up to the moment when they allowed themselves to be carried away in a panic by the mass.' Sir John Lawrence also thought that the blowing away from guns of 120 men was rather a tall order. 'On further reflection, I would not put them all to death,' he advised; 'I do not think that we should be justified in the eyes of the Almighty in doing so,' and he suggested 'destroying from a quarter to a third of them.' Though Cotton found it a little difficult to ascertain the exact views of the Almighty, he felt sure they coincided with those of the Chief Commissioner, and only forty mutineers were picked to die, the rest being sentenced to imprisonment.

On June 10th a great punishment-parade was held at Peshawar. The entire garrison was drawn up, forming three sides of a square, and thousands of spectators had come in from the neighbourhood to witness the ceremony. In the words of the historian, Kaye, 'It was not to be doubted that the time had come when the severity of the hour would be the humanity of all time.' Be that as it may, the spectators saw forty men bound to the mouths of guns; they heard the sharp command, a roar of artillery, and a murmur of horror from the watching troops.

Such scenes as this became common enough; they were the result of fear no less than rage. The occurrences at Delhi and Meerut, bad enough without embellishment, had been exaggerated by report. Women, it was said, had been violated before they were butchered; and many Englishmen, fancying themselves or their women-folk in the hands of the mutinous sepoys, behaved as people do in a panic. Nothing was bad enough for the Pandies. Even Nicholson, who certainly knew no fear, advocated torture, but he exploded with the fury of twenty men, which more than made up for the absence of fear in him. His letters to Edwardes on the subject reveal the mentality of one whose hatred of evil has festered and become malignant; for the devil is re-created in those who hate him, the reformer's zeal is increased by self-hatred, and Satan is aroused to cast out Satan.

'Let us propose a Bill for the flaying alive, impalement, or burning of the murderers of the women and children at Delhi,' wrote Nicholson. 'The idea of simply hanging the perpetrators of such atrocities is maddening. I wish that I were in that part of the world, that if necessary I might take the law into my own hands.' Edwardes was less simple-minded; he could see the effect of such a Bill on the minds of the English humanitarians whose indignation was quickly aroused over the oppressed of every nation but their own; so he let the matter drop. But Nicholson picked it up again: 'You do not answer me about the Bill for a new kind of death for the murderers and dishonourers of our women. I will propose it alone if you will not help me. I will not, if I can help it, see fiends of that stamp let off with simple hanging.' Again Edwardes refused to be drawn, and Nicholson, feeling perhaps that his friend was suffering from religious scruples, helped him over the difficulty: 'As regards torturing the murderers of the women and children: If it be right otherwise, I do not think we should refrain from it, because it is a Native custom. We are told in the Bible that stripes shall be meted out according to faults, and, if hanging is sufficient punishment for such wretches, it is too severe for ordinary mutineers. If I had them in my power to-day, and knew that I were to die to-morrow, I would inflict the most excruciating tortures I could think of on them with a perfectly easy conscience. Our English nature appears to be always in extremes. A few years ago men (frequently innocent) used to be tortured merely on suspicion. Now there is no punishment worse than hanging, which is a very easy death, for atrocities which could not be exceeded by fiends. We have different scales of punishment for different kinds of theft, assault, forgery, and other crimes—why not for murder?' Edwardes managed to survive the controversy and retain the writer's friendship, knowing quite well that Nicholson would not have the patience to draft a Bill and safely assuming that he would feel all the better for relieving his feelings in letters, each of which exhausted him more than a battle.

During the progress of this correspondence Nicholson was accompanying Chute's column from one frontier fort to another. Each fort was garrisoned by detachments of the 64th native regiment together with men from a border regiment, and he discovered that the sepoys were trying to seduce the frontiersmen from their allegiance. Letters had gone to Dost Mahomed, asking for his aid against the British, but the Dost refused to commit himself. 'What will be remains to be seen,' he replied with some truth. Nicholson's messages to Edwardes were not so vague. One of them ran: 'I have got a man who taunted my police on the line of march with siding with infidels in a religious war. May I hang him?' The next morning he reported from Abazai: 'We arrived here all right yesterday, and found the 64th looking very villainous, but of course perfectly quiet. They have been talking very disloyally both to the Ghilzyes' (men of the frontier regiment) 'and people of the country, and the former have ceased to associate with them. The latter have been rather hoping for a row, in the midst of which they may escape paying revenue.' Early in June he obtained permission to disarm all the detachments of the 64th. He was on his way to one post when a sepoy nearly precipitated a mutiny by knocking down a sentry and calling on his comrades to arm: 'Nicholson Sahib is coming,' he shouted, 'and will blow us all away from guns; now is our time!' But his comrades knew the length of Nicholson's arm and refused to be stampeded.

Having struck the first mortal blow at the mutineers and having secured the safety of the frontier, Nicholson returned to Peshawar on June 10th, looking worn from

exposure and, Edwardes thought, much greyer than he
had been, but feeling well. Things were going badly in
every part of India except theirs. The mutineers were
triumphantly established at Delhi; rebellious regiments
marched into the capital every day; British officers
could not cope with the situation, trusting their men
blindly up to the last moment and failing to disarm
them or prevent their escape when the mask was thrown
off. Nicholson and Edwardes knew that much depended
on them. John Lawrence was removing soldiers from the
Punjab as quickly as they could be spared for the army
before Delhi, and the time was not far distant when the
safety of the north-west frontier would rest with the
raw recruits who kept pouring in from the hill country
round about. So Edwardes enlisted men and Nicholson
trained them for dear life: Afghans, Afridis, Mahsuds,
Waziris, Ghilzyes, Pathans, outlaws, desperadoes, escaped convicts, murderers, rogues· and vagabonds, the
cankers of a stormy world and endless wars, men who
were mounted on horses so wild that they could not be
drilled, men who sat upon horses so tame that they would
not march. 'Delhi and loot!' was the cry among them,
and Delhi was their name for Eldorado. Every Punjabi
regiment was increased, new corps were formed to ac-
commodate these "irregulars," and swarms of them had
to be rejected.

While Edwardes and Nicholson were hard at work
turning bandits into soldiers they received an extraordinary letter from John Lawrence, revealing such
weakness, timidity and shortsightedness in the Chief
Commissioner that if it had not been written in his own
hand they would not have believed it his. Lawrence
considered that British rule in India was contingent upon
the recovery of Delhi from the rebels and that everything
should be sacrificed to the needs of the army besieging
it. He therefore proposed that Dost Mahomed should be

asked to occupy the valley of Peshawar with his troops and given an assurance that if he remained true to his alliance the coveted territory would be made over to him in perpetuity. This, said Lawrence, would free the British soldiers and native levies in that region for concentration farther south and release a large number for the capture of Delhi. 'If disaster occurs at Delhi,' he concluded, 'all the Native Regulars and some of the Irregulars (perhaps many) will abandon us. We should, then, take time by the forelock.'

Having recovered from the shock of this communication Edwardes wrote on behalf of Nicholson, Cotton and himself: 'We are unanimously of opinion that with God's help we can and will hold Peshawar, let the worst come to the worst, and it would be a fatal policy to abandon it and to retire across the Indus. It is the anchor of the Punjab, and if you take it up the whole ship will drift to sea. . . . As to a friendly transfer of Peshawar to the Afghans, Dost Mahomed would not be a mortal Afghan —he would be an angel—if he did not assume our day to be gone in India, and follow after us as an enemy. Europeans cannot retreat—Kabul would come again! . . .' Next day he wrote again to say that it would be 'certain ruin' to give up Peshawar; and a week later he was still unable to keep his amazement out of an official letter: 'I don't know anything in this war that has surprised me so much as the judgment you have now formed on this subject. . . .'

But John Lawrence held to his view and soon a wire came from him containing grave news: 'A severe action (at Delhi) apparently with little result. . . . Bareilly mutineers en route to Delhi. Gwalior Contingent have mutinied. Agent has left. If matters get worse it is my decided opinion that the Peshawar arrangements should take effect. Our troops before Delhi must be reinforced and that largely. They must hold their ground.' Lawrence's main fear was expressed in the last phrase. From letters he had received it appeared that the commander of the British force outside Delhi was seriously considering the question of raising the siege. Such an action would have meant the loss of India, and John Lawrence was willing to risk an invasion from the northwest rather than a retirement from Delhi. But the men who were in command of Peshawar could not share his view. They believed that the evacuation of that outpost would be the beginning of the end of British dominion in India, and Cotton as well as Edwardes wrote in strong terms to the Chief Commissioner. 'We may pretend to make friendly presents of provinces,' said Edwardes, 'but we cannot disguise that we have lost them by weakness. India has not yet recovered from our expulsion from Afghanistan. . . . The Empire's reconquest hangs on the Punjab.' Lawrence wrote to the Governor-General giving his reasons in favour of a withdrawal from Peshawar and begging for a speedy decision. Canning's reply, which arrived some weeks later, ran: 'Hold on to Peshawar to the last.' But long before that telegram came Nicholson had left Peshawar.

Early in June Neville Chamberlain was appointed Adjutant-General to the army before Delhi and greatly to the annoyance of many senior officers the command of the Movable Column was conferred upon the man who had suggested its formation, John Nicholson, now raised to the rank of Brigadier-General. On June 14th a telegram requested him to start at once for Rawal Pindi. Before parting the two friends exchanged presents. Nicholson gave Edwardes his little clock, and Edwardes, because he valued it, gave Nicholson his Bannu silver drinking-cup. They bade farewell to one another and after Nicholson had disappeared into the night Edwardes sat down and wrote the words: 'A nobler spirit never went forth to fight his country's battles.' At a later date he amplified this. In the stress of emotion aroused in him by the report of Nicholson's death, he wrote: 'How grand, how glorious a piece of handiwork he was! It was a pleasure to behold him even. And then his nature so fully equal to his form! So undaunted, so noble, so tender to good, so stern to evil, so single-minded, so generous, so heroic, and yet so modest. I never saw another like him, and never expect to do so.'

At Rawal Pindi Nicholson met his old enemy John Lawrence and they disagreed noisily on the subject of Peshawar. 'Rather than abandon Peshawar let us give up Marri and Rawal Pindi,' said Nicholson. As Lawrence was living at the latter and his wife was staying at the former, Nicholson's suggestion did not evoke the Chief Commissioner's enthusiasm. Their meeting lacked harmony and it was not until he had put a considerable distance between himself and Lawrence that Nicholson softened down: 'I forgot before starting to say one or two things I had omitted saying,' he wrote. 'One was to thank you for my appointment. I know you recommended it on *public* grounds, but I do not feel the less obliged to you. Another was to tell you that I have dismissed old grievances (whether real or imaginary) from my mind, and, as far as I am concerned, bygones are bygones. In return, I would ask you not to judge me over-hastily or hardly.' In the course of his reply John Lawrence said, 'I endeavour in all public affairs to be guided by a sense of my duty.' This admirable sentiment was echoed by Nicholson, who, having failed to persuade the Chief Commissioner to move a regiment from Rawal Pindi to Lahore, promptly advised the commanding officer to do so, reported his action to Lawrence, said, 'I should be wanting in my duty if I neglected every means in my power to get what I think right done,' and added, 'I wish I were Commissioner or Deputy-Commissioner for a week.'

Nicholson was now back in the country where he had first won fame. Twelve years after his death General Younghusband was told by a Sikh chieftain, 'To this day our women at night wake trembling and saying they hear the tramp of Nikal Seyn's war-horse.' Such was the effect he had produced in the second Sikh war. He was about to produce a more devastating effect on the sepoys who had helped the British to beat the Sikhs. As a general he had one enormous advantage: he had nothing to unlearn. He was only thirty-four, about half the age of the average general, and he had spent a mere fraction of his life as a professional soldier. He could thus face every situation with the fresh outlook of one who had not studied any situation in a text-book. What little military lore he had ever imbibed he had fortunately expelled. Having watched several famous soldiers in action, he had a pretty clear idea of what to avoid, while his native genius for war prompted that rapidity of movement and exact appreciation of circumstances which are the hall-marks of the born leader.

His appointment was extremely unpopular except among the junior officers or hot-heads like Hodson. The many seniors who had been passed over were naturally furious and went about talking contemptuously of "*Mister* Nicholson." Edwardes wrote to congratulate John Lawrence on the promotion of Chamberlain and Nicholson: 'Amid the ruins of the Regular Army these two Irregular Pillars stand boldly up against the sky, and I hope the Tomnoddies will admire their architecture.' Nicholson had foreseen the heart-burning his elevation would cause, writing to Edwardes: 'I fear that my nomination will give great offence to the senior Queen's officers, but I shall do all in my power to get on well with them. I feel so sorry for the disappointment they must experience, that I think I shall be able to put up with a great deal of coldness without taking offence.'

Perhaps his sorrow was not quite so sincere as he hinted; more likely it was the complacent sympathy of one who curiously inquires after the health of an opponent he has just knocked out.

Chamberlain handed over his command of the Movable Column to Nicholson at Jullundur on June 22nd and then departed for Delhi. There had been a mutiny of sepoys at Jullundur and owing to the incompetence of the military authorities the rebels had got safely away. At the request of the local political officer, Major Edward Lake, the friendly Rajah of Kapurthala had garrisoned the town with his troops; but the weakness displayed by the British had aroused the contempt of the Sikhs, who swaggered about as if the place belonged to them. Lake, however, with no white troops at his disposal, had to swallow his pride in order to remain friendly with the Rajah. The arrival of the Movable Column at Jullundur temporarily strengthened his position, but as the Column might be ordered to leave at any moment he thought it would pleasantly impress the Sikh officers if Nicholson were to meet them. Nicholson agreed and a durbar was arranged in Lake's house. When the ceremony was over a general officer in the Kapurthala army named Mehtab Singh took his leave and marched towards the door. As senior in rank at the durbar it was his privilege to leave the room before any one else. Nicholson, however, got to the door before him and waved him back with an imperious gesture. Mehtab Singh stood aside while the rest of the company filed out. Then said Nicholson to Lake:

'Do you see that General Mehtab Singh has his shoes on?'

In those days natives removed their shoes before entering a room unless they wished to signify disrespect. Even Ranjit Singh received his white visitors with his feet bare and the chief nobles of the land left their shoes at the door when they called on Europeans. But Lake was in a difficult position and did his best to excuse Mehtab Singh.

'There is no possible excuse for such an act of gross impertinence,' said Nicholson. 'Mehtab Singh knows perfectly well that he would not venture to step on his own father's carpet save barefooted, and he has only committed this breach of etiquette to-day because he thinks we are not in a position to resent the insult, and that he can treat us as he would not have dared to do a month ago.'

This was a long speech for Nicholson, too long for Lake, and much too long for Mehtab Singh, who looked extremely uncomfortable and began to stammer apologies. But Nicholson had not completed his observations:

'If I were the last Englishman left in Jullundur, you should not come into my room with your shoes on.'

Then, recalling that it was not his room, he turned politely to Lake:

'I hope the Commissioner will now allow me to order you to take your shoes off and carry them out in your hands, so that your followers may witness your discomfiture.'

Mehtab Singh did not wait for the Commissioner's permission. He meekly removed his shoes and himself.

Nicholson's behaviour had what was called a good moral effect. There were no more swaggerers in the streets of Jullundur. It also had an artistic effect, not perhaps quite so good. Sir Henry Newbolt wrote a poem on the incident. But Lake must have pondered for some time on the inscrutable ways of providence, for his plan to impress the Sikh officers by asking them to meet Nicholson was more of a military than a diplomatic triumph.

The Movable Column consisted of three British units: the 52nd Queen's Light Infantry, a troop of Horse

Artillery under Major Dawes and a Horse Battery under Major Bourchier; Nicholson also brought several hundred Multani horse and foot with him. There were in addition three native units in the Column which outnumbered the Europeans: the 33rd and 35th Native Infantry and a wing of the 9th Cavalry.

On June 23rd the force marched south in the direction of Delhi. Everybody thought that Nicholson was taking a grave risk in letting the two sepoy regiments accompany the Column. It was common talk that they were not to be trusted and few doubted that they would desert at the first opportunity to join the rebels in the capital. In reality his action was extremely prudent. The 33rd regiment was some distance away when the Column started, and had he disarmed the 35th at Jullundur the news would have travelled quickly, provoking a mutiny of the 33rd before he could deal with it. But when the sepoys in the latter regiment heard that they were going to join the Movable Column at a certain spot on the road to Delhi their suspicions were lulled and they walked straight into the trap.

Nicholson chose the fort of Phillaur for the execution of his plan. On the morning of June 25th the British troops at the head of the Column arrived at the camping-ground, unlimbered the guns and got ready for emergencies. Nicholson had already arranged that the bridge of boats over the Sutlej should be cut if firing was heard from his camp, and now he spoke a few words to the English infantry: 'In a few minutes you will see two Native Infantry regiments come round that little temple. If they bring their muskets to the "ready," fire a volley into them without further orders.' The English soldiers were seemingly taking their ease when the 35th regiment appeared, and though the sepoys were halted facing the guns they suspected nothing. Nicholson, leaning over one of the guns, coolly gave his orders, the last of which ran: 'If they bolt, you follow as hard as you can; the bridge will have been destroyed and we shall have a second Sobraon on a small scale.' The order to pile arms came as a shock to the British officers no less than to the Indians, but at least one of the former was relieved, for he muttered, 'Thank God!' The order was obeyed and the arms were taken to the fort. After a reasonable interval, carefully timed by Nicholson, the 33rd regiment arrived and was equally surprised by the order. Its officers indeed still believed that the men were loyal and the Colonel, who had been with the regiment for over thirty years, was aghast: 'What! disarm my regiment? I will answer with my life for the loyalty of every man!' When the order was repeated he burst into tears. Though he would have liked to do so Nicholson did not disarm the wing of the 9th Cavalry, because the rest of the regiment was stationed far away at Sialkot and would have mutinied the moment the news got through.

Before the disarmed sepoys were marched off Nicholson warned them that the penalty of desertion was death. Eight men of the 35th tried to escape, were caught and condemned to death by drum-head court-martial. A hollow square was formed, one side taken up by eight guns, opposite which the 35th regiment was drawn up, the other sides being lined with the remaining troops. The eight guns were loaded with powder only. All being ready, an order was heard, 'Quick march!' and immediately the eight deserters entered the square, the space between each corresponding to the distance between the guns. At the word 'Halt!' each man stopped opposite the muzzle of a gun. 'Right face!' They turned and saw their old regiment at the other side of the square. 'Stand at ease!' Their hands went behind them, and at the same instant their heads flew upwards, their legs fell forward, and their intestines were blown into the faces of their former comrades. It was a remarkable exhibition

H.D.—7

of discipline, courage and coolness; but Nicholson thought it a waste of good powder and soon abandoned the practice in favour of hanging. Characteristically he did not trouble to report his actions to the Chief Commissioner, who heard through other channels that the two native regiments had been disarmed and wrote to complain of the Brigadier's omission. All he got for his pains was the knowledge that Nicholson spoke of him as 'an old woman.'

On June 28th the Column started off to Amritsar, a good central point from which blows could swiftly be delivered at any troublesome regiment in the Punjab. Nicholson had already turned a part of his force into a flying column. At any moment of the twenty-four hours it was necessary to dispatch troops to some place where their presence was instantly required; so he collected as many light carts as possible for the transport of infantry. His system of obtaining intelligence was extremely effective; it kept him informed of what was happening all over the country. Whenever the Column halted the telegraph wires were tapped, and every message that passed from one station to another was transcribed in a small tent by a clerk whose faculties were marvellously sharpened by the certain knowledge that Nicholson would carry out his threat: 'If you let a message pass without taking it off, I will hang you.' A remark like this, made in Nicholson's deep vibrant voice and accompanied by a glance that seemed to perforate the recipient, was never taken as a pleasantry. 'He looks quite through the deeds of men,' might have been written of Nicholson, who somehow knew instinctively when people were lying to him. His soldiers used to wonder whether he ever slept, for he had a nasty knack of appearing suddenly in the most unlikely spots at any time of the day or night. Not content with tapping the wires, he ordered all letters to be intercepted on the road, the native ones being copied and afterwards forwarded to allay suspicion.

Young Roberts (already nicknamed "Bobs"), who had a bright enough spark in him to perceive the flame in the older man, said that Nicholson always knew exactly what to do and the best way to do it. Roberts was serving on the staff of the Movable Column, which he left for Delhi when it got to Phillaur. He hated parting from Nicholson, but he was ambitious and laurels were to be won at the city of the Moguls. When he asked permission to go Nicholson said: 'Well, Roberts, your loss I can't replace; both personally and publicly I regret your going, but at the same time you have more chance of getting on before Delhi.' Roberts had to get someone to take his place before leaving, as Nicholson did not know a single officer serving under him.

A curious incident occurred just before the Column reached Amritsar. The orderly officer for the day was riding ahead to prepare the next camping-ground for the arrival of the force. Bumping along in the darkness, feeling very tired and only kept awake by the frequent stumbling of his horse, he was nearly unseated by a sudden swerve and perceived that his animal had shied at the approach of an elephant. 'Who are you?' he called out in English when the elephant with its riders came abreast of him. There was no answer, so he assumed that the occupants of the howdah were native; and as Nicholson had issued instructions that no native should be permitted to ride by any white man but should be made to dismount and salaam, the orderly officer drew his revolver and shouted in Hindustani: 'Get down, you bloody niggers, and salaam, or I'll fire at you!' There was a rattle of arms, followed by some whispering and then a command, after which the elephant went down on its knees and two figures stepped from the howdah and salaamed.

Some hours later Nicholson's Brigade-Major walked

into the orderly officer's tent and said: 'Here, youngster, the General wants to speak to you; what on earth have you been up to?' They went to the General's tent and found him writing at a table, near which stood a magnificently dressed native, black bearded and whiskered. Nicholson looked up and spoke:

'You met an elephant on the road early this morning and made the riders get down and salaam you. Why did you do it?'

'Your order, sir, that no natives should pass a white man riding without dismounting and salaaming.'

A short but unintelligible conversation took place between Nicholson and the native.

'You owe your life to this gentleman,' said Nicholson, 'for his attendant would have shot you, but he prevented him.'

A further interchange of mysterious gabble. At last:

'You can go,' said Nicholson, 'but before you do so I may tell you what he has just said to me: "No wonder you English conquer India when mere boys obey orders as this one did." '

The orderly officer afterwards learnt that the native was an emissary of Dost Mahomed, who had sent a leading chieftain to assure Nicholson of his loyalty and to offer troops if they should be needed. The fact that the Dost had sent this messenger to Nicholson instead of to John Lawrence was an extraordinary tribute to his reputation on the north-west frontier.

On July 5th the Column got to Amritsar, where Nicholson heard that there had been an outbreak at Jhelum on the northern border of the Punjab. The regiment there had for some time been on the brink of mutiny and John Lawrence had decided that it ought to be disarmed. 'The Chief Commissioner,' wrote Kaye, 'had prepared a plan of operations for taking the sepoys by surprise; but the Colonel, thinking that he knew better than any civilian how to manage an affair of this kind, departed from Lawrence's views, and sketched out a plan of his own. There was, therefore, no surprise.' The business was hopelessly bungled and resulted in a lot of unnecessary bloodshed. Nicholson did not wait for the contagion to spread, and although the native garrison at Amritsar had done nothing to provoke suspicion he took an English company into the fort, surprised the guard, quietly occupied one position after another, marched the sepoys out and disarmed them on the plain. They were too much amazed to offer resistance even if they had intended it.

Bad news continued to come in. Native regiments were disarmed at Rawal Pindi and again the affair had been mismanaged. Then, on July 10th, came the worst news of all. That evening the officers of the Movable Column were seated round the mess-table congratulating themselves on a piece of good fortune. They had not enjoyed a whole night's sleep for weeks. They had been marching in the dark hours and trying to sleep by day, lying down under their beds after piling their clothes on top to keep off the heat of the sun. But sleep beneath an Indian sun in midsummer was at best an intermittent doze and they were tired out. Now at last they could thankfully anticipate a good night's rest and they felt relatively cheerful. About half-way through dinner Nicholson, who according to his custom had not spoken a word since the beginning of the meal, suddenly looked round and said: 'Gentlemen, I do not want you to hurry your dinner, but the Column marches in half an hour.'

He probably rather enjoyed dropping bombs of this kind. He had by now become a 'character' and such things were expected of him. Unconsciously he had created a personality, the effect of which on other people had by degrees made him self-conscious, from which point he had begun to play a part. But the performance was always of a realistic order and never more so than on the night of July 10th, for he had received information that nearly a thousand native horse and foot had mutinied at Sialkot and were streaming southwards towards Delhi.

Sialkot was an important military station situated near the border of Jammu about seventy miles north of Amritsar and Lahore. The commanding officer, Brigadier Frederick Brind, had objected to the removal of European troops from the station to reinforce the Movable Column, but when advised to disarm the sepoys he had refused to do so, believing in their loyalty. The outbreak at Jhelum, together with a command from the King at Delhi that the native regiments should immediately join the Royal Army within the walls, precipitated the crisis at Sialkot. On the morning of July 9th the European residents were awakened by the tumult of revolt, rose hurriedly and rushed in a panic to the only place of safety, an old fort that had once been the stronghold of the Sikh leader, Tej Singh. Some reached it unhurt, a few got there in spite of wounds, most were murdered on the way. Ably assisted by the native servants of the British, the mutineers released the prisoners from the gaol, plundered the treasury, blew up the magazines, sacked and gutted the houses of the white people, and sabred, shot or bayoneted every man, woman and child they came across. Taking all the loot they could carry, and destroying everything they could not, the mutineers then started for the Ravi river, which they had to cross on the way to Delhi. Brigadier Brind was shot in the back and died in the fort, while his butler accompanied the rebels without the least suspicion that he would shortly meet another Brigadier of a more exacting nature than his old master.

News of the Sialkot disaster reached Amritsar shortly after dawn on July 10th. 'The troops here are in open mutiny,' the message ran: 'Jail broke. Brigadier wounded. Bishop killed. Many have escaped to the fort. Bring the Movable Column at once if possible. 6½ a.m. July 9.' The first thing Nicholson did was to disarm the wing of the 9th Cavalry, the remainder of that unit having been among the most bloodthirsty of the Sialkot mutineers. Next he commandeered every pony-cart, bullock-cart and other means of transport in the neighbourhood of Amritsar and Lahore. He sent spies in all directions to keep him in touch with those rumours which travel as fast as the wind through Indian bazaars. His plans were subject to complete alteration at a moment's notice, and although everything was ready for immediate action his final decision was probably made an hour or two before he broke silence in mess that evening. He ignored official instructions, encouraging others in a similar position to do the same. When Robert Montgomery advised Reynell Taylor to disarm the sepoys in his district, adding, 'I send this through Brigadier Nicholson, whose experience may be able to suggest something,' Nicholson forwarded the note with a short addition: 'I can suggest nothing. You and the officers on the spot are the best judges of how you should act. God prosper what you do.'

Having collated all the reports and rumours he had received during the day, Nicholson concluded that the Sialkot mutineers were making for Gurdaspur, half-way between the Ravi and the Beas, where they would try to incite the Irregular Cavalry to mutiny and then plunder the station. Gurdaspur was about forty-four miles north-east of Amritsar and as the rebels had had two days' start Nicholson determined to do the journey in a single forced march.

The Column left camp at 8.30 p.m. and travelled through the night. Having covered twenty-six miles, it halted for two hours at eight next morning, when rations of bread with rum and milk were served out. The remaining eighteen miles were accomplished in a blazing July sun. Nicholson had managed to get horses or pony-carriages for the greater part of his force, which gave the route by which they went the appearance of the Epsom road on Derby Day. Officers and men crowned their helmets with wreaths of green leaves and constructed awnings of tree-branches over the gigs and gun-carriages. Many soldiers who had never been mounted in their lives entertained their more secure companions by falling off their horses at intervals. As usual when British tommies are gathered together there was a good deal of back-chat and humorous ribaldry, interspersed with the singing of sentimental ditties such as "The Girl I left behind me," or songs that came straight from the heart like "Confound our officers!" In fact they made the best of a grilling experience, though many men fell out and had to be carried in dhoolies, some died of heat apoplexy and not a few horses succumbed to the sun.

At the hottest part of the day, with the Column approaching a large grove of trees, several officers suggested that Nicholson should halt for a couple of hours owing to the exhausted state of the men. But Nicholson was anxious above all things to get what he called 'a good bag' and refused. The officers pressed him and at length he yielded. There was plenty of room for the whole force in the shade of the trees; the men dropped as they arrived and were soon fast asleep. When they were roused to continue the journey they saw their General seated motionless on his horse in the middle of the road, in the full glare of the afternoon sun. He had been there all the time, waiting patiently for them to have their sleep out.

The tail of the Column arrived in camp near Gurdas-pur at 6 p.m. on July 11th, having completed the forty-four miles in about twenty-one hours. Nicholson admitted that the march had been 'of unusual length, performed at a very trying season of the year.' Yet he had enough energy left to ride through the town and arrest suspicious characters who might have informed the enemy of his coming. His unfailing memory for faces enabled him to spot two disguised sepoys in the crowd of people selling provisions to the troops. They were quickly put beyond the reach of temptation. His officers were surprised at his apparent inaction at Gurdaspur, but they did not know what he knew: that the Sialkot mutineers had not yet crossed the Ravi, his intention being to wait till they had crossed and attack them when their retreat was cut off by the river at their rear.

At 9 o'clock on the morning of July 12th he learnt that the enemy were crossing the river by a ford some nine miles distant at a place called Trimmu Ghat. At noon he was upon them. Anxious to get his guns within short range of the mutineers, who had the river a mile away behind them and a deep ditch a little way in front of them, he masked his advancing batteries with mounted Punjabis. But the opposing cavalry, stimulated by bhang, charged wildly and the mounted Punjabis did not wait to receive them. In Nicholson's euphemistic phrase, they seemed 'undesirous of engaging.' In actual fact the bhang-excited mutineers frightened them so much that they galloped some ten miles before stopping to consider whether they need have gone so far. Their sudden stampede gave Nicholson a few moments of anxiety, but the fire of his guns soon nullified their defection. The mutineers fought bravely, but their heavy artillery consisted of an old gun which no one but Brigadier Brind's butler knew how to work, and their smooth-bored 'Brown Bess' muskets were no match for the Enfield rifles of the British infantry. In half an hour they were rapidly withdrawing to the river, leaving three to four hundred killed and wounded behind them, as well as all their plunder, arms, ammunition and clothing. At this point Nicholson felt the need of some good cavalry to complete the business. The mounted Punjabis were far away, the infantry were dead beat, and he could not personally polish off five or six hundred desperate if retreating men. Still he did his best, and one of his officers caught sight of him parrying the thrust of a rebel and almost with the same motion cleaving his assailant's head in two. A second later he had disappeared with two Pathan followers into the smoke of battle.

Officers serving with Nicholson were not expected to stop fighting merely because they were wounded. At this engagement a subaltern received a spent bullet in his chest. Seeing a hole in his jacket, he assumed that he had been shot through the lungs and began to make his way towards the rear. The Brigade-Major met him and asked what was the matter. 'I am shot through the lungs,' replied the subaltern, making his voice sound as hearty as wounded heroes are supposed to feel. But his voice sounded a little too hearty for a man whose lungs had been pierced and the Brigade-Major said: 'Turn round and let me see the hole where the bullet came out.' There being no sign of perforation, the heartless Brigade-Major gave him a swipe on the back and ordered him back to the firing-line.

The River Ravi was rising rapidly and what had been a ford was becoming a torrent. Most of the escaping mutineers managed to reach an island in the middle of the river, where they planted their solitary gun and prepared for another fight. The British infantry were too exhausted to follow them and the river was practically unfordable by the time they got to it. Nicholson left a Punjabi guard to keep an eye on the rebels and led his tired troops back to Gurdaspur. He was not, however, content with his victory. A few days were needed to rest his men and obtain boat transport with which to take them across the river. The moment the boats arrived he posted the artillery on the bank opposite the position of the mutineers and while his guns kept the enemy occupied the infantry were quietly landed at the other end of the island, over a mile from the rebels and their gun. Nicholson then led his men forward through the thick brushwood. On such occasions he cast all cares aside, his nature expanded, the prospect of a pleasant battle making him communicative. As he rode along he opened his heart to a young subaltern, speaking of the jolly days he had spent hunting tigers in just such a piece of country as they were traversing, of how the most exciting way of cornering the beast was to gallop round it on horseback at top speed, and of the bracing moment when the alternative to killing it with a single blow was to be torn to death by it.

The rebels were soon informed by their pickets that Nicholson was on the island. They turned their gun towards the advancing line, but in the panic of the moment the makeshift artillerymen failed to depress the rusty screw and the shot went too high. Nicholson did not wait for them to make the necessary adjustment. He swept on at the head of his infantry, leading the attack on the battery. With one exception all the sepoys in charge of the gun died at their post. The man who ran away was caught by Nicholson, who rose in his stirrups and brought his tulwar down slantwise on the rebel's shoulder, cutting him diagonally clean in two at a stroke, one half of the body falling to the right, the other to the left, of Nicholson's weapon. It was a deft piece of work, denoting a sure eye, a firm wrist, nice judgment, accurate timing, and even Nicholson approved it: 'Not a bad sliver that!' he remarked quietly to his aide-de-camp. The fight was over in a few minutes, the

mutineers running to the river's edge, where they stood
their ground and were slain or took to the water and
were drowned.

Thus Nicholson's two actions resulted in the destruction of nearly a thousand men, while his own losses were
forty-six. John Lawrence declared that if other commanders had displayed his energy 'Delhi would long
since have fallen into our hands,' while Lord Canning
wrote that Nicholson, 'sweeping about the country like
the incarnation of vengeance, had struck terror into
wavering hearts.'

The Movable Column now returned to Amritsar,
Nicholson's Multanis, mounted on wiry ponies, surrounding it like a web, riding in couples, each pair
within signalling distance of the next, and so encircling
the force for many miles in every direction. They
recognised no leader save Nicholson, whom they worshipped and blindly obeyed. His passage through the
country was marked by less practical forms of worship,
an English officer recording that a common sight at
evenings was the appearance of Sikhs, who were
admitted to the General's tent in bodies of about a dozen
at a time. They sat on the ground, fixed their eyes on the
object of their adoration for a while, and then made way
for another group. Nicholson went on with his work,
taking no notice of his idolaters, unless their emotions
got the better of them and they prostrated themselves,
when they were soundly whipped and ejected. His
personal attendant, a huge, black-whiskered, black-mous-
tached Pathan, was able to deal with all such intrusions.
This man, whose father had saved Nicholson's life and
whose life had been saved by Nicholson, never left his
master's side, slept across the opening of his tent, served
his food and stood behind his chair with a cocked revolver
in hand. Such precautions were not excessive, as the
following incident will show.

One night the officers of the Movable Column were waiting for their dinner, which was overdue. A messenger was sent to the cooking-tent bringing back word that dinner would soon be ready. About half an hour after the appointed time Nicholson stalked in, saying abruptly: 'I am sorry, gentlemen, to have kept you waiting for your dinner, but I have been hanging your cooks.' Later they learnt what had happened. Nicholson had heard from one of his spies that the soup had been poisoned with aconite, so just before dinner he sent for the soup and arrested the cooks, who denied the accusation; but as they refused to taste it on the ground of caste, he gave some to a monkey, which died. A few minutes later, reported an officer who was present, 'our regimental cooks were ornamenting a neighbouring tree.'

While the Column moved on to Amritsar John Nicholson went to see John Lawrence at Lahore. Appalling news had just been received from Cawnpore, where after a siege in which the British garrison had suffered terribly, the Nana Sahib had promised the besieged men and women a safe passage by water to Allahabad and had treacherously murdered them by firing on their boats; after which the Nana had ordered the surviving women and children to be butchered, and their bodies, in some of which life was not yet extinct, had been flung into a well. This gruesome episode gained for the Nana a singular infamy and he was regarded through the English-speaking world as the authentic Devil incarnate. But the worst that can be said about the Devil, if we accept the authority of Holy Writ, is that he was actuated by a little harmless ambition and a little natural vanity. In these civilised times we should consider the Nana's behaviour as more in tune with that of a modern ruler in Russia or Germany.

Far worse than all the horrors of Cawnpore, for

Nicholson, was the death of Henry Lawrence early in July. Against his own judgment but egged on by the taunts of a braggart named Gubbins, the Director of Intelligence, Henry Lawrence led a force of under seven hundred men from Lucknow to tackle the mutineers who were about to invest the city and whose numbers were anything from ten to fifteen thousand. The expedition was mismanaged, the native gunners deserted, and a defeat would have become a massacre but for the personal bravery of Lawrence, who, having done his best to get killed, was heard to exclaim in an agony of self-reproach: 'My God! My God! And I brought them to *this*!' John Lawrence, one feels, would have expressed himself differently. The siege of the Lucknow Residency began next day and on the following morning, July 2nd, an eight-inch shell burst in the room occupied by Henry Lawrence, almost taking off his left leg and shattering his thigh. He lingered in agony until the morning of the 4th, saying not long before his death: 'I forgive everyone—I forgive my brother John.'

'He was our master, friend, example, all in one,' wrote Edwardes on hearing of Henry's death, 'a father to us in the great earnest public life to which he led us forth . . . our feeling was ever that of the old Cavaliers, who looked for the day when "the King shall enjoy his own again."' When Nicholson felt equal to it he wrote to Edwardes: 'If it please Providence that I live through this business, you must get me alongside of you again, and be my guide and help in endeavouring to follow his example; for I am so weak and unstable that I shall never do any good of myself.'

Such words as "weak" and "unstable" would not have occurred to John Lawrence if he had been asked to describe Nicholson; but then, unlike Henry, Nicholson never forgave brother John and never missed an opportunity of annoying him. Once the Chief Commissioner, anxious to feel assured that the Movable Column was still in the Punjab, sent its leader a peremptory note: 'You are to inform me, without delay, where you are and what you are doing, and to send me a return of courts-martial held upon insurgent natives, with a list of the various punishments inflicted.' Nicholson reversed the note and returned it after writing on the back (1) the name of the place he was at, (2) the date, (3) 'The punishment of mutiny is death,' and (4) his signature. John Lawrence's query concerning courts-martial was certainly justified, for Nicholson had practically dispensed with them, believing that the evidence of his own eyes was more valuable than any evidence sworn before a court.

'Jack,' said a British soldier as the Column marched into Jullundur on July 28th, 'the General's here.'

'How do you know?'

'Why, look there; there's his mark.'

A pair of gallows, from each of which six mutineers were suspended, and several bullock-carts filled with sepoys awaiting their turn, marked the General's presence. It would not have solaced the victims to know that frequently, after ordering executions, Nicholson returned to his tent and burst into tears. Such emotional releases were caused, no doubt, by the sudden change from action to reflection; he could for a while objectify the situation and with the exercise of his imagination he felt remorse.

While Nicholson was at Lahore he did his utmost to increase the strength of the Movable Column before it left the Punjab for Delhi. John Lawrence was only too willing to help him, stripping the province of every available man. But Nicholson was greedy, asked for more, and took what was not given him. Largely owing to his exertions the Punjab was now considered safe and on July 25th the Column started on its march to Delhi.

In defiance of the Chief Commissioner and without asking permission of the Commanding Officer, Nicholson swept a battery into his force, and when asked for an explanation of his conduct apologised curtly in a note, proving the shallowness of his repentance immediately afterwards by carrying off all the artillerymen he could find in the fort at Phillaur. 'I fear you are incorrigible,' wrote John Lawrence, 'so I must leave you to your fate. But, depend on it, you would get on equally well, and much more smoothly, if you worked *with* men rather than by ignoring them.'

Nicholson had put up with a lot from the head of the army in the Punjab, General Gowan, and had even threatened to throw up his job if that functionary went on complaining whenever Nicholson felt it his duty 'for the public good' to move troops directly under Gowan's command without consulting him. In reply to John Lawrence's letter about the Phillaur artillerymen, Nicholson wrote: 'I am very sorry to hear that General Gowan has taken offence again. I don't wish to ignore him or any other superior; I dislike offending anyone, and, except on principle, would never have a disagreement.' (He was, however, a man with many principles.) 'You write as if I were in the habit of giving offence. . . . I fear that I must have given offence to you, too, on the Rawal Pindi question. I can truly say that I opposed my opinion to yours with great reluctance, and, had the matter been of less importance, I might have preserved silence; but when in a great crisis an officer holds a strong opinion on any matter of consequence, I think he fails in his duty if he does not speak it out, at whatever risk of giving offence.'

He had indeed gravely offended the Chief Commissioner, for he had said that the troops at Rawal Pindi as well as those which were protecting the women and children at Marri should join the Column and march to

Delhi. Since John Lawrence's family were at Marri, he could scarcely be expected to relish Nicholson's remark: 'When an Empire is at stake, women and children cease to be of any consideration whatever.'

On August 7th Nicholson arrived at Delhi ahead of his Column because the General in command wished to consult him. He had not been there many days before the General in command showed no wish to consult him.

CHAPTER XI

The Hero of Delhi

As we have seen, the outbreak of the Mutiny had produced a panic among the comfortable classes in Calcutta. The less rich but equally secure residents of Simla behaved in much the same manner. The Commander-in-Chief, General Anson, was 'recreating himself' there in the month of May. He went south to Ambala almost at once, intending to collect a force and march on Delhi. No sooner was his back turned on Simla than a rumour got abroad that a battalion of Gurkhas had revolted and threatened to attack the place. Actually the Gurkhas had no intention of joining the sepoys; they merely wanted their pay, and they did not want to be removed from their native hills. Reassured on these points, they again became loyal. But the rumour frightened a part of the white population of Simla into the bank, 'a point esteemed to be best capable of defence,' while the greater portion, feeling that the bank afforded no security, fled in terror to the plains. 'The incidents of those two days on the Hills are not to be regarded with national pride,' wrote Kaye.

But though the Gurkha difficulty was overcome and the bank was doing business as usual, Anson's troubles were just beginning. He discovered that the various War Departments could only function in times of peace. They were prepared for everything except an emergency. The Adjutant-General, the Quartermaster-General, the Commissary-General, the Chief of the Army Medical Department, were quite incapable of dealing with a crisis. One said that the troops could not be mobilised at once, another that they could not be transported, a third that they could not be fed, a fourth that they could not be physicked. 'It was the speciality of these War Departments that they were never prepared for war,' said Kaye, and there is not much doubt that if Anson had relied on "the system" he would have remained inactive for weeks. But the firmly-worded messages of Lord Canning and Sir John Lawrence gave him no alternative; and whether he liked it or not, whether his troops were ready or not, whether he had sufficient ammunition or not, he was forced to march. On May 25th he started on the road to Delhi; the next day he was down with cholera; he was buried on the 27th. Sir Henry Barnard took command of the army and pressed onwards rapidly. On June 7th he was joined by the Meerut troops under Archdale Wilson. Together they attacked and defeated a large force of mutineers sent out from the rebel city to dispute their progress, and on June 8th the British occupied the long rocky ridge overlooking Delhi.

The siege of Delhi, which lasted for more than three months, was not really a siege at all. That is to say, until the arrival of Nicholson, the British were besieged on their ridge every bit as much as the sepoys were besieged in their city. The ridge is a little over two miles long and from forty to eighty feet high. It runs obliquely from a point within a thousand yards of the north-west corner of Delhi to the River Jumna some four miles north of the city. Thus not more than one-seventh of the city's circumference was invested by the so-called besiegers. The tents of the British were pitched on the left of their position, towards the Jumna, their right being exposed to constant attack. The country around them in every direction afforded good cover to the enemy; while the city, with its seven miles of thick walls twenty-four feet high, its bastions holding nine to twelve guns, its surrounding ditch twenty-five

feet broad and twenty feet deep, its well-guarded gates,
its eastern side secured from attack by the Jumna, seemed
well-nigh impregnable.

In spite of its defences Barnard was keen to assault
the place without delay, and the younger men, Hodson
among them, pressed for a night attack. But the advice
of senior officers like Wilson and Reed, who prophesied
a failure, influenced him and 'guided by military rule'
he awaited reinforcements. All through June the British
on the ridge were kept busy repulsing the night and day
attacks of the mutineers, who had the advantage of
preponderant numbers, superior artillery and large
supplies of ammunition which had escaped the explosion
contrived by Willoughby and his comrades. Every
member of the small British force of three thousand men
had to turn out and defend whatever point of the ridge
was being attacked, and while they grew weaker and
numerically smaller as the summer days dragged by, the
enemy gained in strength and freshness with the regular
arrival of new rebellious units. It soon became apparent
that Barnard was not the man for the job. A brave
soldier, who looked after his men and exposed himself
freely to bullets and sun-rays, he suffered from a want
of self-confidence and a consequent inability to dis-
criminate between the judgments of others. He worried
himself into a condition of insomnia and died suddenly
of cholera on July 5th. Three months before he had
asked Lord Canning: 'Cannot you find some tough job
to put to me? I will serve you faithfully.' The tough
job had killed him inside six weeks, but he had done
his best.

Barnard was succeeded by General Reed, whose departure from Peshawar had given so much pleasure to
Edwardes and Nicholson. Twelve days of responsibility
were sufficient for Reed; his health broke down completely and he left for the hills on the 17th after making

over the command to Brigadier Archdale Wilson, whose
inaction at Meerut had excited the contempt of his
do-or-die subordinates. By this time all hope of taking
the city by assault had vanished. The small British force
had suffered severely from the constant attacks of the
enemy, from sickness and the sun. Reinforcements had
trickled in at intervals, but no heavy artillery had
arrived, and though the enemy had frequently been
driven off with great slaughter the British casualties had
been high and the best officer with the army, Neville
Chamberlain, had been badly wounded.

Wilson was not the man to make the best of such a
situation and he was seriously talking of raising the
siege, or rather of evacuating the ridge, when Baird
Smith, the Chief Engineer, persuaded him to hold on.
'All India,' said Baird Smith, 'would at once believe
that we retreated because we were beaten.' What was
wanted to capture the city was 'a siege-train of sufficient
magnitude and sufficient weight to silence the guns on
the walls of Delhi.' So Wilson agreed to maintain his
position pending the arrival of considerable reinforcements and the necessary artillery. Nicholson brought the
first and by a brilliant battle enabled the second to get
through.

Many men in the camp outside Delhi had heard of
Nicholson but few had seen him. His appearance caused
surprise, few famous men, least of all men of action,
being as imposing in the flesh as they are in reputation.
His imperial air, giant build, grave handsome face, curt
speech and sonorous voice inspired annoyance or confidence at sight. Kaye described him as standing on the
ridge 'taking in all the wonderful suggestiveness of the
scene with that quiet, thoughtful, self-contained solemnity of mien, which distinguished him from all his
contemporaries.' But he did not stand there for long.
Within a few hours he had visited all the posts on

the ridge and had thoroughly inspected the defences.

'Our position is a perfectly providential one,' he wrote to Edwardes; 'we could not have found one better suited to our requirements. Had the ground been of an ordinary character, we must have abandoned it long ago, but the Ridge, with the strong buildings on it in front, and the river and canals protecting our flanks and rear, have saved us. I think Wilson has hitherto had considerable cause for anxiety. Had the enemy had the enterprise to detach a strong force in his rear, he could not have sent more than 500 or 600 men against it. It is too late for them to try that game now, and they know it, and are at their wits' end to devise some new plan of action. ... When the siege-train from Ferozpur arrives, I believe we shall be able to go in.'

Wilson was to have more cause for anxiety, but not for the same reason. In a short while Nicholson's presence would worry him as much as it did the King of Delhi, who had been composing poetry to solace his waking hours, but who gave it up on hearing that the pacificator of the Punjab was within gunshot of him. Others, however, hailed Nicholson's arrival with relief. 'Nicholson has come on ahead and is a host in himself,' wrote Hodson. . . . 'The camp is all alive at the notion of something decisive taking place soon.' Whatever his merits as a host, he was a trying guest. On the evening of August 7th he dined at the headquarters mess and hardly opened his mouth except to put food into it. 'If we had all been as solemn and as taciturn during the last two months,' complained a political officer, 'I do not think we should have survived. Our genial, jolly mess-dinners have kept up our spirits.' Having done what he came to do, Nicholson returned to the Movable Column, which he led into camp on August 14th to the musical accompaniment of a band and the resounding cheers of the army on the ridge.

But while the army cheered, some of its commanders groaned. Nicholson was thirty-four years old, a mere boy in the eyes of the average colonel or general. They thought it grossly unfair that their years of service (mostly in barracks) should have counted for nothing, that this upstart should have been promoted over their heads. They asserted that his appointment was unauthorised by the terms of the Queen's Warrant. It probably was. But when a house is ablaze and the fire brigade breaks down public-spirited people do not wait for the approval of authority before trying to save the suffocating inmates. In this case, however, Archdale Wilson thought it would be best for all concerned to remove the officers of the derelict fire brigade from the command of the only person who could extinguish the flames; and as there was 'a very unpleasant feeling' amongst the senior officers of the 52nd Light Infantry, which had been serving under Nicholson in the Movable Column, that regiment was posted to a different brigade when the Column reached Delhi, while Nicholson's command was chiefly made up of irregular units, the officers of which did not boil with indignation whenever they had to salute their Brigadier.

Strictly speaking, Nicholson had no official position in the camp before Delhi, and as he was careless about his attire he often went from place to place unnoticed; but whenever he was recognised by the men who had been led by him he was given the honours due only to the Commanding Officer; for them he was always 'the General.' Once when he was passing the guard of the 52nd Light Infantry, which had fought with him at Trimmu Ghat, a soldier spotted him, saluted, and called out:

'Jack, here's the General. Present arms!'

Nicholson acknowledged the salute of the guard and said:

'Thank you, but I am not *General*, only Captain Nicholson.'

He had probably heard that the authority of his appointment had been questioned.

If he was 'the General' to the British soldiers who had served with him, he was 'the god' to all those who had felt the strength of his arm on the north-west frontier. A female survivor of the Delhi massacre, after a number of horrible experiences and hair-breadth escapes, was brought into camp by two Afghans, who had concealed her with great difficulty and at considerable danger to themselves ever since the middle of May. Nicholson ordered them to be brought before him. Sitting on his horse in the full glare of the sun, he gazed at the two men. Then he spoke to one of them:

'You were tried at Peshawar three years ago, convicted of felony and sentenced to fourteen years' imprisonment.'

The man fell on his face, exclaiming:

'My Lord and my God!'

Addressing the other, Nicholson detailed his crimes and sentence. He, too, prostrated himself. They were told to get up, and as they had saved a British woman's life Nicholson promised that their lives should be spared on condition that they continued to act faithfully. He had decided to use them as spies, but issued a warning:

'Do you believe that if you are faithless to the trust my arm is long enough to reach you wherever you are?'

The Afghans, visibly trembling, said they believed it.

With the addition of the Movable Column the force before Delhi consisted of about eight thousand men, of whom some three thousand were British. Heavy guns were still required before the city could be assaulted, and a powerful siege-train was on its way from Ferozpur. The rebels fully appreciated the importance of inter-

cepting this and dispatched a force of between five and
eight thousand men with thirteen guns to cut off communication between the British army and the Punjab.

At daybreak on August 25th Nicholson left camp with
sixteen hundred infantry, four hundred and fifty cavalry
and sixteen guns, in pursuit of the rebels. The rain was
falling in torrents and the country was a quagmire. The
road, no better than a bullock-track, could hardly be
traced; all was bog and mud and swamp. The gun-
wheels sank beneath their axles; the artillerymen pushed
and pulled in the mire; the infantry slipped and slid and
fell and fell again, wet to the skin, covered in dirt; the
horses of the cavalry stumbled and swerved, blinding
their riders with the mud they struck up; the baggage-
camels sprawled in the slime. In the midst of one morass
the water was over the backs of the artillery horses and
a certain officer had quite abandoned hope when he
looked ahead, 'saw Nicholson's great form riding
steadily on as if nothing was the matter,' and knew that
all was well. Panting along and cursing as they went,
subject to alternate bouts of fierce sunshine and drench-
ing rain, now breast-high in water, now wallowing in
filth, the men ploughed their way through nine miles of
country before a halt was called.

Nicholson had received instructions as to the route he
should follow. Naturally he disobeyed them and relied
upon his intuition. He had no guides except those he
picked up on the road, no political officer to obtain useful
information. But his instinct did not fail him, for while
his men were resting he learnt that the mutineers were
twelve miles ahead, nearing the town of Najafgarh. He
decided to push on at once. Objections were instantly
raised by one of his colonels, who said that his men were
exhausted and had already done more than should have
been required of them, that he disclaimed all responsibility if they were asked to go on and that they were

already too tired to fight. Nicholson accepted the
responsibility and gave the order to march.

By five o'clock, after more than eighteen miles and
twelve hours of intense effort and discomfort, the men
had waded through a deep ford and flung themselves on
the ground, dead beat. While they were resting Nicholson rode along the front of the enemy's position, which
extended for about two miles, their left touching the
town of Najafgarh, their centre embracing an old serai
in which four guns were posted, their right reaching to
a bridge over a canal. Nine more guns were in position
between the serai and the bridge. The moment the
British troops passed the ford, where the water almost
reached to their shoulders, the enemy opened fire.
Nicholson disregarded the shot and shell, making a
quick but thorough inspection of their position.

The sun was sinking; his men had been limping with
fatigue; but instant action was imperative. The
strongest point was the serai and this he determined to
attack. Sending young Lumsden at the head of some
Punjabis to clear the town of Najafgarh, he rode along
the British line, addressing the men who were lying on
the ground. 'Hold your fire till you are within twenty
or thirty yards of the enemy, then pour your volleys
into them, give them a bayonet-charge, and the serai is
yours.' Following a preliminary burst of artillery fire
the order was given: 'Line advance!' With Nicholson
at their head the men went cheering, ankle-deep in mud,
through a hail of grapeshot and bullets. Two hundred
yards brought them to the serai. The rebels made a
desperate resistance and there was a bloody hand-to-
hand conflict in which the towering figure and death-deal-
ing arm of Nicholson were conspicuous. No sepoy left
the serai alive. The order was then given to change front
to the left and the British swept along the rear of the
enemy's position towards the bridge, capturing all the

guns, killing some eight hundred sepoys and putting the rest to flight.

The victory was complete, but the discomforts of the victors were not over, for the baggage had lagged behind and the men with their leader spent the night in a swamp, starving, soaked through and without shelter. Next day they returned to Delhi, having marched over thirty-six miles and beaten a strongly-posted enemy at least three times their number in less than forty hours, with a loss to themselves of two officers and twenty-three men killed, two officers and sixty-eight men wounded. It was the heaviest blow yet struck at the Delhi mutineers, who never again ventured forth to face the British in the open. A few of the senior officers said that Nicholson had over-marched and thoroughly used up some of the best European troops, but they had to say something. General Wilson thought that 'the exertions of all . . . must have been incredible,' and even Nicholson reported that the troops were 'entitled to great credit for the cheerfulness with which they bore the hardships they were exposed to.' John Lawrence sent congratulations: 'I wish I had the power of knighting you on the spot; it should be done.' By now Nicholson had seen enough of the military bigwigs to make him warm towards the Chief Commissioner, so he replied: 'I would much rather earn the good opinion of my friends than any kind of honorary distinction.' Friends? John Lawrence must have lifted an eyebrow.

The march to Gurdaspur, the affair at Trimmu Ghat, the march to Najafgarh and the ensuing battle, were Nicholson's main achievements as a General, though many of his previous engagements as a political officer were quite as remarkable. The first terrified the Punjab into submission, the second paralysed the mutineers in Delhi. Had Napoleon done either, a thousand text-books would have been written on his bewildering rapidity, his brilliant execution. But Nicholson did not sprawl across the continent of Europe and suffered no great defeats to contrast with his spectacular victories; moreover, he did not enjoy the sheltered life of Napoleon, for he led his troops personally in charges and assaults, shared the discomforts of his men and endured greater fatigues. Such things have limited his reputation, and he will never take his rightful place as one of the greatest leaders of all time because the reading public like to picture their cushioned conqueror with a crown upon his head, bestriding the earth above the conflict, making ample gestures, vociferating far-reaching ideals, perhaps enduring martyrdom, but always being "Cæsar." On hearing of Nicholson's latest exploits Dalhousie, who like most people was more impressed by quantity than quality, called the victor of Najafgarh 'a born soldier' who 'lately has shown many signs of being that most rare creation—*a born general.*' He had proved his capacity for generalship on a hundred occasions in the second Sikh war, but Dalhousie could hardly have been expected to realise that: he was too busy checking the errors of generals who were not born but made.

One of the officers who had been killed at Najafgarh was young Lumsden, to whose brother Harry Lumsden (of the Guides) Nicholson wrote:

'*Before Delhi,*
'1*st September,* 1857.

'MY DEAR LUMSDEN,—It is with great grief I have to communicate news which will be a sore trial to you and Peter. You will not have been wholly unprepared for it, for you know that hard fighting has been going on here for some time.

'Your poor brother was killed at the head of his regiment in action on the 25th. He died nobly doing his duty, and sincerely regretted by the whole army. His last words, as he fell dying to the ground, were ones of encouragement to his men and officers. He was in command of the corps at the time, Coke having been wounded and Travers killed in previous actions.

'We shall assault before the 10th, most probably, and I hope that his and other losses will be amply avenged.

'Give my love to Peter; you have my sympathy with you more than I can express.

> 'Ever, dear Joe,
> 'Yours very sincerely,
> 'J. NICHOLSON.'

Though about two thousand five hundred men of the Delhi Field Force lay sick in hospital on September 1st, there were few grumblers after Nicholson's victory. His coming had revivified the whole camp and expectation was in the air. 'Of all the superior officers in the Force,' wrote Neville Chamberlain, 'not one took the pains he did to study our position and provide for its safety. Hardly a day passed but that he visited every battery, breastwork and post; and frequently at night, though not on duty, he would ride round our outer line of sentries to see that the men were on the alert and to bring to notice any point he considered not duly provided for. John Nicholson was the only officer not being an Engineer who took the trouble to study the ground which was to become of so much importance to us. . . . From the day of the trenches being open to the day of the assault he was constantly on the move, from one battery to another. And when he returned to camp he was constantly riding backwards and forwards to the Chief Engineer endeavouring to remove any difficulties.'

There were indeed few matters that did not receive Nicholson's close attention; he was the (unauthorised) supervisor of the camp; he looked into and looked after everything, taking upon himself the duties of artilleryman, engineer, orderly officer, commissariat officer, political officer and officer of the guard. Nothing escaped his notice and he was to be seen most frequently at the posts of danger. The extreme right of the English position was surmounted by a large, fairly modern building called Hindu Rao's House, after the name of a former owner. It was the most exposed point on the ridge, persistently under gun-fire and frequently attacked in force by the mutineers. Major Charles Reid held it with his regiment of Gurkhas and several companies from other regiments. At first Reid had disliked Nicholson, who asked a number of questions in his abrupt and lofty manner, of which Reid complained to Baird Smith. 'Yes,' said the latter, 'but that wears off. You'll like him better when you have seen more of him.' The prophecy was quickly fulfilled and Reid began to look forward to his visits. Nicholson went there nearly every day, calling up the ladder which led to Reid's 'look-out': 'Have I permission to pass this sentry of yours? He always stops me.' One day they were standing close together in the 'look-out' when a shrapnel shell burst just over their heads, three of the balls hitting the telescope in Reid's hand and wounding two Gurkhas sitting below them. The incident did not affect Nicholson's visits nor the time he spent in the 'look-out.'

His work as an unofficial 'political' went on. He had spies in the city, one of their jobs being to persuade the Sikhs and certain others in the garrison to desert the rebels: 'We have been trying to get over the Sikhs,' he wrote to John Lawrence, 'but without success. They have been formed into a battalion at their own request, and seem inclined to stand their chance. They may possibly think better of it as the crisis approaches. Some of the Irregular Cavalry regiments have indirectly hinted that they are anxious for forgiveness. Now, though I would not pardon a single Pandy in a regiment which had murdered its officers, or perpetrated any other atrocities, I do think that these are corps which it would be neither just nor politic to refuse pardon to. The Irregular Cavalry have, as a rule, everywhere taken a much less active part in this mutiny than either Regular Cavalry or Infanry. They have no love or fellow-feeling with the Pandies. Several of these corps are still serving with arms. We are in great want of cavalry, and are likely to be in still greater. All accounts from below state that want of cavalry prevents Havelock from completing his victories. My own opinion is, that we ought to forgive all regiments which have not committed murder, or played a prominent part in the mutinies. Some, like the 29th at Moradabad, were positively the "victims of circumstance," and could not have held out longer. We cannot, if we would, annihilate the whole force now in arms against us in this Presidency, and it is not wise, all things considered, to make *every* man desperate. I would give no quarter to the leading corps in the mutiny, or to them which have murdered their officers; but I would not refuse it to a corps like the 29th, or some of the Irregular Cavalry. I spoke on this subject yesterday to both Wilson and Chamberlain, and they agreed with me; but Wilson thought his hands tied by the Government Proclamation, prohibiting pardon. I do not think we should allow that notification to be actually binding on us. We cannot now communicate with the Supreme Government, and the state of affairs is different now to what it was when the order was issued.'

On September 4th the heavy guns and mortars, drawn by elephants, together with many bullock-waggons filled with ammunition, came into camp and the erection of batteries between the ridge and the city commenced that night. 'I think we have a right to hope for success,' wrote Nicholson to Edwardes, 'and I trust that, ere another week passes, our flag will be flying from the palace minarets. Wilson has told me that he intends to nominate me Military Governor, for which I am much obliged, but I had rather that he had told me that he intended to give me command of the column of pursuit.' A few days later he heard that John Lawrence had obtained for him the Commissionership of Leia. 'You won't take it now that you are likely to remain a General and get a division,' said a friend. 'A General?' returned Nicholson: 'you don't think I'd like to be a General of division, do you? Look at them! Look at the Generals!'

Much of Nicholson's time was now spent with the Director of Trenches, Alexander Taylor, who was Baird Smith's executive assistant, responsible for the tracing and erection of the batteries. Taylor and Nicholson liked one another on sight and had many long talks together in the trenches while the work was going on. It was strange to hear Nicholson, utterly careless of his personal safety, begging Taylor not to expose himself unnecessarily. 'Caution, caution!' he said whenever the engineer allowed his head and shoulders to be seen by the enemy. They had both been nurtured in a Calvinistic atmosphere and recognised the effect it had produced on their characters; but Nicholson sometimes spoke bitterly of his strict upbringing, of the Sunday observances of his youth, and he had begun to doubt most of the doctrines he had been taught to believe. While the bullets flew past them they rested from work behind a rock or a ruin and talked of home and drank a little claret and agreed that an all-merciful Deity could not have created a world in which only Christians were destined to be saved. Nicholson's scepticism on certain points went too far for Taylor, who nevertheless was greatly struck by the other's open, simple and very truthful nature.

Beneath a cold exterior there was a vein of real tenderness in Nicholson. 'When he first arrived in camp I was on my back, and unable to move,' wrote Neville Chamberlain, 'and only commenced to sit up in bed on the siege-train arriving. Under these circumstances, I was, of course, only able to associate with him when he was at leisure, but out of kindness to my condition he never failed to pass a portion of the day with me, and frequently, though I would beg of him to go and take a canter, he would refuse, and lose the evening air. My recovery, after once being able to sit up, was rapid, and by the time our first battery opened, I was able to go in a dhooly on to the ridge and watch the practice. He would frequently insist upon escorting me, and no woman could have shown more consideration—finding out good places from which to obtain the best view, and going ahead to see that I did not incur undue risks, for he used to say no wounded man had any business to go under fire.'

Few men can have been so just and considerate to his deserving subordinates as Nicholson, who wrote to John Lawrence: 'I offered Randall of the 59th the Adjutancy of Stafford's corps, but he wishes to serve here, though on his bare subaltern's pay. Bear this in mind if anything happens to me, for it is not every man who declines staff employ, that he may serve in the trenches on his regimental allowances and without increase of rank. Randall is, moreover, a very steady, intelligent, conscientious fellow.' Lawrence did not forget, making Colonel Randall one of his aides-de-camp when he became Viceroy. As a youngster Randall's enthusiasm for Nicholson resembled that of Roberts, and like Roberts he never altered his opinion, writing in late life: 'The feelings with which I regard John Nicholson may have been at first engendered by the almost superhuman majesty of the man, acting on impressionable youth.

But the impression was indelible. . . . To me John Nicholson was and is the ideal of all that is noble, great and true—a hero.' Though they stood in awe of him, Nicholson's kindliness was extended to his native servants: 'A poor orderly of mine named Sadat Khan died here of cholera the other day,' he wrote to Edwardes. 'He has a mother and a brother, and I think a wife, in the Yusafzai country. Should I not be left to do it, will you kindly provide for the brother, and give the women a couple of hundred rupees out of my estate?'

While Taylor, the engineers and artillerymen were getting their batteries ready for action under fire of the enemy's guns, Nicholson and Baird Smith were opposing a far more dangerous enemy within their own lines. General Archdale Wilson was living up to the reputation he had gained at Meerut; he was a typical official who hated committing himself to a course of action; he wanted reinforcements and more reinforcements; nothing less than the entire British Army would have satisfied him; and even then he would have liked someone else to give the order for the assault. He had been told again and again that months would elapse before large reinforcements could reach him; he had been told that if Delhi was not taken the Punjab would rise in rebellion; John Lawrence had given him every man who could be spared, including the greatest soldier in India; yet his fears increased as his prospects brightened. Before the coming of the siege-train Nicholson wrote to John Lawrence: 'Wilson says that he will assume the offensive on the arrival of the heavy guns, but he says it in an undecided kind of way, which makes me doubt if he will do so, if he is not kept up to the mark. Do you therefore keep him up to it. He is not at all equal to the crisis, and I believe he feels it himself.' Wilson, however, was not by any means the only incompetent officer in the camp: 'Should I escape the storm and have to go out with a column afterwards, I must—unless you can supply a competent man—be my own political agent. I would rather have 2,000 men and be so, than 4,000 and hampered with an incapable. If you agree with me, you must authorise it, however, for Wilson will take no responsibility on himself, and it seems to me that he is becoming jealous of me, lest I should earn more than my share of *kudos*. He will not even show me the plan of assault now, though I feel pretty sure his nervousness will make him do so before the time comes.'

Baird Smith told the some story: 'The simple truth is,' he wrote, 'that I have such contempt for Wilson's military capacity and found him throughout the siege operations so uniformly obstructive by his dread of responsibility and his moral timidity that I say as little about him as I can. . . . I believe his mind to have been off its usual balance all the time we were at work, and he was literally more difficult to deal with than the enemy. It was only by constantly reminding him that if he interfered with my plans, I would throw the whole responsibility for the consequences on him, that I could get on at all.' Whenever Baird Smith told him a few home-truths, Wilson sulked like a staff officer and refused to deal with his Chief Engineer except through intermediaries. 'I am satisfied Wilson has gone off his head,' said Baird Smith on one such occasion. 'Wilson's head is going,' reported Nicholson: 'he *says* so himself, and it is quite evident that he speaks the truth.' Which was broadly the case, for Wilson had written to Baird Smith: 'I have already more than I can manage, and my head gets into such a state that I feel nearly mad sometimes. For God's sake don't drive me quite so.'

Though fretted almost to breaking-point by the go-ahead promptings of Baird Smith, it was Nicholson who made Wilson's life insupportable. Nicholson endorsed the Chief Engineer's policy with such vigour that Wilson could no longer ignore it; so he did the next best thing and ignored Nicholson, who wrote to John Lawrence: 'The Engineers have consulted me about the plan of the attack, though Wilson has not. They tell me they proposed to him that I should be consulted, and that he maintained a chilling silence. I imagine it is, as I supposed, that he is afraid of being thought to be influenced by me. I care little, however, whether he receives my suggestions direct, or through the Engineers. Like Barnard, he talks about the "gambler's throw." ' Wilson had at any rate one achievement to his credit: he turned Nicholson into a letter-writer.

'The game is completely in our hands,' wrote Nicholson to John Lawrence: 'we only want a player to move the pieces. Fortunately, after making all kinds of objections and obstructions, and even threatening more than once to withdraw the guns and abandon the attempt, Wilson has made everything over to the Engineers, and they, and they alone, will deserve the credit of taking Delhi. Had Wilson carried out this threat of withdrawing the guns, I was quite prepared to appeal to the army to set him aside and elect a successor. I have seen lots of useless generals in my day; but such an ignorant, croaking obstructive as he is, I have never hitherto met with; and nothing will induce me to serve a day under his personal command after the fall of this place. The purport of his last message in reply to the Engineers ran thus: "I disagree with the Engineers entirely. I foresee great, if not insuperable, difficulties in the plan they propose. But as I have no other plan myself, I yield to the urgent remonstrances of the chief engineer." The above are almost the very words used by him, and yet he never even examined the ground on which the Engineers proposed to erect the breaching batteries. I believed the Meerut catastrophe was more his fault than Hewitt's; and by all accounts he was driven into fighting at the Hindan, and could not help himself. The same may be said now. He is allowing the Engineers to undertake active operations, simply because the army will not put up with inactivity.'

But Wilson did not submit to the engineers until Nicholson had done something that he should never have been allowed to do. About five hundred yards to the north of the Kashmir Gate, between the city and the ridge, there was a modern mansion called Ludlow Castle. It was held by the enemy, whose battery constantly harassed the British pickets, and Alexander Taylor had crept round it at night-time before preparing a report proving the necessity of its capture as a preliminary to the assault on the city. Wilson would not accept this report because it was based on a personal inspection of the ground and he refused to believe that Taylor had made it. Nicholson at once volunteered to go over the position with Taylor in order to check the accuracy of his report. Wilson agreed, and a most valuable but foolhardy excursion was made. At midnight Nicholson accompanied Taylor not only to Ludlow Castle but to an old summer-palace of the Moguls almost beneath the walls of the city. They found Ludlow Castle temporarily unoccupied, but every step they took was within the territory of an enemy capable of silent movement and sharp hearing. As Nicholson would have been quite irreplaceable, Wilson's permission to let him go almost suggests that he would not have died with grief if there had been a mishap. Nicholson's full approval of Taylor's report resulted in the capture of Ludlow Castle and the planting of a battery that greatly simplified the assault on the city. 'Had it not been for his going down that night,' wrote Neville Chamberlain, 'I believe we might have had to capture at considerable loss of life the positions which he was certainly the main cause of our occupying without resistance.' Nicholson himself gave all the credit to Taylor, and when he heard that the headquarters staff were criticising the work of the engineers he indignantly declared: 'If I live through this I shall let the world know who took Delhi, that Alex Taylor did it.'

Concerning the midnight visit to Ludlow Castle, there is no doubt. With regard to a similar story, the authority must be specified because of its fantastic nature.[*] The only possible comment is that if it had been recorded of any leader in history except Nicholson it would instantly be dismissed as fabulous. The leader of the attacking force had to know the exact lie of land between the Kashmir and Lahore Gates, those being the eastern and western points of the assault. Nicholson could trust no eyes but his own and late one night, probably aware through his spies that the guns on the walls were temporarily manned by Sikhs, he calmly traversed the walls through the batteries in his usual dress, having made no attempt to disguise himself. He went all the way from the Lahore Gate to the Kashmir Gate and had the astonishing good fortune to meet no sepoy on the way. The Sikh gunners, when they saw the massive figure of the man they worshipped approaching them, had the fright of their lives and prostrated themselves reverently as he passed by. Incredible though the story seems, it is not so remarkable as that of the same man who paralysed into peace the most lawless district in India and made it unnecessary that any forts should be maintained in Bannu for the protection of its people from neighbouring tribes of bandits.

---

[*] *An Unrecorded Chapter of the Indian Mutiny,* by Reginald G. Wilberforce, 3rd edition, 1895. After the publication of my book in September 1939, Major-General H. R. Davies informed me that many of Wilberforce's statements had been disproved; so the story here printed must be accepted with reserve.

Yet while Nicholson, Taylor, Hodson and others were risking their lives every day, General Wilson would not risk his reputation by issuing the order to assault, and at last Nicholson decided on a course of action as daring as it was original. A Council of War had been called and it happened that Frederick Roberts was with Nicholson in his tent just before he set out to attend it. Nicholson had been talking, according to Roberts, 'in confidential terms of personal matters,' from which we may guess that the Old Testament prophecies had been under discussion, but suddenly he switched over from Jeremiah to Wilson: 'Delhi must be taken,' he said, 'and it is absolutely essential that this should be done at once; and if Wilson hesitates longer, I intend to propose at to-day's meeting that he should be superseded.' Roberts was 'greatly startled, and ventured to remark that, as Chamberlain was *hors de combat* from his wound, Wilson's removal would leave him, Nicholson, senior officer with the force.' Nicholson smiled as he answered: 'I have not overlooked that fact. I shall make it perfectly clear that, under the circumstances, I could not possibly accept the command myself, and I shall propose that it be given to Campbell of the 52nd; I am prepared to serve under him for the time being, so no one can ever accuse me of being influenced by personal motives.' There is not the least doubt that Nicholson would have made good his threat, and there is very little doubt that Wilson saw what was coming if he continued to shilly-shally. Nicholson's face at the Council of War frightened him more than the prospect of certain failure which he envisaged; he gave way and agreed to the assault.

By September 12th the heavy artillery of the British was battering the walls and bastions of Delhi. Gaps soon appeared in the walls and the bastions were partially reduced to ruins. Though the rebels tried hard to repair the breaches and replace the guns that had been silenced, Taylor was able to assure Wilson on the 13th that the assault was feasible. All that day Nicholson was on the move. In the morning he visited Hindu Rao's House to make final arrangements with Reid, who was to fight his way through the western suburbs to the Lahore Gate, which Nicholson promised to open to him from within. The assault had been provisionally fixed for daybreak on the 14th, but Wilson still delayed the final order and Nicholson rode over to Chamberlain's tent several times on the 13th to get him to exert his influence with the General. That evening Nicholson repaired for the last time to headquarters in order to beg Wilson not to delay the assault. Then he made a final round of the batteries, in one of which he said to the gunners: 'I must shake hands with you fellows; you have done your best to make my work easy to-morrow.' An hour later he was in his tent explaining to his officers exactly what they had to do once they were over the walls of the city. He was in a jubilant frame of mind because Wilson had not only made him leader of the storming columns, but had promised that after the fall of Delhi he should command the pursuing force which was to relieve Agra and then join the army under the new Commander-in-Chief, Sir Colin Campbell. In talking over his future plans Nicholson said to a friend: 'I am certain that old ass Colin will put me under arrest before I have been twenty-four hours with him.' He did not feel at all confident that any one but himself could succeed in crushing the Mutiny, but in the event of failure 'I hope,' he said, 'that the British will drag down with them in flames and blood as many of the Queen's enemies as possible.'

Darkness had fallen when he went down to inspect the walls near the Kashmir Gate, and though the engineers reported that the breach close to the bastion was not as wide as it ought to have been, Nicholson, impatient of further delay, said that it could be carried by escalade and strongly supported Baird Smith, who urged upon Wilson the necessity of immediate action. Still protesting, Wilson gave the order, and the night was spent in feverish preparation.

'There was not much sleep that night in our camp,' wrote an officer : 'I dropped off now and then, but never for long, and whenever I woke I could see that there was a light in more than one of the officers' tents, and talking was going on in a low tone amongst the men, the snapping of a lock or springing of a ramrod sounding far in the still air, telling of preparation for the coming strife. A little after midnight we fell in as quietly as possible, and by the light of a lantern the orders for the assault were then read to the men. They were to the following purport : Any officer or man who might be wounded was to be left where he fell; no one was to step from the ranks to help him, as there were no men to spare. If the assault were successful he would be taken away in the dhoolies, or litters, and carried to the rear, or wherever he could best receive medical assistance. If we failed, wounded and sound should be prepared to bear the worst. There was to be no plundering, but all prize taken was to be put into a common stock for fair division after all was over.* No prisoners were to be made, as we had no one to guard them, and care was to be taken that no women or children were injured. To this the men answered at once by "No fear, sir." The officers now pledged their honours on their swords to abide by these orders, and the men then promised to follow their example. At this moment, just as the regiment was about to march off, Father Bertrand came up in his vestments, and, addressing the Colonel, begged for permission to bless the regiment, saying: "We may differ some of us

* Perhaps it is unnecessary to add that the men were cheated of their prize-money by the East India Company.

in matters of religion, but the blessing of an old man
and a clergyman can do nothing but good." The Colonel
at once assented, and Father Bertrand, lifting his hands
to Heaven, blessed the regiment in a most impressive
manner, offering up at the same time a prayer for our
success and for mercy on the souls of those soon
to die.'

Five columns, each about a thousand strong, were in
position before dawn. It was the duty of the first three
columns under Nicholson to storm the northern wall of
Delhi, of the fourth column under Major Reid to effect
an entrance to the west of the city, and of the fifth
column under Brigadier Longfield to render assistance
where required. Nicholson personally led the first
column, and before he gave the signal to advance Roberts
saw him from the wall of Ludlow Castle and wondered
what was passing through his mind: 'Was he thinking
of the future, or of the wonderful part he had played
during the past four months? At Peshawar he had been
Edwardes's right hand. At the head of the Movable
Column he had been mainly instrumental in keeping the
Punjab quiet, and at Delhi every one felt that during the
short time he had been with us he was our guiding star,
and that but for his presence in the camp the assault
which he was about to lead would probably never have
come off. He was truly "a tower of strength." Any
feeling of reluctance to serve under a Captain of the
Company's army, which had at first been felt by some,
had been completely overcome by his wonderful personality. Each man in the force, from the General in
command to the last-joined private soldier, recognised
that the man whom the wild people on the frontier had
deified . . . was one who had proved himself beyond all
doubt capable of grappling with the crisis through which
we were passing—one to follow to the death. Faith in
the Commander who had claimed and been given the

post of honour was unbounded, and every man was prepared "to do or die" for him.'

Further evidence of the change of heart among the senior officers on the ridge was supplied by General Sir Henry Daly (then a Captain, who had brought the Guides to Delhi, riding 580 miles in twenty-two days): 'Only those who remember the too frequent attitude of superiority adopted by the officers in the Queen's service towards those in that of "John Company"* will realise how great the tribute to a dominating personality was the fact that officers commanding such regiments as the 9th Lancers, the 6th Dragoon Guards and the 60th Rifles, should have been willing to serve under this regimental Captain in the Company's service, this General by grace of God, who had ridden into camp like a King coming into his own, and though with strangely little official position, had virtually assumed the command of the Force; for it was an open secret that it was *his* will that the ostensible General was constrained to obey, and that it was his leading that the army was prepared to follow.'

During the night the enemy had partially repaired the gaps in the walls and with the dawn the British guns opened a cannonade. The sun was up when the batteries fell silent and Nicholson gave the signal to advance. As the troops emerged from the scrub in which they had been concealed a storm of bullets met them from the walls. Many fell before they reached the ditch, and until the scaling-ladders came up the survivors were subjected to a hail of stones thrown by the defenders. Nicholson was the first to ascend the breach; he drove the mutineers from the wall and followed by his men captured house after house. Following his action the Kashmir gate was blown in, another column making its entrance there.

* The East India Company.

It was of primary importance that the ramparts should be cleared and held as far west as the Lahore Gate. After an hour's fighting the British commanded the walls for two-thirds of the distance, their flag flying on the Kabul Gate. A little way beyond they suffered a check, and when Nicholson arrived, after fighting his way through the northern part of the city and cutting down every mutineeer who came within his reach, he found that the enemy were making a stand in considerable numbers at the Burn bastion, stopping the British advance on the Lahore Gate. He had promised Major Reid that he would open that Gate for the fourth column and though unaware that Reid's advance through the western suburbs had been held up he did not intend to break his word. The distance from the Kabul Gate to the Burn bastion was about two hundred yards, the connecting lane having the city wall and rampart on its right and a number of flat-roofed parapeted houses on its left. Not more than four men could go abreast down this lane, which was open to frontal artillery fire from the Burn bastion and to the musket fire of the mutineers who swarmed along the tops of the low houses on the left. Up this narrow passage the British troops had advanced again and again, each time recoiling before the fusillade that ploughed down their best officers and thinned their ranks. They were attempting to rally from one of these shattering reverses when Nicholson arrived on the scene.

As a leader of men Nicholson had every virtue it is possible to enumerate; as a master of strategy he had two grave defects: he was rashly impetuous in action, and, tirelessly brave himself, he expected the same quality in those he led. The men who had just fallen back before a tempest of lead were not only worn out by the morning's fighting but were in a feeble physical condition after months of nervous strain and the pestilential atmosphere of the camp. Nicholson himself had endured far more than any man there, but his body and spirit had been shaped for endurance; and when warned by the Major in command that the men could do no more, his body stiffened, his spirit flared out, and sending the officers to the front he ordered another thrust up the alley of death. Once more the men followed their leaders, but again they could not face the hurricane of shot and came reeling back towards the Kabul Gate, leaving many of their comrades dead.

Had Nicholson stopped to think he would have realised that progress was only possible by breaking through the houses on the left of the lane, but the hours of strenuous exertion under a brazen sky which exhausted other men excited him and, yelling the order for yet another advance, 'One more rush and we'll get that gun!' he charged up the centre of the lane brandishing his tulwar. His Brigade-Major, having no option in the matter, followed him, and the few surviving officers, hugging the left wall, trailed along in his wake. But the soldiers by now were completely demoralised and hung back, some of them taking cover in the archways along the right wall, others disappearing in the opposite direction. Nicholson, glancing over his shoulder, perceived this, and stood for a moment in a towering rage, his back to the enemy, his tulwar flashing in the air as he shouted scornful encouragement at the British soldiers. In that attitude he presented an easy mark, and a sepoy, lying on a roof a few yards away, took careful aim and fired, the bullet entering his exposed right side beneath his uplifted arm and penetrating his lung. He did not fall at once, but the thud of the heavy bullet as it struck him was audible above the prevailing din and an officer said, 'You are hit, sir.' Irritated by such an unnecessary remark, Nicholson answered impatiently, 'Yes, yes.' Then his knees began to give way, and propping himself against the nearest wall he ground his teeth with fury as he sank slowly to the earth.

An officer gave him some brandy and offered with the assistance of a sergeant to move him to a place of safety. 'The men who would not follow me shall not lift me from the ground,' said Nicholson, adding, 'I will remain here till Delhi is taken.' But his pain increased and when about half an hour later an officer with whom he had quarrelled, named Captain Hay, came to look for him he gasped: 'I will make up my difference with you, Hay; I will let you take me back.' Hay had not been among those who had failed him in the lane. At the Kabul Gate he was placed in a dhooly and some native carriers were ordered to take him to the field hospital below the ridge; but they met temptation on the way. What happened has been related by Lord Roberts:

'While riding through the Kashmir Gate, I observed by the side of a road a dhooly, without bearers, and with evidently a wounded man inside. I dismounted to see if I could be of any use to the occupant, when I found, to my grief and consternation, that it was John Nicholson, with death written on his face. He told me that the bearers had put the dhooly down and gone off to plunder; that he was in great pain, and wished to be taken to the hospital. He was lying on his back, no wound was visible, and but for the pallor of his face, always colourless, there was no sign of the agony he must have been enduring. On my expressing a hope that he was not seriously wounded, he said: "I am dying; there is no chance for me." The sight of that great man lying helpless and on the point of death was almost more than I could bear. Other men had daily died around me, friends and comrades had been killed beside me, but I never felt as I felt then—to lose Nicholson seemed to me at that moment to lose everything.

'I searched about for the dhooly-bearers, who, with

other camp-followers, were busy ransacking the houses and shops in the neighbourhood, and carrying off everything of the slightest value they could lay their hands on. Having with difficulty collected four men, I put them in charge of a sergeant of the 61st Foot. Taking down his name, I told him who the wounded officer was, and ordered him to go direct to the field hospital.'

Late in the afternoon Nicholson entered the hospital where he met his brother Charles, whose right arm had just been amputated close to the shoulder. The surgeon saw at once that Nicholson's case was hopeless; nothing could be done to stop the internal hæmorrhage. Having made him as comfortable as possible, the surgeon asked if there was anything else he could do. 'Nothing now,' replied Nicholson. He was then removed to the camp on the ridge and was placed for a while in Captain Daly's tent, where Chamberlain found him, 'stretched on a charpoy, helpless as an infant, breathing with difficulty, and only able to jerk out his words in syllables at long intervals and with pain. . . . He asked me to tell him exactly what the surgeons said of his case; and after I had told him, he wished to know how much of the town we had in our possession, and what we proposed doing. Talking was, of course, bad for him, and prohibited, and the morphia, which was given to him in large doses, to annul pain and secure rest, soon produced a state of stupor.'

Next evening Chamberlain returned, thought Nicholson seemed much better and began to hope 'it was not God's purpose to cut him off in the prime of manhood.' The camp on the ridge was very silent; nearly every one was fighting in the city; and another caller at Daly's tent was depressed by what he saw: a man lying on a couch with the ghastly pallor of death on his face, a native servant standing motionless beside him, a miserable candle flickering in the gloom. As the visitor approached the couch Nicholson turned his eyes and in a sepulchral voice asked, 'Who are you?' The visitor gave his name and murmured a few words of sympathy. There was a long pause. The lips of the wounded man opened and with a great effort he said, 'I thank you.' Then he closed his eyes. The following day Chamberlain managed to get him removed to cooler quarters in a sergeant's bungalow, a portion of which had not been destroyed by the mutineers on May 13th.

Throughout his struggle against death his main interest in periods of consciousness centred on the conflict in the city. Bad news made him fearfully excited, which brought on the hæmorrhage. He insisted on knowing everything and was told of the heavy casualties in the first day's fighting, of the failure of Reid's column, of the temporary cessation of hostilities due to the drunkenness of many soldiers, the enemy having designedly left cases of strong liquor in their way, and of Wilson's intention to retire from the city. The last item of news threw him into a paroxysm and lifting himself slightly with a terrible effort he burst forth: 'Thank God I have strength yet to shoot him if necessary!' Between spasms of agony he dictated a letter to John Lawrence imploring him to supersede Wilson and appoint Chamberlain in his place. Fortunately Baird Smith, when asked by Wilson whether they could hold what they had won, replied 'We *must* hold on.' Wilson, wisely, did not call on Nicholson to seek his advice. Had he done so he would almost certainly have been shot. Weak though he was, and suffering torments when fully conscious, Nicholson could still lift a pistol. The day after he was laid low his Multani horsemen were anxiously jabbering outside his tent; he sent word ordering them to be silent as he wished for quiet; his order was obeyed for about twenty minutes, when their concern for him got the better of them and the jabber recommenced; so he picked up a pistol from the table by his bed and fired it through the side of the tent; after which there was silence.

Chamberlain went to see him as often as duty permitted and one day Nicholson dictated a message for Edwardes: 'Tell him I should have been a better man if I had continued to live with him, and our heavy public duties had not prevented my seeing more of him privately. I was always the better for a residence with him and his wife, however short. Give my love to them both.' When Edwardes heard that his friend was dying he wired to Chamberlain: 'Give John Nicholson our love in time and eternity, and read him Acts xvi. 31 and Rom. x. 9. God ever bless him. I do not cease to hope and pray for him as a dear brother.' Edwardes was seriously concerned over Nicholson's soul, for the passages he wished the dying man to ponder show clearly that Nicholson had been drifting far from the old beliefs: (1) 'Believe on the Lord Jesus Christ and thou shalt be saved,' (2) 'If thou shalt confess with thy mouth the Lord Jesus, and shalt believe in thine heart that God raised Him from the dead, thou shalt be saved.' John Lawrence was also anxious about Nicholson's future, telegraphing to Chamberlain: 'Give my love to Nicholson and say how deeply we shall deplore his fall. He is a noble fellow. Tell him to think of his Saviour and pray for His aid which alone can save him.' Nearly all these Punjab officials were bibliolaters, Nicholson being perhaps the only one among them who would not have endorsed Robert Montgomery's explanation of how the Mutiny was quelled: "It was not policy, or soldiers, or officers, that saved the Indian Empire to England, and saved England to India. The Lord our God, He it was.'

On September 20th Nicholson learnt that Delhi had fallen. 'My desire was that Delhi should be taken before I die and it has been granted,' he said to his servant. The capture of the city broke the back of the Mutiny, and though much remained to be done there was no longer any doubt as to the result. One of Nicholson's last utterances was, 'Remember to tell them that Alex Taylor took Delhi,' but the truth is that fifty Taylors could not have taken it if Nicholson had not been there to get the siege-guns through, to help the engineers and to bully the General in command. Without him, as John Lawrence said, Delhi could not have fallen.

Chamberlain heard on the afternoon of September 22nd that Nicholson was sinking and immediately went to see him. Chamberlain had been kept very busy on the ridge while the army was fighting in the city and expressed his sorrow that he had been unable to see more of his friend. 'I knew that your duty to the service required your being at headquarters, and I was glad to think that you were there to give your counsel,' replied Nicholson.

'I found him much altered for the worse in appearance, and very much weaker,' wrote Chamberlain to Edwardes; 'indeed, so weak that, if left to himself, he fell off into a state of drowsiness, out of which nothing aroused him but the application of smelling-salts and stimulants. Once aroused, he became quite himself, and on that afternoon he conversed with me for half an hour or more, on several subjects, as clearly as ever. He, however, knew and felt that he was dying, and said that this world had now no interest to him. His not having made a will, as he had proposed doing the day before the storm, was the source of some regret to him, and it was his wish not to delay doing so any longer, but as he said he then felt too fatigued from having talked so much, and was too weak to keep his senses collected any longer, he begged me to leave him to himself until the evening, and then arouse him for the purpose. On this afternoon he told me to send you this message: "Say that if at this moment a good fairy were to give me a wish, my wish would be to have him here next to my mother." Shortly after writing down the above to his dictation, he said: "Tell my mother that I do not think we shall be unhappy in the next world. God has visited her with a great affliction, but tell her she must not give way to grief."

'Throughout those nine days of suffering he bore himself nobly; not a lament or a sigh ever passed his lips, and he conversed as calmly and clearly as if he were talking of some other person's condition and not his own.'

Late that evening he was asked if he could dictate his will; he felt too weak to do so, saying he hoped to be stronger in the morning. But the next morning at half-past nine he turned once on his side and died without a sigh.

Throughout India, except perhaps at Simla whither the whole headquarters staff at once repaired, the news of his death was received with sorrow and consternation. It was felt that even the fall of Delhi had been purchased at too high a price. John Lawrence, who burst into tears, believed that 'as long as an Englishman survives in India the name of John Nicholson will not be forgotten.' Edwardes was prostrated with grief: 'I feel as if all happiness had gone out of my public career,' he wrote: 'Henry Lawrence was as the father, John Nicholson was the brother, of my public life. . . . Never, never again can I hope for such a friend.' He longed to receive Chamberlain's account of Nicholson's last days, 'to know whether our dear friend was blest at last by the grace of God to see things free from doubt, and to be happy in resting on his Saviour. . . . Nicholson was the soul of truth. If he doubted, it was sincerely. If he melted at the last, it was sincerely. And I think it most of all probable that his dear mother's prayers were not permitted to be unanswered, nor his own.'

On the morning of the 24th the body of John Nicholson was borne on a gun-carriage in silence to the new burial ground near Ludlow Castle, opposite the Kashmir Gate and the breached wall he had been the first to ascend. No band played a Dead March, no volleys of musketry were fired. Neville Chamberlain was there and many English officers and men, some with sunburnt faces, others with faces bleached white by fever and sickness, their khaki uniforms contrasting with the picturesque dresses of Pathans, Afghans and Multanis. These last, who believed that a man who cried deserved to be whipped by women, could not contain their anguish when the coffin was lowered into the grave, throwing themselves on the ground and weeping without restraint like lost children. They owed allegiance to no one but Nicholson, recognised no leader but him, no service but his, and returned to their homes after his funeral with as much loot as they could carry.

AUTHORITIES

A NOTE ON KAYE

Few people read the works of Sir John Kaye nowadays, so I wish to mention my indebtedness to him. His Histories of the War in Afghanistan and the Sepoy War are among the greatest chronicles in the English language. Without the detachment of Gibbon, the eloquence of Macaulay, the dramatic sense of Carlyle, the industry of Parkman or the picturesqueness of Prescott, he had some of all their qualities, together with a humour of his own, an acute feeling for the significant, and that primary virtue: a readableness that grips the attention.

A History of the Sepoy War in India, by John William Kaye, 3 vols., 1864–76.

History of the War in Afghanistan, by John William Kaye, 3 vols., 1857–8.

Lives of Indian Officers, by John William Kaye, 2 vols., 1867.

Kaye's and Malleson's History of the Indian Mutiny, 6 vols., 1889.

The Indian Mutiny of 1857, by Colonel G. B. Malleson, 1891.

The Life of John Nicholson, by Captain Lionel J. Trotter, 1904.

The Life of Hodson of Hodson's Horse, by Captain Lionel J. Trotter (Everyman edition, 1927).

Twelve Years of a Soldier's Life in India, being Extracts from the Letters of the late Major W. S. R. Hodson, 1859.

Forty-One Years in India, by Field-Marshal Lord
     Roberts, 1898.

Rise and Fulfilment of British Rule in India, by Edward
     Thompson and G. T. Garratt, 1934.

The Other Side of the Medal, by Edward Thompson,
     1925.

A History of the Sikhs, by Joseph Davey Cunningham,
     1918.

*The Military Operations at Kabul, with a Journal of
     Imprisonment in Afghanistan,* by Lieut. Vincent
     Eyre, 1843.

*Memorials of the Life and Letters of Major-General Sir
     Herbert B. Edwardes,* by his Wife, 2 vols., 1886.

The Punjab in Peace and War, by S. S. Thorburn, 1904.

Bannu, by S. S. Thorburn, 1876.

A History of the British Army, by the Hon. J. W. For-
     tescue, vol. XIII, 1930.

Life of Sir Henry Lawrence, by Sir H. B. Edwardes and
     Herman Merivale, 2 vols., 1872.

Private Letters of the Marquess of Dalhousie, edited by
     J. G. A. Baird, 1910.

Life of Lord Lawrence, by R. Bosworth Smith, 1912.

An Unrecorded Chapter of the Indian Mutiny, being the
     personal reminiscences of Reginald G. Wilberforce,
     1895.

Letters from India 1829-32, being a selection from the
     Correspondence of Victor Jacquemont, translated
     with an introduction by Catherine Alison Phillips,
     1936.

Scinde in the Forties, being the Journal and Letters of
     Colonel Keith Young, edited by Arthur F. Scott,
     1912.

Men and Events of my Time in India, by Sir Richard
     Temple, 1882.

Reminiscences of Forty-three Years in India, by Lieut.-
     General Sir George Lawrence, 1874.

Life of Field-Marshal Sir Neville Chamberlain, by G. W. Forrest, 1909.

Reynell Taylor, by E. Gambier Parry, 1888.

Lawrence of Lucknow, by J. L. Morison, 1934.

Honoria Lawrence, by Maud Diver, 1936.

Richard Baird Smith, by Colonel H. M. Vibart, 1897.

The Life and Campaigns of Hugh, First Viscount Gough, by Robert S. Rait, vol. 2, 1903.

Eight Months' Campaign, by Colonel George Bourchier, 1858.

Old Memories, by General Sir Hugh Gough, 1897.

From Cadet to Colonel, by Sir Thomas Seaton, 2 vols., 1866.

Miss Eden's Letters, edited by Violet Dickinson, 1919.

Incidents in the Sepoy War, compiled from the Private Journals of General Sir Hope Grant, 1874.

Up the Country, Letters written by Emily Eden, with an introduction by Edward Thompson, 1930.

Letters from India, by Emily Eden, vol. 2, 1872.

Court and Camp of Ranjit Singh, by the Hon. William G. Osborne, 1840.

Lumsden of the Guides, by General Sir Peter S. Lumsden and George R. Elmsie, 1899.

The Punjab and Delhi in 1857, by the Rev. J. Cave-Browne, 2 vols., 1861.

History of the Siege of Delhi, by An Officer Who Served There, 1861.

Memories of My Indian Career, by Sir George Campbell, vol. 1, 1893.

The Life of Lord Roberts, by Sir George Forrest, 1914.

Letters Written during the Indian Mutiny, by Fred Roberts, afterwards Field-Marshal Earl Roberts, 1924.

Diary and Correspondence of the late Colonel Keith Young, 1902.

Life of General Sir Alex Taylor, by A. Cameron Taylor, 1913.

Memoirs of General Sir Henry D. D. Daly, by Major H. Daly, 1905.

The Revolt in Hindustan 1857–9, by Sir Henry Evelyn Wood, 1908.

Earl Canning, by Sir H. S. Cunningham, 1891.

Field-Marshal Sir Donald Stewart, by G. R. Elmsie, 1903.

Life of Charles Lord Metcalfe, by Edward Thompson, 1937.

Selections from the Letters, Despatches and other State Papers preserved in the Military Department of the Government of India, 1857–8, edited by George W. Forrest, vol. 1, 1893.

Selections from the Records, Punjab Annual Administration Reports, 1849–50, 1855–6.

Blackwood's Magazine, February, 1898.

Friend of India, October 18th, 1860.

The Dictionary of National Biography.

INDEX

NAVIGATION ON THE ROAD?

When the *Queen Mary* enters a busy port, she and all the other vessels obey the recognized lights and signals on which safe navigation depends.

We, too, obey lights and signals — and rely on them for safety — when we drive or ride or walk on the roads.

We are, in fact, "road navigators." Modern traffic simply could not work without a set of rules which we all accept.

Why, then, are there still accidents — far too many?

Partly because we don't all know and understand the rules and principles of Road Navigation. And even if we know them, we forget or ignore them. And partly because some of us don't yet realize that the rules apply to *everyone* — walkers as well as cyclists and drivers. *Any* of us can cause an accident in which we or other people get killed or maimed.

If we all understood the principles of good Road Navigation (based on the Highway Code) and obeyed them *all the time*, traffic would flow faster and more smoothly. We should all get about more easily and, above all, *more safely*. By learning to be skilful Road Navigators, we can help ourselves and everyone else to *get home safe and sound*.

GET HOME SAFE AND SOUND

Issued by the Ministry of Transport